Public Relations
South African Perspectives

Editors

RS Rensburg
M Cant

www.heinemann.co.za

Published by Heinemann Publishers (Pty) Ltd
66 Park Lane, Sandown 2196
www.heinemann.co.za

First published 2003
07 06 05 04 03
8 7 6 5 4 3 2 1

ISBN 0 79620 318 0

Typeset in 10.5 on 13 pt Dutch by Daleen Behr
Illustrations by Daleen Behr
Cover design by Karen Brink
Reproduction by Castle Graphics
Printed by Clysons

Contents

Contributors

Mr C Bothma, Department of Business Management, University of South Africa (Chapter 7).

Prof M Cant, Head: Marketing and Retail Section, Department of Business Management, University of South Africa (Chapter 2).

Ms A Crystal, Department of Communication, Rand Afrikaans University (Chapter 1).

Mr M du Toit, Department of Business Management, University of South Africa (Chapter 8).

Ms C Gerber-Nel, Department of Business Management, University of South Africa (Chapter 8).

Mr R Machado, Department of Business Management, University of South Africa (Chapter 5).

Ms I Niemann, Department of Communication, Rand Afrikaans University (Chapter 1).

Prof R Rensburg, Head: Department of Marketing and Communication Management, University of Pretoria (Chapters 3 and 9).

Ms C Swart, Department of Communication, Technikon South Africa (Chapter 4).

Prof S Verwey, Head: Department of Communication, Rand Afrikaans University (Chapter 6).

Preface

Public Relations: South African Perspectives revisits the concept of public relations within the South African environment while keeping in mind current global phenomena and developments.

A recent publication, *The fall of advertising and the rise of PR,* by marketing guru Al Ries and consulting partner Laura Ries (published in 2002), contends that public relations has quietly become one of the most powerful disciplines of our time. It is a more cost-effective tool than advertising, and through its use of publicity, interpersonal communication and relationship building, public relations is rapidly moving away from its 'tainted past' to become a credible strategic management tool in the hands of public relations practitioners across all organisational spectra.

The public relations practitioner of the past was primarily a *technician*, who used public relations mainly at the implementation level of public relations programmes or campaigns. Although this traditional role will still be acted out – particularly in developing countries and learning organisations – the new millennium will see public relations utilised as the 'closer' instrument that turns a budding relationship with stakeholders into a lasting union. The 'new' strategic management role of public relations will emphasise the initiation, construction and maintenance of *inter-relationships* (a deeper connectivity) by organisations with all stakeholders.

Public relations has become a serious academic discipline over the last decade and a variety of learning and training offerings are available at tertiary institutions across the globe. Public relations as practice is also regaining prominence in today's integrated communication toolbox and is being utilised with new vigour by organisations. Thus the power of public relations to enhance integrated brand experiences that build profitable, long-term stakeholder relationships is illustrated. Brand image is a promise made and recorded in the hearts and minds of stakeholders. Brand equity (where the value is) is that promise kept through multiple contacts over a period of time that creates and builds positive stakeholder experiences and relationships. True brand building is in many ways about trust building. Building trust in this *Enron-ic* or *Andersonian* and *continuously changing* age is not an easy task. Nor should it be – trust must be earned. This is where strategic and ethically tenable public relations programmes or campaigns are becoming driving forces in communication plans and strategies that deliver exceptional value to organisations.

With all the choices available today in the integrated communication toolbox, why is public relations enjoying a rejuvenation? There is more than one reason, but first and foremost public relations can create great stories. Not just stories that appear in the print or electronic media, but stories that are told and shared among stakeholders, prospects and centres-of-influence about products, services, causes and organisations. Opinions are passed along to others on what they have heard, seen and experienced. Word-of-mouth endorsements, and these days word-of-modem, are tremendous brand building opportunities. There is no better way to create, cultivate and circulate the seeds of those narratives than through public relations as a strategic management tool.

Effective stakeholder interrelationships can build brand ambassadors and even apostles. And there is no better way to combat misinformation or negative narrative than by getting the truthful, accurate information out to the stakeholders in order for them to feel confident about their brand relationships. As part of an integrated communication plan and strategy, public relations should deliver great opportunities. But public relations practitioners and organisations must ensure that public relations is treated as a strategic management tool and executed effectively in order to deliver value.

More enlightened organisations these days are planning and budgeting for public relations initiatives as a higher priority than ever, instead of treating them as *ad hoc* items. This book attempts to illustrate the immense value and application of public relations education, science and practice in a South African environment. If this book can succeed in persuading students, scholars, practitioners or organisational managers and leaders to think critically but also positively about the field of public relations, the authors have succeeded in 'getting their stories out'.

Ronél Rensburg (co-editor)

October 2002

Section 1

Theoretical Background to Public Relations

Section 1 provides a theoretical platform for the topics under scrutiny, namely the concept of public relations as a field of study, an area of research and a profession. This section also investigates the key concepts of integrated marketing communication (IMC), the interrelationship between marketing and public relations, and the role of public relations in the organisation, in the business environment and in society. This section therefore sets the scene for and acts as backdrop to the sections that follow.

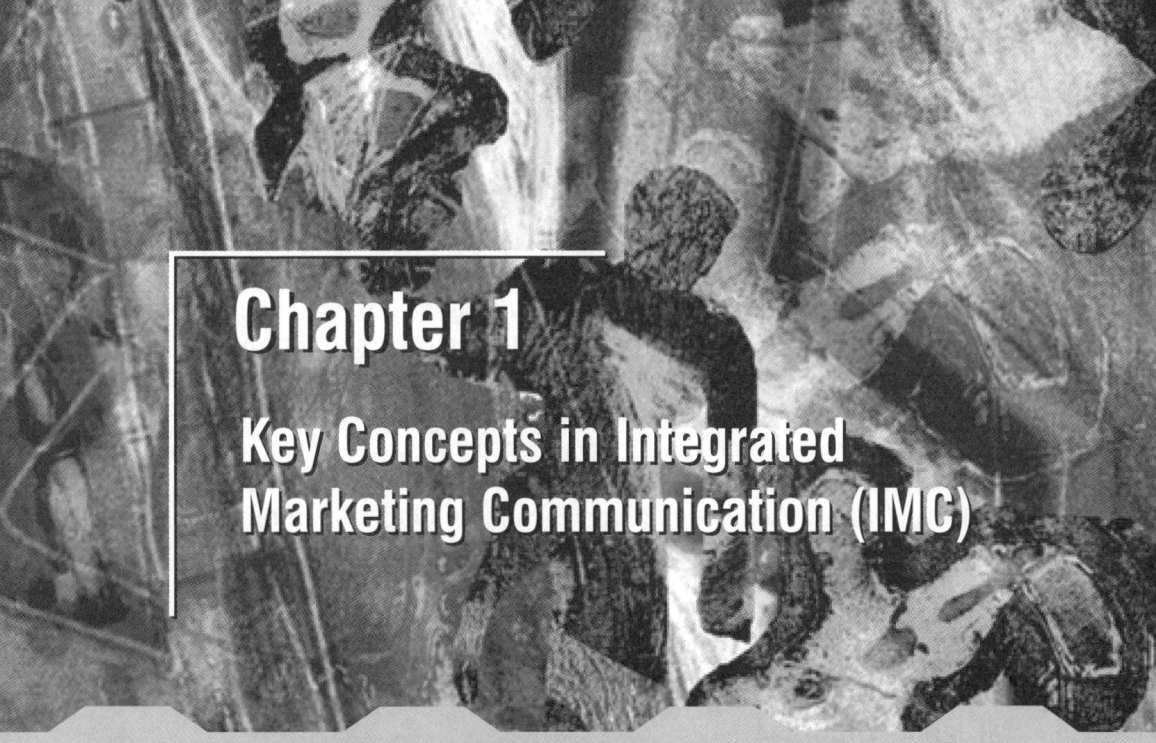

Chapter 1

Key Concepts in Integrated Marketing Communication (IMC)

LEARNING OUTCOMES

After studying this chapter, you should be able to:

▲ show an understanding of the concept IMC

▲ contextualise IMC by relating it to similar concepts in the field

▲ define IMC and identify significant contributions of each definition

▲ show an understanding of the shift from the traditional promotional mix to integrated marketing communication

▲ provide an overview of trends, both inside and outside organisations, that facilitated the development of IMC

▲ demonstrate the levels of IMC.

Introduction

In an era of significant product and brand parity, it has become more important than ever to ensure that a brand achieves market and perceptual penetration in order to break through the clutter. One approach to achieving this is integrated marketing communication (IMC). In this regard, Moriarty states, 'Integrated marketing communication is enjoying a growth in awareness, particularly among larger companies. More than half (54 per cent) of the 179 polled say their companies are implementing some form of integrated marketing communication, and 75 per cent of large companies are doing so.' The value of IMC is that it changes the focus from the four Ps (product, price, place and promotion) to a more customer-centric orientation and emphasises strategic consistency rather than independent brand messages.

IMC contextualised

To understand integrated marketing communication, it is essential to have a fundamental understanding of a number of important concepts related to the field. For this reason, the following section explains the basic elements of marketing, the marketing mix, the promotional mix, marketing communication and integrated marketing communication.

Marketing

Marketing, as an academic and practical discipline, is a product of the twentieth century (Kitchen, 1999:20). The American Marketing Association's (AMA) definition of the word *marketing* introduces a number of key concepts: 'the process of planning and executing the conception, pricing, promotion, and distribution of ideas, goods and services to create exchanges that satisfy individual and organisational goals' (Bennett, 1995:244). In addition, Evans and Moutinho (1999:4) refer to marketing as 'the process of creating and providing what customers want in return for something they are willing to give (money, time, or membership)'. According to these definitions, marketing involves the setting of an expectation or expectations with customers and management, and the creation of reciprocal satisfaction through exchange processes. The marketer has a number of tools to hand – the instruments of the marketing mix.

The marketing mix

The AMA's definition of marketing given earlier contains a list of activities or marketing strategy areas that, together, are called the *marketing mix*. Traditionally, the instruments included in the marketing mix are divided into four components, called the four Ps of the marketing mix. These four Ps determine how goods or services are manufactured or provided, the pricing of the goods and services, the distribution thereof, and how the organisational communication presents it (Duncan, 2001:14). The four Ps of the marketing mix are:

1. product (design and production)
2. place (distribution)
3. price
4. promotion.

4 Ps

Promotion, the final element of the marketing mix, also consists of various elements that comprise the promotional mix. Therefore, although promotion is part of the marketing mix, it is also a mix in its own right.

The promotional mix

The fourth P, promotion, is the most visible instrument of the marketing mix (Pelsmacker, Geuens & Van den Bergh, 2001:3). Promotion involves communication instruments through which the organisation communicates with its target groups and stakeholders to promote its products or the organisation as a whole. Cross (1998:80) and Koekemoer (1998:2) state that the promotional mix consists of six elements:

1. advertising	4. personal selling
2. sales promotion	5. direct marketing
3. public relations	6. sponsorship.

6 elements

However, as a result of the evolution in the marketing sphere whereby marketing evolved into a more tailored, personalised approach, the emphasis is more on communication and its functionality within marketing. This shift introduced a movement towards the communication mix in preference to the use of the term promotional mix (Howard, 1997:32). The communication mix not only focuses on six elements (like the promotional mix), but includes at least 12 communication elements. These include:

1. advertising	7. sales promotion
2. sponsorship	8. public relations
3. point-of-purchase	9. exhibitions/trade fairs
4. direct marketing	10. personal selling
5. interactive marketing	11. personal communication
6. mass communication	12. image/theme communication.

12 elements

The communication mix is therefore a wider mix of elements than the promotional mix.

Marketing communication

In the more contemporary views of the 1990s, the role of communication in organisations has become broader and, to a greater extent, is focused on creating dialogue (Gronstedt, 2000:7). This implies that the customer can now also initiate communication and the organisation will respond to it, or vice versa should the organisation initiate communication. Marketing communication is characterised by:

▲ **two-way communication**, not only by dispensing information

▲ **inclusiveness** – this is the collective term for all the communication functions used in marketing a product or a service (Rotzoll & Haefner, 1996:31); the emphasis here is on the use of the words *collective* and *all* (an organisation seldom uses just one of the marketing communication functions – most often, it uses a different combination thereof)

▲ **communication with all stakeholders** – this can include communication with internal audiences, company stakeholders and external audiences other than customers and consumers

▲ **strategic processes** – the components of the marketing communication mix vary widely. The extent to which each marketing communication function is used varies greatly, depending on the specific product or service and situation.

The concept of integrated marketing communication has evolved from the concept of marketing communication.

What is integrated marketing communication?

In the 1990s, confusion abounded as to the exact definition of integrated marketing communication. Some people referred to it as 'one-stop shopping' (Swan, 1993:42), while others regarded it as one consistent message (Duncan & Everrett, 1993:31). Integrated marketing communication has further been depicted as a management philosophy (Stewart, 1996:149; Cornelissen, 2000:3), an educational movement (Hutton, 1996:159) and a unifying business practice (Burnett & Moriarty, 1998). These inconsistencies in describing IMC have prevented the development of a cohesive research stream in this area (Low, 2000:29). Wolter (1993:12) describes the consequences of this inconsistency as follows: 'People are having trouble defining integrated marketing communication because the concept lacks a good, solid theory from which to start. Current integrated marketing communication practice suffers from superficiality …, ambiguity …, and a blurred focus.'

In order to try to clarify the concept, various definitions of IMC are presented below in chronological order. The main concepts of each definition are identified, after which the common elements amongst all of them are highlighted.

The 1980s

At its earliest application in the 1980s (Spotts & Lambert, 1998:211), integrated marketing communication was described as the integration of various communication vehicles within a specific campaign. From this initial description of IMC, the line dividing it and marketing communication was *integration*. The introduction of integration immediately takes the notion of marketing communication one step further in not only *combining* various communication functions, but also *integrating* these functions. Based on the description by Spotts and Lambert (1998:211), IMC is therefore not merely a combination of communication instruments, but an integration of those instruments. According to this description, the premise of IMC can be referred to as *synergy*. Synergy can be achieved when all such communication works in concert, as it ensures that stakeholders are exposed to *consistent* and *complementary* messages.

In addition to the description offered by Spotts and Lambert (1998:211), one of the first definitions of integrated marketing communication was proposed by the American Association of Advertising Agencies in 1989. This definition focused on using more than just advertising, public relations and direct marketing communication to achieve maximum communication impact:

> … [Integrated marketing communication is a] concept of marketing communication planning that recognizes the added value of a comprehensive plan that evaluates the strategic roles of a variety of communication disciplines – general advertising, direct response, sales promotion, and public relations – and combines these disciplines to provide clarity, consistency, and maximum communication impact (Caywood, Schultz & Wang, 1991:3).

The contribution of this definition is that it views integrated marketing communication as a strategic process that adds value to the communication by combining various communication disciplines to create a powerful, clear and consistent message. By applying 'clarity' and 'consistency' in combination, it implies synergy, as stated in the description by Spotts and Lambert (1998:211). The limitation of the definition proposed by the American Association of Advertising Agencies is the inclusion of only traditional promotional mix elements, excluding a broader array of communication instruments.

The 1990s

Schultz (1991) uses the following definition of integrated marketing communication: 'The process of managing all sources of information about a product or service to which a customer or prospect is exposed which behaviourally moves the consumer toward a sale and maintains customer loyalty'. The key contribution of this definition is that it focuses on IMC as a *process* that should be *managed* actively, and therefore implies that it is not something that just happens. Furthermore, there are three more contributions:

1. By including 'all sources of information' to which customers are exposed, the definition by Schultz (1991) focuses on a broader variety of communication functions available, in contrast to the definition by the American Association of Advertising Agencies, which is limited to the traditional promotional mix elements.

2. This definition adds the need for a *conscious, behavioural outcome* from consumers when communicating with them.

3. The maintenance of 'customer loyalty' implies that the outcome is not limited to a sale; in other words, it does not stop there. By referring to customer loyalty, the definition indicates that there is a shift towards being a *customer-centric* organisation, where the focus is more on the importance of the customer than on the organisation.

In addition to the definitions stated above, Tannenbaum (1991:3) views integrated marketing communication as follows when stating that:

> ... [Integrated marketing communication is] a renewal of a forgotten commitment made to consumers. It is a return to the day when the consumer was approached with respect. The customer conversation [is] two-way ... It combines every form of communication – the price of the product, where the product is sold, how it is displayed, labelling, packaging, what is said about it in the advertisements, direct marketing, public relations. It even includes what a company's employees say about the product – in sale pitches, telephone conversations, [at] cocktail parties ... Integrated marketing communication is a return to building brand loyalty by building brands that deserve loyalty.

Contributions of this definition include:

▲ An **internal focus**. Internal communication and actions also contribute to the communication efforts of an organisation, not only the traditional audiences of the organisation previously included.

▲ An emphasis on **dialogue** (a prominent feature of marketing communication), by moving away from the transactional style to focus on a conversational style.

▲ The idea of **two-way communication** as a key characteristic of the concept of a *customer-centric* organisation, as implied by the definition by Schultz (1991), since a lack of two-way communication will damage an organisation's affiliation with customers and will ultimately destroy its customer-centricity.

▲ Similar to the definition by Schultz (1991), an emphasis that **all sources of information** about the organisation should be **integrated** (Tannenbaum, 1991).

▲ **Brand loyalty as a behavioural change**, which is required as an outcome.

In addition, Keegan, Moriarty and Duncan (1992:631) view integrated marketing communication as the 'strategic co-ordination of all messages and media used by an organisation to collectively influence its perceived brand value'. Their definition highlights:

▲ the use of *'strategic co-ordination'*, which implies synergy through the co-ordination of complementary messages

▲ similar to the definition by Schultz (1991), the concept that *all* messages and media should be used collectively to create a greater *impact*

▲ that the focus is more on influencing the *perception* of the brand, which results in more of an *attitudinal* change.

More recently, Duncan (1997) defines integrated marketing communication as 'the process of strategically controlling or influencing all messages and encouraging purposeful dialogue to create and nourish profitable relationships with customers and other stakeholders'. Duncan's (1997) definition is useful for the following reasons:

▲ The notion of *controlling messages strategically* is similar to the idea of managing all messages, as stated in the definition by Schultz (1991), and is equivalent to the idea of strategic co-ordination of messages used in the definition by Keegan et al. (1992:631).

▲ The focus is more on *relationship building* as the outcome of the approach.

▲ The use of *'profitable' stakeholders* reflects that some stakeholders are more profitable than others. Furthermore, adding 'stakeholders' to the definition moves the concept of IMC beyond the consumer target audiences to include all the relevant parties with a direct or indirect impact on or stake in organisational operations and profitability.

Following on Duncan's (1997) definition, Harris (1998:7) defines integrated marketing communication as '… a cross-functional process for creating and nourishing profitable relationships with customers and other stakeholders by strategically controlling or influencing all messages sent to these groups and encouraging purposeful dialogue with them'. The contribution of this definition is:

▲ The idea that integrated marketing communication involves a *cross-functional process*. The outcome of this process will then be not only to create (as stated by Duncan's (1997) definition), but also to nourish profitable relationships through 'purposeful dialogue' between the organisation and the stakeholders.

▲ The use of 'all messages' in a *two-way* communication process.

▲ That *action* is required in the form of 'creating and nourishing profitable relationships'.

The 2000s

In one of the most recent definitions of integrated marketing communication, Duncan (2001:8) defines it as 'a cross-functional process for creating and nourishing profitable relationships with customers and other stakeholders by strategically controlling or influencing all messages sent to these groups and encouraging data-driven, purposeful dialogue with them'. Duncan (2001:8) includes all the key elements already mentioned as contributed by the other authors, but most importantly adds that the focus on two-way communication should be 'data-driven'. This is brought on by an increasing amount of communication taking place between the organisation and the stakeholder, based on information obtained and captured into a database.

Following on the various definitions stated above, the main elements of integrated marketing communication can be identified as follows:

▲ synergism

▲ creating and nourishing stakeholder relationships

▲ identifying profitable customers

▲ long-term relationships:

△ strategic consistency

△ a cross-functional process

△ strategically controlling or influencing all messages

△ encouraging purposeful dialogue

△ data-driven communication.

To clarify the concept of integrated marketing communication even further, its origin is discussed in the following section.

From the traditional promotional mix to the four Ps vs. the four Cs

According to Duncan and Moriarty (1997:xi), traditional marketing can no longer justify its existence. Organisations can no longer just make a product, price it, place it, promote it and expect to continue to exist in this linear fashion, using what is referred to as inside-out thinking.

Traditional promotional mix variables such as product development, pricing, form and type of distribution or channels are no longer as effective as they were. The developments in computers and communication technology, the expansion of the global marketplace, the growing competition among the various internal departments and external agencies, the move from an economy based on manufacturing to a service-based one, the increase in mergers and acquisitions, and the increase in customer demands, requires that organisations completely transform how they communicate with customers and sell their products. In a less developed, less sophisticated, less informed marketplace, traditional marketing communication concepts worked well. Today, the traditional promotional mix variables on which marketers conventionally relied (a better product design, more production efficiency, restricted or limited product availability, willingness to take a lower margin on sales) have lost their value as competitive weapons (Duncan & Moriarty, 1997:xi; Schultz, Tannenbaum & Lauternborn, 1994:43). According to Duncan and Moriarty (1997:xi), the new competitive arena is *brand value*, which creates long-term, profitable brand relationships.

Thus the fundamental view of marketing has shifted to a large degree from the four Ps of the 1960s – product, price, place and promotion, to the four Cs of the 1990s – consumer, cost to satisfy need, convenience to buy (including negotiating terms and conditions) and communication (dialogue between field sales, the corporate office and the customer) (Anchrol, 1991:82). Table 1.1 summarises the contrast between these two approaches.

Four Ps: Inside-out focus		Four Cs: Outside-in focus
Product	→	Customer
Price	→	Cost to satisfy need
Place	→	Convenience
Promotion	→	Communication

Table 1.1 Moving from the four Ps to the four Cs

In most organisations, changing from a focus on the traditional four Ps to more of a customer focus requires a major change in the corporate culture and marketing strategy. In other words, an organisation must move from using inside-out thinking to using outside-in thinking, that is, focusing externally on customers' needs and wants (Duncan, 2001:14). Inside-out thinking starts with the organisation's needs, whereas outside-in thinking starts with the customer's needs (Schultz, 1993a:8). Schultz (1993a:8) summarises the outside-in approach as follows:

▲ Always start with the customer – the key is knowledge of the customer as a person.

▲ In this approach, the marketers are constantly trying to build a relationship with the customer, to get and keep a customer over time.

▲ Value the customer in some way. Then the marketers know which customers they want to keep and which ones they want to let go.

▲ Marketers are driven by effectiveness, not just efficiency, by knowing the value of the customer.

The four Cs are not designed to replace the four Ps, but rather to refocus, redirect and examine the true market engine: the customer (Reich, 1998:27). The four Cs model can be seen as a simplified way of demonstrating how the integrated marketing communication focus is different from the traditional marketing focus. This does not mean that the four Ps are unimportant, but rather that they have an external dimension that must be taken into consideration and managed when building a brand (Duncan, 2001:15).

In essence, this implies that the old traditional linear production-based value chain needs to be replaced by the non-linear, interactive value field – a brand relationship environment (or customer-centred environment) containing many stakeholder groups, extensive brand contact points, after-market support, the reputation of the organisation, customer recourse and relationship-sensitive factors (Duncan & Moriarty, 1997:xii).

The primary differences between traditional marketing communication (the inside-out approach) and integrated marketing communication (the outside-in approach) concepts are best summarised in table 1.2 on the next page, as suggested by Duncan and Moriarty (1997:xii), and Duncan and Caywood (1996:21).

The focus of traditional marketing communication	The focus of integrated marketing communication
• Transaction	• Relationships
• Customers	• Stakeholders
• Mix of marketing communication tools	• Strategic consistency in brand messages
• Mass media (monologue)	• Interactivity (dialogue)
• Cause marketing	• Mission marketing
• Adjust prior year's plan	• Zero-based planning
• Specialisations	• Core competencies
• Functional organisation	• Cross-functional organisation
• Mass marketing	• Data-driven marketing
• Stable of agencies	• Communication management agencies

Table 1.2 Differences between traditional marketing communication and integrated marketing communication

Based on the shift to outside-in thinking, Duncan and Moriarty (1997:16–19) propose ten drivers of brand relationships:

1. **Create and nourish relationships rather than just make transactions.** Traditionally, marketing communication has been a process of developing and sending out brand messages to create sales, that is, transactions (Duncan, 2001:62). Organisations have learned, however, that they can be more profitable by focusing on building customer relationships rather than on just transactions. It is increasingly costly to acquire a new customer (Harris, 1998:4). Therefore, organisations are finding that putting more investment into growing current customers is more cost-effective (Duncan & Moriarty, 1997:16). The more organisations know about current customers, and the more they can use this information when communicating with these customers, the more credibility their communications will have and the stronger the relationship between the organisation and the customer will become.

2. **Focus on stakeholders rather than only on customers and/or shareholders.** Integrated marketing should not be limited to managing relationships with customers but should also be used for planning and monitoring relationships with all stakeholder groups. By definition, all the stakeholders

have a vested interest in the success of the organisation. What the organisation does affects them, and what the stakeholders do affects the organisation.

3. **Maintain strategic consistency rather than independent brand messages.** Recognising the communication dimensions of all brand contacts and the sources of these messages is critical because these impact positively or negatively on the behaviour of customers and other stakeholders. The more the brand's position is strategically integrated into all the brand messages, the more consistent and distinct will be the organisation's identity and reputation. The more a 'big idea' is emphasised, the more likely it will be that all the marketing communication efforts will have integrity.

4. **Generate purposeful interactivity rather than just a mass media monologue.** Interactivity is itself a form of integration (Duncan & Moriarty, 1997:17). A balance between mass, personalised and interactive media is used to enrich feedback from customers (referred to as feedback loops), and to reach them. The more customer feedback and dialogue is facilitated, the more the customers can be integrated into the organisation's planning and operations. This means the organisation achieves more listening and learning, and less telling and selling.

5. **Market a corporate mission rather than just product claims.** According to Duncan (2001:31), the only way a genuine mission makes a positive contribution to an organisation is when it is integrated into everything that the organisation does, regardless of the department or programme.

6. **Use zero-based planning rather than alter last year's plan.** Zero-based communication planning means that all communication objectives and strategies must be justified in terms of what needs to be done to manage relationships better, as opposed to simply adjusting the previous year's allocations and programmes (Duncan & Moriarty, 1997:18).

7. **Use cross-functional rather than departmental planning and monitoring.** Organisationally, integration is about linking expertise and sharing information (Aakar & Biel, 1993:1). A cross-functional management process for planning and monitoring relationships provides a way to link (rather than merge) specialty departments and functions, allowing them to maintain their specialisation but eliminating their isolation (Duncan, 2001:763).

8. **Create core competencies rather that just communication specialisation and expertise.** All marketing communication professionals should have a basic understanding of the strengths and weaknesses of major marketing communication functions. Experts are needed in the organisation to produce materials, but communication generalists are needed to plan and manage an integrated marketing communication programme.

9. **Use an integrated agency, rather than a traditional, full service agency.** A communication management agency takes responsibility for co-ordinating a brand's total communication programme. It handles the planning and routine executions internally, but when communication expertise is needed, it has relationships with other specialist agencies that can provide it. It continues to monitor the work of the specialist agencies to see that they remain focused on strategy and execute at the appropriate level of quality (Duncan & Moriarty, 1997:19).

10. **Build and manage databases to retain customers rather than acquire new customers.** Information is the bloodstream of integration (Duncan & Moriarty, 1997:19). How customer and other stakeholder data are collected, organised and shared determines whether or not an organisation has a record of its stakeholders' transactions and interactions. Without a programme of building and using databases, it is difficult for the organisation to create personalised communication (Duncan, 2001:62) or to be a learning organisation.

Gronstedt (2000:5–8) describes this shift from the traditional marketing communication approach to the integrated marketing communication approach as a shift of focus from the production-based approach, where the emphasis is on 'selling what we make' (tell and sell approach), to the consumer-based approach, where the emphasis is on 'make what customers want'.

In this consumer-based century, integrated marketing communication is a concept and an interactive process not only for acquiring, but also more importantly, for retaining and maximising the lifetime value of brand relationships. It is based on the fact that everything an organisation does, and sometimes what it does not do, sends a message. It recognises and responds to the fact that everyone in the organisation increasingly has the potential to 'touch' the customer at a contact point (Gronstedt, 2000:6). Related to this is the notion that customers integrate messages automatically, so it is important for the organisation to try to manage/control this process.

Duncan identifies four types of messages that an organisation needs to be aware of, so it can control or influence, namely: planned, inferred, maintenance and unplanned messages.

1. **Planned messages**, as the name implies, are messages that the organisation plans such as advertising, sales promotions, annual reports, notices in payslips, etc.

2. **Inferred messages** are all the messages sent by a product's design, performance, pricing and distribution (Duncan, 2001:131). For example, what message does a shop's physical location and layout send out?

3. **Maintenance messages** are primarily communicated through service. These include the attitudes of frontline staff, as well as the organisation's induction programme.

4. **Unplanned messages** include, for example, news stories, gossip, rumours and word of mouth. Such messages are hard to control as they come from sources outside the organisation.

This shift from the traditional promotional mix to the integrated marketing communication approach has occurred as the result of a variety of trends that have developed.

Trends that have necessitated new ways of communicating

This shift from the traditional promotional mix with its emphasis on transactions, to integrated marketing communication with its emphasis on brand relationship building, is driven by trends and situations. These trends, both inside and outside organisations, have made relationship building a critical element of any organisation's success. These trends include internal or organisational changes, and external or marketplace changes.

Internal or organisational changes

Integration in an organisation must exist internally if the organisation is to communicate effectively with the stakeholders. However, there are internal situations that cause marketing communication efforts to disintegrate:

▲ **Departmentalisation:** As organisations grow bigger and bigger, they find themselves composed of highly separated departments and divisions that have been grouped in order to maintain accountability and control. With each new department and division in the organisation, increased competition for budgets, staff and recognition occurs. Senge (1990:24) explains this as follows: 'Functional divisions grow into fiefdoms, and what was once a convenient division of labour mutates into the "stovepipes" [departmental silos] that all but cut off contact between functions. The result: "Analysis of the most important problems in the organisation, the complex issues that cross functional lines, becomes a perilous or nonexistent exercise".' This means that unless organisations integrate operations that communicate with customers and other key stakeholders, they will have little success in building profitable brand relationships (Duncan, 2001:30).

▲ **Increasing mergers and acquisitions of marketing communication agencies:** Many top public relations firms are presently owned or merged with an advertising agency (Duncan & Caywood, 1996:15–16). For example, Twilight Advertising & Promotion Holdings (Anon., 1999:11) and TinCan

Communication (Olwagen, 2001) were both previously public relations firms that merged with advertising agencies in order to provide a full marketing communication function to clients. Although mergers have resulted in few clients moving all their communication business under one roof (Reich, 1998:27), their mergers have underlined that certain advertising agencies recognise that these other forms of marketing communication are important and will comprise an increasing portion in their clients' marketing communication activities (Duncan & Everett, 1993:33). Consequently, many agencies have evolved from advertising agencies to marketing communication agencies.

▲ **Increasing pressure on bottom lines:** The financial community continues to look at quarterly earnings of public organisations, thus driving managements to force marketing to do more with less, and give priority to short-term rather than long-term results (Reich, 1998:27; Duncan & Caywood, 1996:16). The impact of this on marketing communication is that marketing communication professionals now have smaller budgets to create more effective, tangible results. Furthermore, this also means that they must be accountable for actions taken for, and on behalf of, the organisation.

▲ **Decreasing cost of using databases:** The drastic cost reduction, coupled with the increased sophistication of audience segmentation, has provided marketers with a whole new way to reach target audiences more efficiently (Reich, 1998:27). According to Duncan and Caywood (1996:15), in the mid-1970s in the United States of America, the cost of storing and retrieving a single name and address was about $1.50; today, it is less than one cent (US).

External trends

There are nine external situations in the marketplace that affect brand relationships and call for the development of more integrated forms of marketing communication:

1. **Decreasing message impact and credibility:** Sacharin (2001) suggests that not only are consumers becoming more insensitive to commercial messages, but the growing number of commercial messages also makes it increasingly difficult for a single message to have an effect. The reason for this trend is that people are overwhelmed by the explosive growth in the new media forms (Rice, 1995:1). Advertisements are everywhere – not just on television, radio and billboards, and in the print media, but also in bathrooms, on luggage, on taxis and even on fruit and vegetables. This ongoing bombardment of messages has desensitised people (Duncan & Everett, 1993:30). Sacharin (2001:ix) states that the constant 'noise' is leading to 'an entire

society with a form of attention deficit disorder'. It is more difficult than ever before for new messages to break through people's perceptual barriers because of this 'techno-splosion' (Chiocchi, 1999–2000:3).

2. **Increasing client expertise:** Clients are not only pressing on their agencies to be more cost-effective today, but are also no longer accepting the idea that television advertising should be the traditional medium to reach consumers (Duncan, 2001:29). At the same time, organisations are realising that besides customers, other stakeholders and publics are often just as important to communicate with (Rice, 1995:1; Kitchen & Schultz, 1999:21).

3. **Increasing 'mass' media costs:** While database costs were falling, increases in mass media costs far outpaced the consumer price index throughout most of the 1980s (Kitchen & Schultz, 1999:21). This trend has continued throughout the 1990s and into the new millennium (Duncan, 2001:278). Mass media endeavours are increasingly expensive, while database management remains cost-effective, with the added bonus of rapid development in technology, in spite of the low cost (Mader & Semenchuk, 1999–2000:2).

4. **Increasing media fragmentation:** Although the number of newspapers decreased, the number of radio stations, television stations and magazines increased between 1980 and 1990, thus increasing the competition for consumers' attention (Brody, 1994:20; Chiocchi, 1999–2000:3; Schultz, 1993b:20; Schultz et al., 1994:21). According to the Lord Group study (1999) – that won the ARF David Ogilvy Research Award – it took 38 years for radio to obtain 50 million users, 13 years for television to reach 50 million users, and only five years for the Internet to do the same. A process that used to be gradual has become accelerated in today's marketplace (Rice, 1995:1). Products introduced to the marketplace have a better opportunity to 'find their market' more quickly (Duncan & Caywood, 1996:15–16). While it is still the survival of the fittest, the gestation period has been shortened (Reich, 1998:27).

5. **Increasing audience fragmentation:** With the assistance of technology and more sophisticated research methods that resulted from technology, organisations have increasingly been able to segment and target specialised audiences such as teenagers, affluent retirees and emerging markets more accurately (Duncan & Caywood, 1996:15–16; Reich, 1998:27). In turn, this has placed more emphasis on finding media that can efficiently reach these niche markets (Rose & Miller, 1994:14).

6. **Misuse of new communication technology:** Computer-driven databases have made interactive, one-to-one marketing possible, moving away from mass marketing. The Internet, too, has opened up new lines of communication. There are also automated voice response systems and automated e-mail

responses. However, organisations often use these technologies at the customers' expense. For example, automated voice response systems often make callers move through various menus but do not offer them the option they desire. All of these new communication technologies are utilised to save organisations money and/or to increase sales efforts, with little regard for those doing the physical responding.

7. **Increasing number of 'me-too' products:** With the increased ability to analyse and match successful competitive products, manufacturers have continued to flood retailers with new products that are nearly identical to many already existing products on the shelves (Rice, 1995:1). The fact that many of the new products have few, if any, significant differences, means that marketing communication must either create a strong brand image or deliver enough commercial messages to gain attention and sales (Schultz, 1996:15; Reich, 1998:27).

8. **Increasing power of the retailer:** The power of the present retailers and the instant information provided by scanner data have resulted in retailers now having both the influence and knowledge to dictate to suppliers the kind of products and promotions they want and when they want them (Kitchen & Schultz, 1999:21). Most suppliers cannot afford not to co-operate (Duncan & Caywood, 1996:16; Rice, 1995:1).

9. **Increasing global marketing:** Nearly every major organisation is involved in global marketing in some way today. Even if an organisation is not selling outside its native country, it must be aware that its competitors will increasingly be foreign-based (Kitchen & Schultz, 1999:21). These changes underline the increase in competition and the necessity for organisations to concentrate on maximum efficiency in all their operations (Gonring, 2000–2001:2).

Based on internal and external trends, the collective trend regarding new ways of communicating in business is towards integrity. One of the most important changes in society in recent years is the increasing demand for integrity in the business world. In an era of customer and other stakeholder distrust, increasing the perception of a brand's integrity is essential (Paine, 1994:107). Integration produces integrity since an organisation that is seen as a 'whole', rather than as a collection of autonomous pieces and parts, is perceived as being more sound and trustworthy, a prerequisite for sustaining relationships. Integrity also has a nuance that connects with values and moral principles, characteristics for any brand that is concerned with social responsibility. In order to guarantee such integrity, it is the duty of the organisation to ensure that there is consistency between what it says, does and promises.

The concept of integration in marketing communication and in the entire organisation is in tune with these trends. Ten years ago, the business world was not quite ready to embrace the principles of integrated marketing communication, but as the marketplace has developed over the past decade, so IMC has grown in stature (Gonring, 2000–2001). In a business environment where all these trends affect the operations of the marketing communicator, following the IMC principles of knowing the customer, building the brand and measuring effectiveness can put organisations ahead of their competitors. For organisations that currently embrace IMC, these trends translate into opportunities. The highly competitive marketplace has made relationship building paramount in the operations of an organisation. It is through relationship building that IMC can strategically place the organisation in this changing marketplace, since it is the best way to communicate more directly with individual consumers and customers.

To be able to achieve total integration in the environment sketched above, the organisation needs to evolve through various levels of integrated marketing communication. These levels are discussed in the following section.

Multiple levels of integrated marketing communication

Organisations facing changing markets and societal expectations have to re-examine their organisational structure and processes. They must undertake some form of re-engineering, restructuring, transformation or realignment to equip them better to respond to these changes (Smith, 1993:17).

The approach to organisational integration outlined below follows an evolutionary process. The process assumes that organisations can integrate their marketing communication activities over time. It also assumes that managers will gain experience at each stage, permitting them to increase the level of performance. IMC begins at an awareness level and may advance through several stages to a general integration of new ways of conducting business. Duncan and Caywood (1996:21–33) suggest a model with seven stages to indicate the various stages an organisation has to go through in order to be fully integrated. These are:

1. awareness

2. image integration

3. functional integration

4. co-ordinated integration

5. consumer-based integration

6. stakeholder-based integration

7. relationship management integration.

At each stage of the model, the communication strengths and weaknesses of each medium are weighed and balanced to create the best mix. A fully integrated strategy will permit each form of communication to contribute to the success of the corporate mission.

Stage one of integration – awareness

The first stage of integration is awareness. Awareness of the changing business environments – social, technological, political and cultural – creates the demand for new business systems to respond to the market. The trends already discussed have contributed to management's recognition that these changes force marketing managers to adapt to the new marketplace. Awareness assumes that change reinforces the opportunity for developing an integrated management and marketing system. Caywood (1998:xvi) states that while most managers caution their consultants and programme speakers about these marketplace trends – 'Don't tell me that the market has changed, tell me what to do about it', organisations can still be ignorant about specific changes in the market or trends they do not recognise. For instance, car manufacturers in the United States developed round cup holders for drinks consumed in transit. While this boded well for industries marketing drinks packaged in round containers, and that were suited to travel, it presented challenges for competing products that did not share these characteristics. Dairy products did not meet these demands and, in the United States, have been slow to create packaging to suit the needs and lifestyles of consumers, which developed with the advent of automotive cup holders. While car manufacturers fought for the greatest number of cup holders in their products, the dairy industry neither responded with rounded packaging that suited the cup holders, nor did it offer packaging that performed satisfactorily (by remaining cold) when travelling. Having square pegs for round holes, the dairy industry involuntarily competed with juice and other cold-drink manufacturers.

This awareness stage of integration in integrated marketing communication forces an assessment of the changes in the environment and provides the motivation for a more integrated approach. For example, each of the increasing number of media alternatives – from compact disc, audio tape, Internet and interactive point-of-purchase coupons to still traditional print and video – must be constantly assessed for its possible contribution to an organisation's management and communication programmes (Gronstedt, 2000:8). The basic shift in market power, taste, access and diversity demands new organisational strategies and tactics to communicate with customers and to establish new relationships with customers and other stakeholders.

Stage two of integration – image integration

The second stage towards a more completely integrated organisation is the integration of the organisation's image. According to Duncan and Caywood (1996:21–33), Sirgy (1998:6–7) and Caywood (1998:xv–xxiv), stage two of integration recognises the value of having a consistent message, look and feel for an organisation. Organisations focus in this early stage of IMC on the importance of having common colours, graphics and logo treatments throughout the organisation's communication materials. Within those organisations that define integrated marketing communication to mean a common look, the approach to IMC planning can be described as follows: a centralised or corporate group gives guidelines, and the makers of all communication materials are asked to develop their materials accordingly. Thorson and Moore (1996:137) refer to this approach as the 'one look' approach.

Efforts to integrate logically focus initially on the appearance of integration or the lack of integration. For example, for many years IBM has placed its focus on the precise representation of the IBM logo. The appearance of the logo in appropriate communication vehicles (brochures, advertising, media stories) was controlled by IBM communication professionals. As the organisation expanded its relationships with what IBM calls 'IBM partners' or business allies, the use of the logo was closely monitored to control the way in which IBM product resellers and service organisations used it (Caywood, 1992:31). Another company that achieves a successful 'one look' is Nandos – from its menus, to packaging, to clothes that staff wear. The corporate image reflected in the icons of trademarks and corporate symbols can be an important element of consistency in the look of communication. However, the tone of the message and the quality of the message production across the media are also important. Potential criticism of this stage of integration is that it is as a relatively superficial level of integration (Duncan & Everett, 1993:33).

Stage three of integration – functional integration

Stage three moves the process of integration to a greater degree of involvement among the still traditionally separated areas of communication responsibilities. The process of integration at this stage begins with a strategic analysis of the strengths and weaknesses of each of the functional communication areas, including – but not limited to – public relations, advertising, sales promotion, sponsorship and direct marketing. For example, public relations permits a product/service or organisation to use third-party credibility with careful targeting and placement of newsworthy stories in the media. Advertising (with sufficient budget) allows a message to be repeated. Promotional marketing may capture the consumer at the point of purchase better than other communication, while direct marketing permits constant testing of various offers to the consumer. Strategic exercises – such as planning and developing programmes that are a link between the organisation's goals and capabilities and changing marketing opportunities – may be developed within a cross-functional team to identify in detail the strengths and weaknesses of each area, according to the specific project to be marketed. Drawing from each functional area of communication allows the practitioner to develop tactics to meet the goals of the marketing team. For example, with the introduction of the new Volkswagen Beetle, Volkswagen won early support of key auto trade and business media by inviting them to participate in background sessions on the car during the pre-production stage. The car was introduced using video news releases and interactive satellite feeds that resulted in 800 individual television segments in the United States. Such media coverage provided a powerful third-party endorsement that was then merchandised with clever advertising tag lines such as 'Less flower. More power.' (Wilcox et al., 2000:311).

According to Caywood (1998:xviii), this integrated stage of functional integration seems to be most controversial with the communication professionals who manage the still separated activities of the traditional promotional mix elements. A national study commissioned by the American Association of National Advertising Agencies and the Association of National Advertisers in the United States in 1990 found that one of the significant barriers to integrated marketing and communication was the so-called functional silos. As a result of years of 'command and control' management (Duncan & Moriarty, 1997:35), these organisations consist of highly separated departments and divisions, each being assigned a certain function in the overall process. As organisations grow, the problem of integration worsens because departments are further subdivided in order to maintain accountability and control. The 'threat' of a more integrated strategy to communication was the pressure to join strategies, programmes and budgets for the overall benefit of the organisation and its stakeholders and shareholders (Caywood et al., 1991:5).

Stage four of integration – co-ordinated integration

At the fourth stage of integrated marketing communication, all the communication functions are equal in their potential to contribute to the marketing effort. Each functional specialty recognises that it must co-operate in the development of a communication programme or risk not participating at all. Shared budgets, shared performance measures and outcomes rule the process. For example, IBM found that its communication agencies followed an all-or-nothing approach to the campaign budget until the organisation redirected the agencies to integrate their plans and tactics before presenting their ideas to the firm's managers (Caywood, 1992:12).

This stage of the marketing effort accentuates personal selling. Personal selling and the sales management process are emphasised in the function as their connection to the customer and marketing becomes more direct. For example, direct mail can be helpful in cultivating individualised relationships with customers, although it is important to supplement postal mail with faster, electronic forms of interaction to enable customers to make more immediate contact with the marketer (Peppers & Rogers, 1999:105). The interpersonal communication aspect of the selling process is included in the integrated plan. This also refers to the idea of relationship marketing – that it is important to know what the customer wants out of a relationship with the organisation. In business-to-business marketing and consumer marketing, a key marketing objective is to develop a communication strategy that increases the customer's tendency to buy with several carefully directed communication tactics, and uses the best communication tools (Hayes, 1994:34). This refers to the concept of communication by objectives. Communication drives relationships or, as Duncan and Moriarty (1997:9) put it: '… the fuel that drives relationships – personal or commercial – is communication'. It is also important to note that, according to the relationship marketing theory, with every interaction, the organisation must have specific and different objectives.

Also evident in this stage may be elements of an emerging database. The database may initially consist of simple and accurate contact information, including names, titles, addresses and e-mail addresses, as well as phone and fax numbers. As the database is strengthened through marketing-driven contacts, information about past purchases, competitive purchases, capital expenditures and service expenses is added. Also included are details of what forms of communication the customer responds to.

Stage five of integration – consumer-based integration

As each step of integration is mastered and accepted, the elements begin to work together. The original objectives of integration – to manage the marketing communication process more efficiently by wasting fewer resources – become a matter of practising greater marketing effectiveness. In consumer-based integration, only the most important consumers of the organisation are reached with the strongest and most effective media and through the most precise channels of communication. In a more fully developed marketing communication process, the customer and consumers are rediscovered, as marketing is planned from the outside-in, as opposed to the inside-out approach (Lauterborn, 1999:13; Reich, 1998:29). Both customers and prospective customers/consumers are included in the formula.

The lessons learned from earlier stages of integration document the value of a refined customer and prospect database. Experience with sales and communication information, combined with marketing research, increases predictions as to a prospect's readiness to buy. Attitudinal data related to business trends, collected through surveys of customers and prospects, may add insight about the customer.

The consumer's contact with the brand and organisation is carefully uncovered in this stage of integration. Each contact point, whether initiated by the customer or the organisation, is identified. For example, all customer contacts with an airline – from the travel agent, to the baggage handler and counter service representative, as well as experience with airport signage, airplane cleanliness, on-time flights, safety and so on – are considered part of the contact points with the airline. Each point of contact is a message, a form of marketing communication that reinforces the customer's business opinion of the organisation (Duncan, 1997).

Carefully collected behavioural data recording the customer's and prospect's response to marketing communication can assist the marketer to plan better. Eventually, the database may reveal the buying stage or readiness to buy of the prospective customer (Schultz, 1995:5).

Rather than constantly replacing customers – following the leaking bucket theory (Peppers & Rogers, 1999:6) which proposes that there are always enough customers to replace defecting ones – attention is given to holding and building the correct customer base in this stage of integration. Issues of customer loyalty are examined as organisations create a marketing plan that builds and maintains relationships with current customers. An organisation should therefore focus more on the retention of current customers than on the acquisition of new customers, which is in accordance with the outside-in approach (Duncan, 2001:62). Increased customer satisfaction and subsequent increased purchases are the goals in this stage of integrated marketing communication (Duncan & Caywood, 1996:30).

Stage six of integration – stakeholder-based integration

The evolution of integration suggests that the success of each stage may lead to new dimensions in the next stage. Beyond the customer and consumer are numerous publics and stakeholders that have a stake in the outcome of the success or failure of an organisation. Integrated marketing communication moves to a more broadly defined integrated communication, as it expands the communication to other stakeholders, including employees, the community, the government, the press, vendors and suppliers, and all individuals or groups which can affect or be affected by the organisation.

In the advanced stages of integration, public relations (PR) plays a more dominant role (Caywood, 1998:xxii). Public relations is the management, through communication, of perceptions and strategic relationships between an organisation and its internal and external stakeholders (PRISA, 2000). This accentuated role of PR at advanced levels occurs because PR is the active management of the relationships that organisations have with stakeholders. As such, it has led to the development of what is referred to as marketing PR. While the attention to stakeholders other than customers or consumers is practised at many levels of integration, the full benefit of a mature integrated process can be applied at this stage of integration (Stepanek, 1999:30).

The concept of stakeholder management is an advanced approach in management and public relations to understanding how organisations relate to a rich mix of individuals and groups. Those organisations and individuals can be approached with the same level of targeted intensity as customers who are targeted by using database systems previously built for marketing. For example, the ability to reach investors quickly under conditions of a takeover or bid for an organisation can be more easily accomplished with data from data organisations, such as Georgeson in the United States. The organisation provides subscription or list services of shareholders, with or without the street name designation, to appeal directly to the shareholders (Burnett & Moriarty, 1998:196).

Integrated communication begins with careful stakeholder identification, with hundreds of possible groups and individuals being labelled as important to the future success of the organisation. The process demands that managers or staff be 'assigned' to each stakeholder group to monitor and track their actions relevant to the firm (Reich, 1998:27).

Stage seven of integration – relationship management integration

The development of a fully integrated communication strategy to reach customers and stakeholders brings the communication professional into direct contact with the full range of management functions in businesses and other complex organisations. Integration implies – and a managerial approach to communication demands – that communication be regarded as a strong element in the total management process. The process has become a full range of relationship management, both internally and externally (Duncan & Moriarty, 1997:11; Schultz, 2000:14).

In general, the fully integrative model should place communication professionals at management level and redefine their roles from staff to management. Thus, there is a definite shift from integration at a 'technical' level to integration at a 'strategic' level. This shift is in line with the definitions of integrated marketing communication presented by Keegan et al. (1992) and Gronstedt (2000), which stress the importance of strategic thinking in IMC.

Each stage of integration contributes to the performance of communication in the management process. As integration is proven both internally and externally to be a logical framework for managing the communication and relationships of an organisation, it will prove to be an integral part of the management effort.

Case study

British Airways (BA)

BA is an example of a company that utilises IMC successfully. A consistent approach is to communicate through various communication vehicles. BA's advertising campaigns use a variety of media (beyond the promotional mix only) such as television, radio, print, outdoor, CD-ROM, banner ads, and a website. For example, a recent campaign used various media to focus on the world's first fully flat, full-size bed for BA's Club World and first class passengers. Traditional mass media were used to create general awareness about the new benefits of the fully extendable seat. Brochures were distributed to all major travel agencies, as well as to existing members of BA's Executive Club. At the same time, their website supported the campaign by providing detailed information. In addition, sales promotions were aimed at Executive Club members, whereby they could win two Club World return tickets to London and other specials if they made use of the new product offering. This was over and above their frequent flier miles offer for loyal customers. Fold-out, life-size posters were also incorporated into the campaign.

BA also targets specific consumers through direct marketing techniques. Here it is able to personalise the message sent. Niche publications (specific travel magazines) are also included in the communication bouquet. In addition, BA has its own magazine for Club members only, as well as an in-flight magazine. Club members can also obtain an electronic ticket by utilising the call centre. This ensures too that the traveller receives a telephone check-in the day before departure.

The corporate identity is used consistently through all communication. The logo is found on all points of contact – from BA's buildings to adverts to brochures. 'The world's favourite airline' is also used in a consistent manner. BA's marketing department reflects an IMC philosophy as the team consists of various functional specialists such as:

▲ business and relationship managers

▲ e-business roles

▲ sponsorship

▲ customer relations

▲ communication and project management.

Furthermore, BA believes in creating long-term relationships, thus focusing on retention of existing customers through the development and effective use of a database and relationship marketing efforts. Products and services in World Traveller, Club World, First, World Traveller Plus and the Executive Club ensure that different customers are treated differently, depending on their monetary worth to BA and the needs of the consumer. The BA Executive database consists of more than one million customers.

Conclusion

A totally integrated communication programme comprises *all* types of messages, synergised to achieve maximum communication impact. Therefore, every contact point that a stakeholder has with an organisation is a communication opportunity.

The various messages need to be related to each other in a coherent way and should come together by applying consistency and interactivity, and by using the company's mission to guide all communication.

The following quotes provided in Shimp (2003:6) capture the essence of IMC:

The marketer who succeeds in the new environment will be the one who coordinates the communication mix so tightly that you can look from ... medium to medium, from programme event to programme event, and instantly see that the brand is speaking with one voice.

The basic reason for integrated marketing communications is that marketing communications has been and will be the only sustainable competitive advantage of marketing organisations in the 1990s and the 21st century.

Questions for self-evaluation

1. How do the terms *marketing, promotional mix, communication mix* and *marketing mix* relate to each other?

2. Why is a marketing communication orientation better than a promotional mix orientation?

3. How has the concept IMC evolved over time?

4. What are key characteristics of IMC?

5. How have various authors contributed to a final definition for IMC?

6. How would you define IMC? Why?

7. Why has there been a shift from the 4Ps to the 4Cs?

8. What are the differences between traditional marketing communication and integrated marketing communication?

9. What are the ten drivers of brand relationships?

10. What trends, both inside and outside organisations, have made relationship building a critical element of any organisation's success?

11. How does the IMC seven stages model work?

12. Why can BA be regarded as a company that practises IMC?

References

Aakar, DA and Biel, AL 1993. *Brand Equity and Advertising*. Hillside, NJ: Lawrence Erlbaum.

Achrol, RS 1991. Evolution of the marketing organisation: New forms for turbulent environments. In *Journal of Marketing,* 77–93.

Anon. 1999. In brief. In *PR and Communications Africa,* 6(2):5.

Bennett, PD 1995. *Dictionary of Marketing Terms*. Chicago: American Marketing Association.

Brody, EW 1994. PR is to experience what marketing is to expectations. In *Public Relations Quarterly,* 39(2):20–23.

Burnett, J and Moriarty, S 1998. *Introduction to Marketing Communication: An Integrated Approach*. Upper Saddle River: Prentice Hall.

Caywood, C; Schultz, DE and Wang, P 1991. Integrated marketing communications: A survey of national consumer goods advertising. Northwestern University report.

Caywood, CL 1992. Integrated marketing communications: A competitive weapon in today's marketplace. In *Marketing Review,* 45(29):30–32.

Caywood, CL 1998. *The Handbook of Strategic Public Relations and Integrated Communications*. New York: McGraw-Hill.

Chiocchi, R 1999–2000. Inductive vs. deductive marketing: The paradigm shift. In *Journal of Integrated Communications*. Website: http://www.medill.nwu.edu. imc.studentwork.pubs/jic/journal/1999-2000/chiocchi.htm (Date of access: 5 June 2001.)

Cornelissen, JP 2000. Theoretical concept of management fashion? Examining the significance of IMC. In *Journal of Advertising Research,* 40(5):7–16.

Cross, R 1998. *Customer Bonding: Pathway to Lasting Customer Loyalty.* Lincolnwood: NTC.

Duncan, T 1997. Integrated marketing communication. Unpublished paper delivered as part of the course on IMC at Rand Afrikaans University. Johannesburg: RAU.

Duncan, T tduncan@colorado.edu 2001. Discussion of possible sources. (E-mail to Niemann, I. in@lw.rau.ac.za June 12.)

Duncan, T 2001. *IMC. Using Advertising and Promotion to Build Brands.* New York: McGraw-Hill.

Duncan, T and Caywood, C 1996. The concept, process and evolution of integrated marketing communications. In *Integrated Communications: Synergy of Persuasive Voices.* Thorson, E and Moore, J (Eds.) Hillside: Erlbaum.

Duncan, T and Everett, SE 1993. Client perceptions of integrated marketing communications. In *Journal of Advertising Research,* 33(3):30–39.

Duncan, T and Moriarty, S 1997. *Driving Brand Value: Using Integrated Marketing to Manage Profitable Stakeholder Relationships.* New York: McGraw-Hill.

Evans, M and Moutinho, L 1999. *Contemporary Issues in Marketing.* London: Macmillan.

Gonring, MP 2000–2001. Global megatrends push IMC concepts to forefront of strategic business thinking. In *Journal of Integrated Communications.* Website: http://www.medill.nwu.edu/imc/studentwork/pubs/jic/journal/2000/gonring.htm (Date of access: 5 June 2001.)

Gronstedt, A 2000. *The Customer Century. Lessons from World-class Companies in Integrated Marketing and Communications.* New York: Routledge.

Harris, TL 1998. *Value-added Public Relations. The Secret Weapon of Integrated Marketing.* Lincolnwood: NTC Business Books.

Hayes, HB 1994. The agency-within-an-agency approach swells in ad shops. In *Washington Business Journal,* 13(11):34.

Howard, CM 1997–1998. Marketing communications: Teamwork and sophisticated sequencing will maximize results. In *Public Relations Quarterly,* 42(4):23–26.

Keegan, W; Moriarty, S and Duncan, T 1992. *Marketing.* Englewood Cliffs: Prentice Hall.

Kitchen, PJ 1999. *Marketing Communications: Principles and Practice.* London: International Thomson Business Press.

Kitchen, PJ and Schultz, DE 1999. A multi-country comparison of the drive for IMC. In *Journal of Advertising Research*, 39(1):21–42.

Koekemoer, L 1998. *Promotional Strategy. Marketing Communications in Practice*. Kenwyn: Juta.

Lauterborn, RF 1999. Truly integrated marcomm inevitable in new millennium. In *Advertising Age's Business Marketing,* 84(11):13–14.

Low, GS 2000. Correlates of integrated marketing communications. In *Journal of Advertising Research,* 40(3):27–40.

Mader, R and Semenchuk, J 1999–2000. From production to connection: The new model for market organization. In *Journal of Integrated Communications.* Website: http://www.medill.nwu.edu/imc/studentwork/pubs/jic/journal/1999-2000/maderandsemenchuk.htm (Date of access: 5 June 2001.)

Olwagen, N 2001. Verbal communication with the author. Johannesburg.

Paine, LS 1994. Managing for organizational integrity. In *Harvard Business Review,* 12:105–117.

Pelsmacker, PD; Geuens, M and Van Den Bergh, J 2001. *Marketing Communications*. Essex: Pearson Education Limited.

Peppers, D and Rogers, M 1999. The short way to long-term relationships. In *Sales and Marketing Management,* 151(5):24–26.

PRISA 2000. Code of professional standards for the practice of public relations. In *PR & Communications Africa,* 6(2):41.

Reich, K 1998. IMC: Through the looking glass. In *Communications World,* 15(9):26–29.

Rice, B 1995. The new face of marketing. Website: http://www.researchsurveys.co.za/papers/newface.htm (Date of access: 22 September 2000.)

Rose, PB and Miller, DA 1994. Integrated communications: A look at reality instead of theory. In *Public Relations Quarterly,* 13–16.

Rotzoll, KB and Haefner, JE 1996. *Advertising in Contemporary Society. Perspectives toward Understanding.* Urbana: University of Illinois Press.

Sacharin, K 2001. *Attention. How to Interrupt, Yell, Whisper and Touch Customers*. New York: John Wiley & Sons.

Schultz, DE 1993a. Maybe we should start all over with an IMC organization. In *Marketing News,* 27(22):8.

Schultz, DE 1993b. We simply can't afford to go back to mass marketing. In *Marketing News,* 27(4):20.

Schultz, DE 1995. It's the data-base question time of year. In *Marketing News,* 29(8):5–6.

Schultz, DE 1996. Be careful picking database for IMC efforts. In *Marketing News,* 30(6):14–17.

Schultz, DE 2000. Maxims for maximum customer relations. In *Marketing News,* June 5:14.

Schultz, DE; Tannenbaum, SI and Lauterborn, RF 1994. *The New Marketing Paradigm. Integrated Marketing Communications*. Lincolnwood: NTC Business Books.

Senge, PM 1990. *The Fifth Discipline: The Art and Practice of the Learning Organization*. New York: Doubleday Currency.

Shimp, TA 2003. *Advertising, Promotion and Supplemental Aspects of Integrated Marketing Communications*. Ohio: Thomson.

Sirgy, MJ 1998. *Integrated Marketing Communications: A Systems Approach*. Upper Saddle River: Prentice Hall.

Smith, PR 1993. *Marketing Communications. An Integrated Approach*. London: Clays.

Spotts, HE and Lambert, DR 1998. Marketing déjà vu: The discovery of integrated marketing communications. In *Journal of Marketing Education,* 20(3):210–219.

Stepanek, M 1999. Effective relationship links in consumer marketing. In *Business Week,* 22:30–31.

Stewart, DW 1996. Market-back approach to the design of integrated communication programmes: A change in paradigm and a focus on determinants of success. In *Journal of Business Research,* 37(3):147–153.

Swan, A 1993. One-stop debate. In *Marketing,* April 1: 42–43.

Tannenbaum, S 1991. Integrated marketing communication: Outside perspectives. In *Sales & Marketing Strategies & News,* 59(1):3–7.

Thorson, E and Moore, J 1996. *Integrated Communications. Synergy of Persuasive Voices*. Chicago: Lawrence Erlbaum Associates.

Wilcox, DL; Ault, PH; Agee, WK and Cameron, GT 2000. *Public Relations Strategies and Tactics*. New York: Longman.

Wolter, L 1993. Superficiality, ambiguity threaten IMC's implementation and future. In *Advertising Age,* 27(19):12–13.

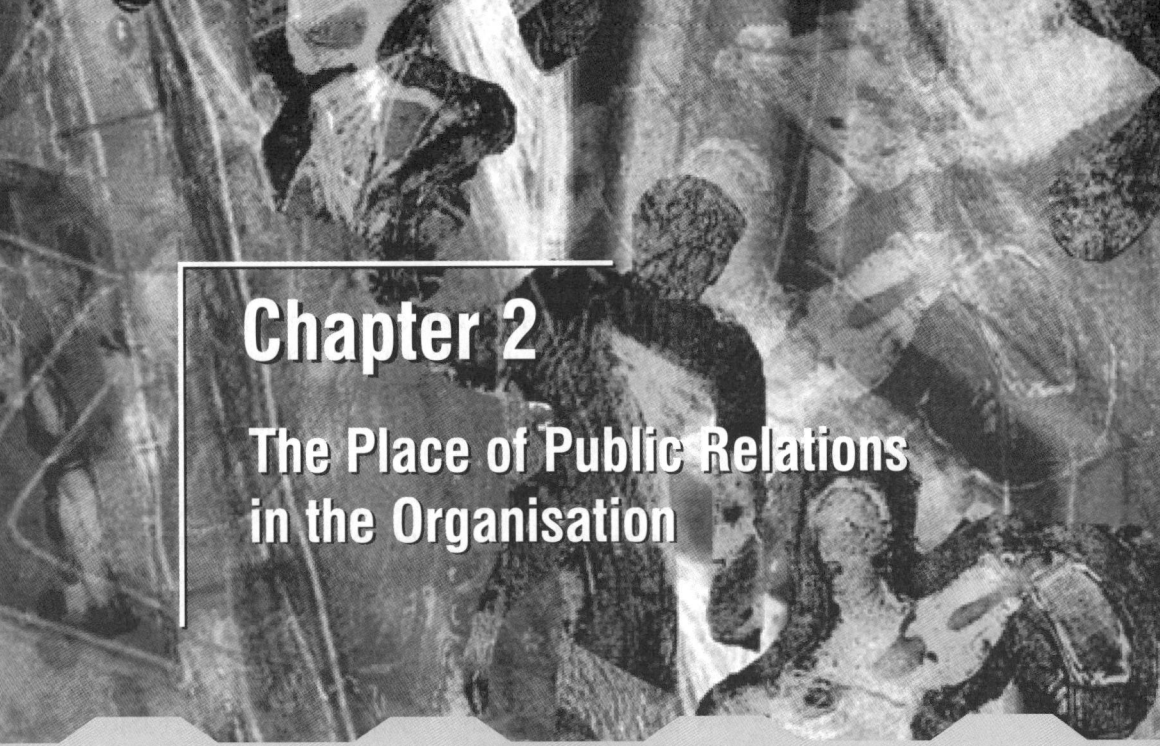

Chapter 2

The Place of Public Relations in the Organisation

LEARNING OUTCOMES

After studying this chapter, you should be able to:

▲ define what is meant by public relations

▲ explain the role of public relations

▲ discuss how public relations evolved over time

▲ discuss public relations in terms of the other management functions in the organisation

▲ describe the public relations process

▲ discuss the place of public relations in the organisation.

Introduction

People establish and maintain relationships with others. These relationships require varying degrees of interaction and interdependence and, therefore, different levels of social, political and economic exchanges. Modern society consists of increasingly interdependent, complex, and often conflict-laden relationships.

Human relations and *interpersonal relations* describe the study and management of relations among *individuals*. *International relations* deals with relationships among *nations*. *Public relations* applies when the area of concern is the relationships of an *organisation* with others.[1]

The term *public relations* is used to refer to many things, and it does not always conform to the concise definitions which exist for it. This chapter defines public relations (PR), reviews the evolution of public relations, discusses the nature and role of public relations, and defines the place of public relations in the organisation.

Defining public relations[2]

Public relations is found in every company and institution, irrespective of whether or not the company or institution wants it. The aim should always be to establish good public relations, which work positively for the company.

Public relations affects almost everyone who has contact with other people. All of us, in one way or another, practise public relations daily. For an organisation, every phone call, every letter, every face-to-face encounter, is a public relations event. As the field has increased in prominence, so has it also grown in professional stature. While the primary objective of marketing is to sell an organisation's products and services, the primary objective of public relations is to market the company itself.

The main focus of advertising, as a paid form of communication, is to sell the products of a company. In the case of public relations, what is said about a company and its products cannot be bought; it must be earned. The credibility derived from sound public relations work may far exceed that gained through paid advertising.

Definitions of public relations will always differ, but all agree that good public relations requires a firm base of theoretical knowledge, a strong sense of ethical judgement, solid communication skills and, above all, an uncompromising attitude of professionalism.

What, then, is public relations? Many people seem to have a fairly good idea, but few seem to agree. The reason for the confusion is understandable. It results largely from the fact that the scope of activities taken on by public relations professionals is limitless. The duties performed by public relations practitioners in one organisation will in all likelihood be quite different from those of a practitioner in another organisation, even though both are engaged in the practice of public relations.

In 1923, Edward Bernays described the functions of a public relations practitioner as 'information given to the public, persuasion directed at the public to modify attitudes and actions, and efforts to integrate attitudes and actions of an institution with its publics and of publics with those of that institution'. Today, although a generally accepted definition of public relations still eludes practitioners, there is a clearer understanding of the field.

The traditional definition of public relations

While a variety of books define public relations, perhaps the most comprehensive definition is that offered by the *Public Relations News*:[3]

> [Public relations is] the management function which evaluates public attitudes, identifies the policies and procedures of an organisation with the public interest, and executes a program of action (and communication) to earn public understanding and acceptance.

As per the definition, public relations is a management function. Management should be used in its broadest sense, in that it is not limited only to business management but also includes other types of organisations and extends to profit and non-profit institutions and organisations.

This definition of public relations defines a process that requires a series of stages, including:

▲ the determination and evaluation of public attitudes

▲ the identification of policies and procedures of organisations with a public interest

▲ the development and execution of a communications programme designed to bring about public understanding and acceptance.

It is clear from the above that this process does not take place at just one point in time. A continuous effort is required if an effective public relations programme is to be established.

This definition also indicates that public relations is more than selling a product or service. The public relations programme may (and should) involve some of the promotional programme elements, but may use them in a different way and for a different purpose. For example, a social responsibility programme may be announced by means of a press release, which is mailed to all the major media, whereas special events at schools may be organised to create goodwill in the community, while advertising may be used to explain an organisation's view on socially or politically sensitive issues.

The definition adapted by the Public Relations Institute of Southern Africa (PRISA) resembles the above definition in that it describes the role of public relations:[4]

> Public relations is the deliberate, planned and sustained effort to establish and maintain mutual understanding between the organisation and its various publics – both internal and external.

More recently, in 2002, the following definition was adapted by PRISA:

> Public relations is the management through communication of perceptions and strategic relationships between an organisation and its internal and external stakeholders.

The first definition contains the following key terms or concepts: deliberate, planned, sustained, establish, maintain, mutual understanding, publics, internal and external. Each of these concepts or terms is discussed below.

▲ **Deliberate**

All public relations efforts are deliberate efforts at achieving the specific aims of an organisation. The areas in which these aims are to be achieved are clearly defined, as are the publics they are aimed at. The messages are carefully evaluated in terms of the overall aims of the organisation.

Public relations is a process of communicating deliberately with target publics. It seeks to receive feedback from its target publics and creates the relationship deliberately.

▲ **Planned**

The nature of public relations ensures that activities are meticulously planned to address all relevant problems or issues and to take appropriate steps to solve them. Many companies have specific crisis plans in action to cover eventualities that may have grave consequences if not addressed properly. These plans, as well as any other plans, must involve a conscious evaluation of all spheres of the organisation's activities that may have a bearing on its reputation. These plans must consider the short-, medium- and long-term objectives of the company.

▲ **Sustained**

For public relations to be meaningful and effective, a continuous analysis of the environment and the ways to communicate with the market is required. Once the communication process has been initiated and established between an organisation and its publics, it must be maintained, which necessitates a sustained effort from the organisation. First contacts are seldom successful, which emphasises the need for sustainability.

▲ **Establish**

The primary aim of public relations is to establish a climate of mutual understanding between an organisation and its publics – new or existing.

▲ **Maintain**

It is essential that once a positive relationship has been established, it be maintained. As the environment in which businesses operate is ever changing, any positive perception that exists must be nurtured and maintained over time. Maintaining the relationship implies that the organisation must listen to the feedback received from target publics and act upon it.

▲ **Mutual understanding**

For communication to be effective between an organisation and its target publics, it is essential that they understand each in the way it was meant to be. In this way, agreement and harmony can be reached and a positive relationship can be built.

▲ **Publics**

Any group that influences an organisation or its operations, or that is important to an organisation, is regarded as a public. These groups can be either internal or external or both.

▲ **Internal and external**

The internal publics of an organisation are usually its employees and the external publics are groups outside the organisation such as unions, financial institutions, the media, shareholders, and the community.

The role of public relations

Traditionally the role of public relations in an organisation was to focus on communicating with the publics and to maintain good relationships with them. Today, public relations has taken on a broader role. Part of its function, where possible, is to market the organisation's products and services. This role is more apparent in smaller companies that have a small marketing/public relations budget.

In larger companies there is a tendency for the marketing and public relations departments to work more closely together. The higher the synergy that exists in these departments, the better the cumulative effect will be in the organisation.

Integrating public relations into the promotional mix

A challenge for many companies is to integrate all the elements of the marketing mix (product, price, promotion and distribution) and public relations. Smaller companies usually accommodate public relations as part of promotion or marketing communication, while larger companies form a separate department for the public relations function. A number of alternative organisational designs are possible: either marketing or public relations is the dominant function, or both have equal but separate functions, or the two perform the same roles. While each of these designs has its merits, in this text we consider public relations as a promotional programme element. This means that, while a broader role is defined, traditional responsibilities must still be assumed.

Public relations involves relationships with all of an organisation's relevant publics. In other words, most PR activities do not involve marketing per se but rather deal with general management concerns. This more encompassing aspect of public relations can be called general PR. Interactions with employees, stockholders, labour groups, citizen action groups, and suppliers are typically part of a company's general, non-marketing public relations.[5]

Public relations as part of the marketing mix can be used effectively in various ways. In the area of product introductions or product revisions, it is integrated with other marketing elements to give a product additional exposure, newsworthiness, and credibility. While advertising and personal selling claims are sometimes dubious, product announcements by a newspaper editor or television broadcaster are notably more believable. Consumers are less likely to question the motivation underlying an editorial-type endorsement.

Like advertising and personal selling, the main purposes of marketing-oriented publicity are to enhance a brand's equity in a twofold manner: first, by facilitating brand awareness and, second, by augmenting brand image by forging strong and favourable associations with the brand in consumer's minds. For example, Isuzu intended its brand to be perceived as caring and compassionate through its alliance with the Mozambique government, in its efforts to rid the country of guns and mines which are still hoarded in the rural areas.

Organisations obtain publicity using various forms of news releases, press conferences, and other types of information dissemination. They usually forward information on new products, large export contracts, technological breakthroughs, and so on, to news editors who decide on its newsworthiness and if it will be published. Press conferences announce major news events of interest to the public. Photographs, tapes, and films are useful to emphasise any of these newsworthy items and to enhance their impact. In the final analysis, the decision to publish the information or not rests with the media itself but, by increasing the volume and quality of information to the media, the chances of it being published are greatly enhanced.

Negative publicity can hit a company at any time. The lesson to be learned is that quick and positive responses to negative publicity are imperative. Negative publicity is something to be dealt with head-on, not denied. When done effectively, publicity can virtually save a brand or a company. A corporate response immediately following negative publicity can lessen the inevitable loss in sales.

The evolution of public relations

Public relations is much younger than many other disciplines. The relative youthfulness of the practice means that the field is still evolving, and its status is continuously improving. Indeed, the professionals entering the practice today are by and large superior in training and even experience to their counterparts decades ago.

> The strength of the practice of public relations today is based on the enduring commitment of the public to participate in a free and open democratic society. At least four trends are related to the evolution of public relations: first, the growth of large corporate institutions; second, the nature of change and conflict internationally and locally, and of confrontation in society; third, the heightened awareness and sophistication of people everywhere as a result of technological innovations in communications; and fourth, the increased importance of public opinion in the twenty-first century for positive democratic means.[6]

Each of these trends are discussed in more detail in section 3.5.

Developments in public relations

1. The **size** of today's society has played a significant role in the development of public relations. The days of the mom and pop grocery store, the tiny community college, and the small local bank are rapidly disappearing. In their place have emerged mass marts, home depots, and super stores, etc. As institutions have grown larger, the public relations profession has evolved to interpret these large institutions to the publics they serve.

2. The increasing incidence of **change, conflict, and confrontation** in society is another reason for the evolution of public relations. Women's rights, gay rights, animal rights, consumerism and environmental awareness; down-sizings and layoffs, and the resultant

unhappiness with large institutions; and the extraordinary growing impact of the Internet and cyberspace have all contributed materially to the need for more and better communications, and to the existence of more and better communicators.

3. Another factor in the development of public relations has been the **heightened awareness** of people everywhere. First came the invention of the printing press. Later followed the pervasiveness of mass communications: the print media, radio, and television. Then came the development of cable, satellite, videotape, video discs, video typewriters, portable cameras, word processors, fax machines, the World Wide Web, and all the other communications technologies that have assisted in fragmenting audiences and in creating Marshall McLuhan's 'global village'.

4. In a world where the image of a lone protester blocking a line of tanks in Beijing's Tiananmen Square can be flashed around the world to be seen on the evening news; where the September 11 horror attack in New York can be witnessed in real time by people in their living rooms around the world; where a dictator in the Persian Gulf can be interviewed live by a reporter in Washington; there can be no doubt that the **communications revolution** has arrived.

5. Finally, the adoption of democracy in Latin America, Eastern Europe, the former Soviet Union, and South Africa has heightened public opinion throughout the world. Just as increasing numbers of people made their voices heard through the civil rights movements, various consumer movements, the women's rights movement, and political movements throughout the ages, so too have oppressed peoples around the world risen up and spoken out. Accordingly, the practice of public relations – as a facilitator in understanding more clearly and managing more effectively in the midst of such democratic revolution – has increased in prominence.

(*Source:* Adapted from Seitel, FP 2001. *The practice of public relations.* Prentice Hall:23–25.)

Early history of public relations[7]

Public relations has evolved over many years to become a discipline, but only recently – in the last century – has it received more prominence in the corporate world. However, this does not mean that the application of public relations principles, in an unsophisticated form, did not exist. In fact, these types of principles have been with humankind for thousands of years in different ways.

Efforts to communicate with others and to deal with the force of opinion go back to the earliest times. For example, in ancient Egypt, the Pharaohs proclaimed their achievements through word pictures on impressive monuments, and staged elaborate festival parades at certain times of the year. While these actions mainly had a religious significance, at the same time they served to impress and entertain the people, and so to win their support for the ruling class.

In the Roman Empire, with its slogan of *Vox populi, vox dei* (people's voice, God's voice), this form of persuasion was continued by orators such as Cicero and Cato. The Romans went further, and some tyrants laid on free shows and parades to win support.

The twentieth century

Public relations, as it is practised today, originated in the United States. To a large extent, the development of public relations in the rest of the world has been influenced by developments in the United States. For example, American politicians have used press agents and other publicity methods for some time. This has led others to follow this trend and to 'manufacture news' and use stunts and gimmicks to gain attention.

Public relations was later employed to defend powerful United States business interests against negative journalism and government regulation. The emphasis was on 'telling our story' in order to ensure that the public do see the other side of a story. This resulted in more organisations hiring journalists in order to obtain positive publicity.

The concept of public relations as one-way persuasive communication continued to dominate as the United States entered World War I and created the Committee on Public Information. Headed by George Creel, the Committee was responsible for uniting public opinion behind the war effort through an extensive, nationwide propaganda campaign. During these early years, public relations was viewed as a publicity effort to influence others. Various communication media, such as advertising, films and exhibitions, were used – to such an extent that people eventually talked of 'the words that won the war'.

This concept of public relations as 'persuasive publicity' still lingers on, so that even present-day public relations practitioners find themselves dealing with managers and clients who hold this concept of the public relations function.

Europe and the international scene[8]

The route of public relations in America created the trend for the post-war development of public relations in Europe. The period from 1955 to 1980 is described as a 'remarkable period of transformation' in the history of European public relations. At its start, comparatively few pioneers were practising public relations and the profession was heavily indebted to American know-how. By the 1980s, however, almost every country in modern Western Europe had an established public relations body. The profession began organising itself into associations at approximately the same time in most of these countries.

The most important international organisation in public relations is the International Public Relations Association (IPRA), which was founded in London in 1955. It is a worldwide professional and fraternal organisation, which furthers the continuing development of 'the highest possible standards of public relations ethics, practice and performance'. The IPRA Code of Conduct was accepted in Venice in 1961 and, in 1965, IPRA accepted the Code of Athens, which was compiled by Centre Européenne des Relations Publiques (CERP) and is based on the principles of the United Nations Declaration of Human Rights. IPRA also publishes the *International Public Relations Review*.

South Africa

After World War II, public relations gained prominence in South Africa. The first public relations practitioner in South Africa was appointed by the South African Railways in 1943, while the first public relations consultancy opened in Johannesburg in 1948.

The Public Relations Institute of Southern Africa (PRISA) was established in Johannesburg in 1957 and today has more than 4 000 members. PRISA's vision is 'to be the professional body for the practice and development of public relations in Southern Africa' and its mission is 'to serve the interests of the public relations profession'.

The Accreditation and Ethics Council of PRISA

A major step in the professionalisation of the public relations industry in South Africa was the launching of the Public Relations Council of South Africa (PRCSA) in Johannesburg in 1985. The PRCSA, which previously operated independently of PRISA, served as a self-regulatory control for the profession, i.e. it guarded the interests of both the general public and the ethical members of the public relations profession.

At the annual general meeting of the PRCSA, held in May 1992, it was decided to rename the Council as the Accreditation and Ethics Council of PRISA. The objectives of this Council are:

▲ to set standards for the professional registration of public relations practitioners, these being a combination of appropriate academic qualifications, plus relevant practical public relations experience, which may include the teaching of public relations

▲ to examine applicants who meet these requirements by way of written and oral examinations, based on the Council's own published standards

▲ to maintain an enforceable code of professional conduct and to apply this code

▲ to award the right to use the title 'Accredited in Public Relations (APR)'

▲ to create an awareness and positive perception among opinion leaders of the role and value of the accredited public relations practitioner.

As part of its objectives, the Council initiated a process of formalised accreditation in 1986. This process took place in two phases: Phase 1 – the so-called grandfather phase – lasted until the end of May 1987, and its purpose was to enable practitioners to apply for accreditation without undergoing formal examinations; Phase 2, which commenced in June 1987, required applicants to undergo the accreditation examination.

Accreditation enables a practitioner to use the designation APR (Accredited in Public Relations) as a symbol of professional status. The Council has a Code of Professional Standards for the Practice of Public Relations (the same as PRISA's Code) and, in the event of a breach of this Code, it implements a particular disciplinary procedure.

Public relations matures[9]

As noted earlier, public relations really came of age as a result of the confluence of four general factors in our society:

1. the growth of large institutions and their sense of responsibility to the public

2. the increased changes, conflicts and confrontations among interest groups in society

3. the heightened awareness of people, brought about by increasingly sophisticated communications technology everywhere

4. the spread of global democracy.

Growth of large institutions

The public relations profession experienced perhaps its most important impetus when business confidence suffered its most severe setback. The economic and social upheaval caused by the Great Depression of the 1930s provided the trigger for corporations to seek public support by telling their stories. In South Africa, most major companies now have a fully-fledged public relations department, as do most mining houses and financial institutions. It is also becoming increasingly important for the larger companies to ensure that their publics are informed as to what they do and what they are involved in.

Change, conflict and confrontation

Perhaps one of the more significant influences in South Africa can be attributed to the social and political upheavals of the post-apartheid era in the nineties. Apartheid caused major polarisation and created a divided society. The Truth and Reconciliation Commission (TRC) began to look pointedly at the implications of the apartheid era. Environmentalists, worried about threats to the environment and to water sources by business expansion, began to support groups opposed to urban development, such as at Chapman's Peak in Cape Town. Homosexuals, senior citizens, birth control advocates and social activists of every kind began to challenge the legitimacy of large institutions.

Heightened public awareness

Post-1994 brought a partial resolution of these problems. Many of the solutions came from the government in the form of affirmative action guidelines, senior citizen programmes, consumer and environmental protection acts, aids to education, equity in the labour force, and a myriad other laws and statutes.

Most major businesses today are involved in various social upliftment programmes and contribute to charities. The general policy of corporations confronting their competitors has been replaced with a more empathetic and compromising attitude of assisting communities. This new policy of social responsibility has continued into the new century in South Africa. Companies realise that their reputations are a valuable asset to be protected, conserved, defended, nurtured, and enhanced at all times.

A shift has taken place in the ways publics are reached today. The Internet and e-commerce is used increasingly to reach a wider public, faster and constantly.

Global democracy in the twenty-first century

As the world moved into the twenty-first century, democracy came to the fore. This was evident in the changes which took place in eastern Europe when the Berlin Wall was demolished and the once powerful USSR was dissolved. In 1993, Nelson Mandela and the last 'apartheid' president of South Africa, FW de Klerk, stood together to share the Nobel Peace Prize and free elections were held in South Africa in 1994. Today, with many parts of the world now truly 'safe for democracy', the public relations challenge has grown in intensity.

Public relations in relation to the other management functions[10]

An organisation embarks on a variety of activities in order to meet the needs of its various publics. Some of these activities, such as production and the marketing of goods and services, are directly related to the primary function of the organisation, while others are supporting functions, such as human resources and public relations. These activities are co-ordinated in order to accomplish the organisation's goals and objectives within a constantly changing environment.

The various activities can be divided into seven broad categories or functional areas of management. These include:

1. the **general management function**, which formulates policy and develops strategies for the effective utilisation of all the resources at an organisation's disposal

2. the **marketing function**, which entails all those activities and responsibilities required for the successful marketing of the products or services of an organisation

3. the **financial function**, which includes all those activities that facilitate the acquisition, utilisation and control of the money an organisation needs to finance its activities and to purchase necessary materials and equipment

4. the **production or operational management function**, which includes the group of activities concerned with the physical production of products and the output of services

5. the **purchasing function**, which is responsible for the acquisition of all products and materials required by the organisation to function profitably, namely raw materials, components, tools, equipment and, in the case of the dealer, the inventory

6. the **human resources management function**, which is responsible for the appointment, development and maintenance of the human resources of an organisation

7. the **public relations function**, which is to establish good relations with those directly and indirectly concerned with an organisation and its products or services.

The position of the public relations department on an organisation chart does not normally provide an indication of its interactive and supporting role throughout the entire organisation. Public relations is a staff function and essentially acts as a support for all the other management functions in the organisation. It is the only function, apart from general management, that interacts with all the publics of the organisation, either directly or indirectly.

For this reason, the role of public relations should be clarified in the organisational dynamics to prevent it from overlapping with other functions, causing confusion and ineffectiveness.

Most functions of the organisation interact primarily with a specific public, for example the marketing function is directed towards customers, the purchasing function towards suppliers, the financial function towards the financial community, and the human resources function towards employees and the labour market. However, the public relations function interacts with all of these publics, either by way of direct communications or by assisting and advising the other functions with regard to their communications policy towards their specific publics. For example, in viewing the interactive role of public relations with the purchasing function, public relations should be involved, either directly or indirectly, in improving supplier relations with the organisation. By being directly involved, public relations can research supplier attitudes towards the organisation, and prepare and distribute information – such as welcome booklets for sales representatives and news bulletins – to suppliers. Indirectly, public relations can act in an advisory capacity to the purchasing function by formulating a communications policy which the purchasing department can implement.

Public relations and marketing

Public relations and marketing are the two functions that are most often confused, with public relations typically being subsumed by the larger, more powerful marketing function. It is a debate that is likely to continue for years to come.

In 1989, in San Diego in the USA, four leaders in marketing and public relations (Kotler, Ehling, Jackson and Jones) formed a panel to discuss and clarify the basic concepts behind the two management functions. Their conclusions were as follows:

▲ **Public relations** and **marketing** both deal with organisational relationships and employ similar processes, techniques and strategies.

▲ The two functions have to be separated by mission or goal. Public relations has the goal of attaining and maintaining accord with social groupings on whom the organisation depends in order to achieve its mission. Marketing has the goal of attracting and satisfying customers on a sustained basis in order to achieve an organisation's economic objectives.

▲ Every organisation needs a marketing function and every organisation needs a public relations function. Both marketing and public relations are essential to organisational survival and success.

Confusion between the two functions exists because the techniques of public relations, such as publicity and interpersonal communication, are often used in support of marketing theory, while the techniques of marketing, such as advertising and controlled communication, are often used in support of public relations theory. It is also common practice for public relations departments and consultants to undertake 'marketing communication' and to 'market public relations' while marketing departments offer 'public relations' to assist in promoting products (for example, product publicity). The right of both of these functions to utilise these techniques cannot be disputed, but the focus or goal should differ for each function. Where marketing concentrates on *quid pro quo* relationships with customers, public relations deals with all publics vital to an organisation's mission.

Public relations also deals with a whole host of relationships, based on mutual accord and positive behaviours, between an organisation and its environment. Marketing, however, is charged with attracting and satisfying long-term customers or clients to achieve an organisation's economic objectives. Building and maintaining relationships between an organisation and the people on whom the organisation depends is a common responsibility. Marketing concentrates on customers, while public relations manages other relationships which affect the way an organisation operates: employees, shareholders, public officials, neighbours and consumer groups.

The public relations process[11]

Public relations, as one of an organisation's management functions, must involve itself in planning on both a strategic and a tactical level, formulating strategies and plans that will ensure the continued existence of the organisation. All strategic and functional strategies of an organisation, as well as its actions, have the potential to impact on public opinion, and the task of public relations – as the function concerned with public opinion – is to guide the organisation proactively and reactively to full public acceptance. Whether public relations reacts to a problem or guides the organisation proactively through emerging or potential issues, a certain process is followed. This process is made up of four distinct but interrelated and interdependent phases: research, planning, communication (implementation) and evaluation. Table 2.1 on page 50 illustrates this process. Problems are solved and issues managed by applying the four basic steps in the public relations process. These steps are also all part of a strategic planning process.

Identifying public relations problems or seeking emerging issues that can impact on the organisation and its publics is done through **research and**

fact-finding, and is the first phase in the public relations process. Public relations management must constantly be aware of situations within and outside the organisation that may affect the organisational goals. These situations can manifest themselves in a number of ways, for example, sluggish new investments, decreasing sales, high employee or management turnover, negative publicity, unusually slow delivery of stock or raw materials, unfounded rumours, etc. By listening and making value judgements that something may be wrong, or by continuous fact-finding, management can become aware of these problems. The process then becomes an objective and systematic research task, which should be designed to describe all the facets of the problem. Management decisions are based on the conclusions drawn from the research phase.

In order for the organisation to achieve its goals, the public relations function must strategically manage emerging issues by operating in a preventive mode. In the past, public relations operated in a reactive mode and the public relations practitioner was called in only once a problem was out of control and the damage to the organisation's public image had already been done. Public relations, as part of an open system, and itself taking the open-systems approach, places an emphasis on the early detection of problems or potential problems. An open-systems approach refers to a system where actions are open to scrutiny from publics at any time. This early detection of a problem is often the result of unsystematic observation and news-gathering undertaken while informally monitoring the environment. This forms the starting point for a more systematic gathering of information. As can be seen from table 2.1 on page 50, strategic planning uses research to define and redefine the perceived problem by undertaking a situation analysis which includes the internal and external environments of the organisation.

The second phase, **planning and programme development**, includes setting goals and objectives to overcome the identified problems or to manage the emerging issues, identifying the publics impacted on by the problem or issue, assessing the way in which they are or will be impacted on, and finally developing procedures and strategies. One of the most important aspects of planning is the setting of objectives. These objectives form the criteria for evaluation of the entire programme. Public relations objectives, based on the identified problem or issue, should underwrite the organisational goal and objectives. The nature of the problem will determine who is, or should be, involved. For example, where investment is low, existing and potential investors, stockbrokers and the financial media would be relevant publics. Relevant publics, for which specific objectives are set, should be analysed in terms of their communication needs, which cover aspects such as the contents of the message, appropriate media or channels, and timings and frequencies. The information gathered in the research phase forms the basis for the strategies and programmes that need to be developed to solve the identified problem or issue. Planning and programme development also entail budgeting, and the allocation and scheduling of tasks and responsibilities in the public relations department.

In the third phase, **action** needs to be taken and **communication implemented** in order to achieve the objectives set for the specific programme. The importance of the selection of the correct message and media strategies becomes evident in this phase as, once plans are implemented, the suitability of messages and media are quickly ascertained. Adjustments to these plans may become necessary as new information or feedback becomes available. Further research may even be required. Feedback on communications in the implementation phase is an important initial measure of the success of a programme, for example, an organisation may continue to receive negative publicity on an issue such as its labour relations, even in the face of ongoing news releases by the organisation to correct misconceptions. Issues such as a poor relationship between media representatives and the organisation's public relations staff may be the cause and have gone undetected in the initial research. The operational aspects of implementing plans and programmes on a day-to-day basis include frequent (monthly, weekly, daily) scheduling of tasks and allocation of responsibilities and financial and other resources.

Finally, in the fourth phase, **evaluating** the results of a programme, or assessing its effectiveness and modifying it for future use, completes the public relations process. This assessment determines to what extent the objectives of the programme have been met. The evaluation techniques are determined in the research and planning phases. The results of the evaluation can lead to new programmes being formulated as new issues or problems may become evident in the evaluation phase of the public relations process. This reflects the cyclical nature of the four phases of the public relations process, since the planning, implementation and evaluation steps are guided and motivated by the information and insight gained in the first step. These phases also overlap since the process is in a continuous state of adjustment to a changing environment.

Four-step process for public relations	Strategic planning process steps and outline for programme plan

1 Defining public relations problems or issues through research	1 The problem or issue
	2 Situation analysis – background information, data, evidence
	  a Internal factors/forces
	  b External factors/forces

2 Planning and programming	3 Programme goal
	4 Publics
	  a Who is involved/affected?
	  b How?
	5 Programme objectives – for each public
	6 Action programme – for each public
	7 Communication programme – for each public
	  a Message strategies
	  b Media strategies
	8 Implementation plans
	  a Assignment of responsibilities
	  b Schedules
	  c Budget

3 Taking action and communicating	9 Implementation
	  a Day-to-day operationalisation
	  b Constant feedback and programme adjustment

4 Evaluating the programme	10 Evaluation of success of completed programme

Table 2.1 Public relations strategic planning process

(*Source:* Adapted from Broom & Dozier, 1990:25)

The publics of public relations[12]

The responsibility of any public relations practitioner is to communicate with many different publics – not just the general public – each with its own special needs and requiring different types of communication. The differences between these publics are not always clear-cut and a huge overlap takes place. As a result of this, it is important that the publics are organised in order of priority (see figure 2.1 on the next page).

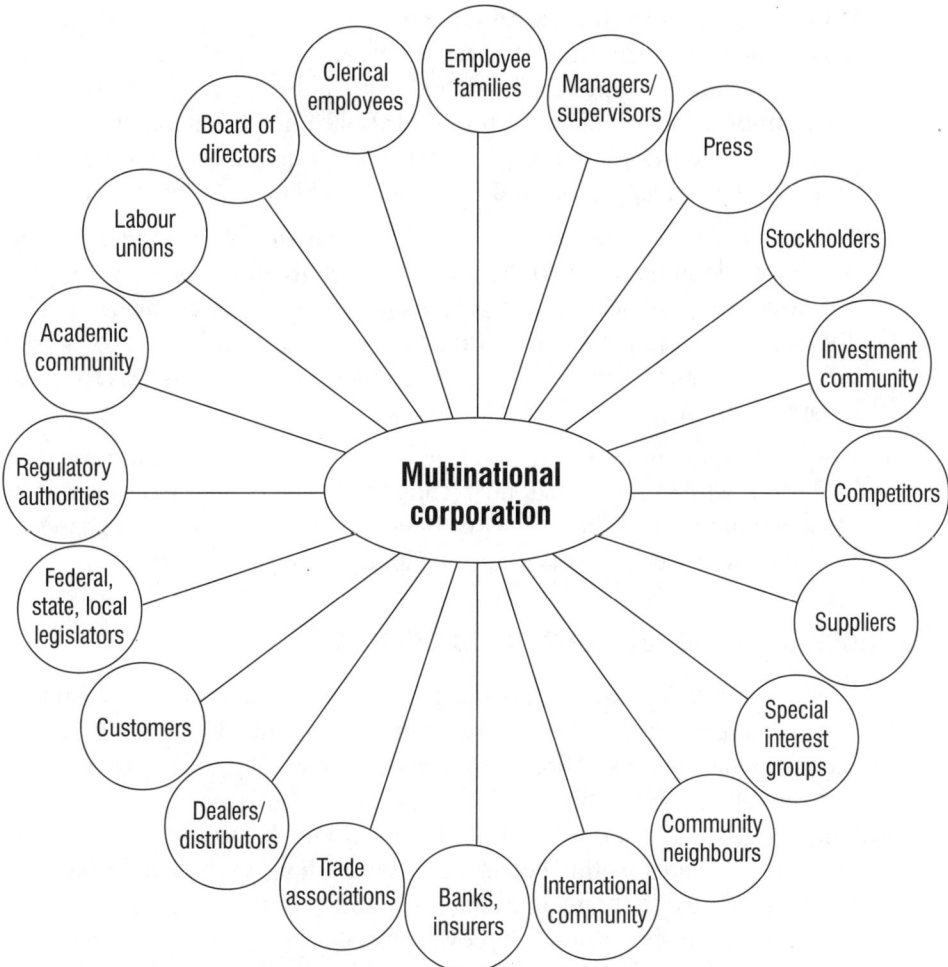

Figure 2.1 Twenty key publics of a typical multinational corporation[13]

Definitions differ on precisely what constitutes a public. One time-honoured definition states that a public arises when a group of people, first, face a similar indeterminate situation; second, recognise what is indeterminate and problematic in that situation; and third, organise to do something about the problem. In public relations, more specifically, a public is a group of people with a stake in an issue, organisation, or idea.

Publics can also be classified into several overlapping categories:

▲ **Internal and external.** Internal publics are inside the organisation: supervisors, clerks, managers, stockholders, and the board of directors. External publics are those not directly connected with the organisation: the press, government, educators, customers, the community, and suppliers.

▲ **Primary, secondary, and marginal.** Primary publics are those which can make a major contribution towards an organisation's efforts – or hinder them. Secondary publics are less important, and marginal publics are the least important of all. The Competition Board, for example, would be a primary public for a large retailer that intends taking over another large retailer, whereas legislators and the general public would be secondary.

▲ **Traditional and future.** Employees and current customers are traditional publics, while students and potential customers are future ones. No organisation can afford to become complacent in dealing with its changing publics. Today, an organisation's publics range from women to minorities to senior citizens to homosexuals. Each might be important to the future success of an organisation.

▲ **Proponents, opponents, and the uncommitted.** An institution must deal differently with those who support it and those who oppose it. For supporters, communications that reinforce beliefs may be in order, but changing the opinion of sceptics calls for strong, persuasive communications.

The place of public relations in the organisation[14]

The theory of public relations stresses that public relations is a management function on a par with all the other major functions of the organisation such as marketing management and financial management. Ideally, the public relations department of an organisation will have a public relations manager or director with input in the formulation of corporate policy and decision-making authority. The subordinates in this department, over whom the manager has line authority, will provide the technical support in the implementation of public relations programmes. In practice, however, the role of public relations is often viewed in terms of its technical aspects and is relegated to a minor status in the organisational structure.

In some organisations, the public relations officer or executive is minor – perhaps reporting to the marketing director – and deals with only the most rudimentary communications, such as arranging a factory tour or welcoming guests to the organisation's premises. In such organisations, the public relations officer or executive rarely participates in the management decision-making process. However, in other organisations public relations is given a more prominent role, with the public relations director more involved in management decision making and probably reporting to the managing director. The public relations manager initiates communications projects, which may include reaching employees through newsletters and meetings, co-ordinating relationships with the media through writing news releases and arranging media interviews, orchestrating interaction with the community through open houses and tours, managing relations with the investment community, managing corporate advertising, co-ordinating special events, and counselling management.

The placement of the public relations function and its effectiveness is also a matter of debate in the literature, where ongoing research relating to the departmentalisation issue questions the scope of public relations work in relation to the organisation's structural arrangements. The contention is that the more responsive the public relations department is to the organisation's overall strategy and structural arrangements, the broader its scope of operations and impact will be. Conversely, the weaker the fit between the public relations unit and the organisational structure and strategy, the more limited the scope of public relations.

Public relations does not operate only within the confines of an organisation but has a second home, namely that of the public relations consultancy, where consultants provide public relations services to client firms or organisations. The overall purpose of a consultancy is to provide advice and perform certain technical services according to the clients' needs and wishes, based on an agreed-upon public relations programme. The public relations consultancy may provide services to an organisation's public relations department or, if no such department exists, may conduct the entire public relations effort.

Types of organisational structures

An organisation that makes use of a functional organisational scheme classifies its activities into functions such as purchasing management, operational management, marketing management, public relations management, and so on. Here the emphasis is on the similarity of specialised skills and responsibilities, irrespective of particular goals. Figure 2.2 indicates this type of organisational structure.

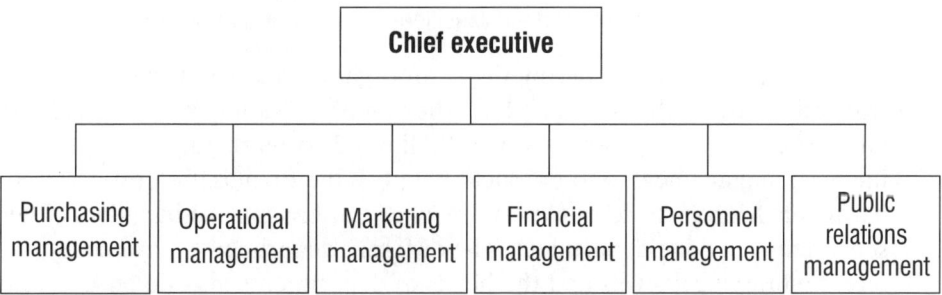

Figure 2.2 An organisational classification according to function

Product departmentalisation is the process whereby an organisation groups its activities according to its different products or services, for example a banking institution may have departments for housing loans, cheque accounts and savings. This can also be referred to as market departmentalisation. In a public relations consulting firm, divisions could be responsible for product promotion, special events, conferences, financial public relations, crisis communication, and so on (see figure 2.3). In other words, all the specialists involved with a product or service or a group of products or services are grouped together into a department or division. The motivation for this type of departmentalisation is that there is a significant difference between the specialised knowledge required, for example, to arrange conferences and that needed to conduct financial public relations programmes.

Departmentalisation according to geographic location groups together all those activities conducted in a specific region where business is done.

Where an organisation focuses on the needs of specific customers or groups of customers, departmentalisation according to customers occurs. In a public relations consulting firm, this structure is organised around clients and client needs.

Public relations consulting firm

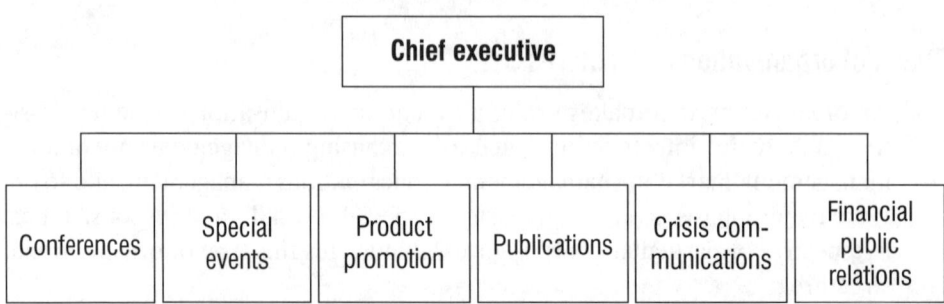

Figure 2.3 An organisational classification according to product

The number of major departments in an organisation is determined by the size and nature of the organisation. When an organisation is established, the number of major departments may be limited to marketing management, financial management, and production, but as the organisation expands, departments for human resources and public relations may be included, either separately or as one department. The different departments may occupy different hierarchical levels and the heads of departments may lie on different managerial levels, which has implications for their authority and decision-making responsibility.

In a number of organisations, public relations is placed as a sub-department of a major department such as marketing, as illustrated in figure 2.4. The placement of any department or function in an organisational scheme suggests the following:

▲ the importance and value ascribed to the function or department

▲ the relationship between the various departments, which has implications for co-ordination, communication and authority relationships

▲ the relative importance of the department or function as viewed by top management, which has implications in terms of accessibility to top management, and impact of the function on strategic decisions and strategy formulation.

Figure 2.4 Public relations as a sub-department of marketing

Organising the public relations department

Once organisational departmentalisation has taken place, the departments themselves are structured. Major departments are divided into a number of subordinate departments.

Grunig and Hunt have outlined six possible configurations for organising public relations, based on horizontal dimensions, that is, where the characteristics of roles, tasks and co-ordinating mechanisms are described on each level:

1. **Structure by public:** The public relations department is organised around major categories of publics such as media relations, employee relations, community relations, etc.

2. **Structure by management process:** The public relations components refer to such processes as planning, communication, research and evaluation.

3. **Structure by communication technique:** The public relations department has production units for techniques such as press services, audiovisual production or publications.

4. **Structure by geographic region:** Public relations units are set up to serve branch or subsidiary locations.

5. **Structure by organisational subsystem:** The subsystem structure is used when an organisation assigns different employees to serve each division, product line, etc. Practitioners serve as account executives for different subsystems of the organisation.

6. **Account executive system:** This relates to the agency (public relations consulting firm) model, where the structure is organised around clients and clients' needs.

An organisation's activities, its internal and external environment, and its significant publics, dictate the structure of the public relations department. This structure determines the interaction between the public relations department and top management, marketing and other management functions.

Van Leuwen examined the scope of the public relations function and the responsiveness of the public relations departmental arrangements to the organisation's overall strategy and structure. This was then matched to the approach taken by top management in departmentalising the organisation, and to that taken by the public relations department in allocating its staff and work. Van Leuwen tackled this by proposing a 2×2 public relations departmentalising matrix, formed by the four combinations of the function and product/market departmentalising concepts. This matrix is presented in figure 2.5 on the next page.

The first combination indicates that the organisation is departmentalised by function (for example marketing, operations, purchasing, finance), and the public relations operations are departmentalised by function (for example media services, research, visitors' programmes, audio-visual production or publications). Note that this form of public relations departmentalisation by function closely parallels Grunig and Hunt's structure by communication technique.

Structuring of the organisation

<table>
<tr><td rowspan="2">Structuring of the public
relations department</td><td></td><td>Function</td><td>Market or public</td></tr>
<tr><td>Function</td><td></td><td></td></tr>
<tr><td></td><td>Market or public</td><td></td><td></td></tr>
</table>

Figure 2.5 Departmentalisation of the organisation and public relations department

The second combination indicates that the organisation is departmentalised by market or public, that is, the organisation is departmentalised according to its products and services relating to specific target audiences, but the public relations operations are departmentalised by function.

The third combination indicates that the organisation is departmentalised by function, but the public relations operations are departmentalised by market or public. Note that this market or public departmentalisation closely parallels Grunig and Hunt's structure by organisational subsystem. Here organisations assign different employees to serve each division, product line, etc.

The fourth combination indicates that the organisation is departmentalised by market or public, and the public relations operations are departmentalised by market or public.

From the research conducted, it became evident that some differences exist in the scope of public relations operations for each combination illustrated in the matrix. These differences are related to the organisational departmentalisation plan, as well as to the public relations departmentalisation plan:

▲ It would appear from the research that the public relations departments of organisations that were departmentalised by market or public showed a greater range of interdepartmental or interfunctional co-operation than those departmentalised by function. This meant that more joint projects were undertaken, dual reporting was undertaken, and other mechanisms were used to link public relations with marketing, human resources, etc.

▲ When public relations operations are departmentalised by market or public, there is greater involvement in strategic planning and decision making at departmental, product group and organisational level.

▲ In organisations where public relations is departmentalised according to function, it would appear that proportionately more time goes into the technical aspects of public relations work. In contrast, when the public relations function is departmentalised by market or public, it would appear that practitioners spend more of their time in consulting and planning roles, and less on hands-on technical detail.

▲ It would appear that the type of programmes conducted may also be related to the type of public relations departmentalisation. This research showed that where public relations was departmentalised according to market or public, more attention was given to media relations, product publicity, trade promotions and other aspects of marketing communication. Where departmentalisation was according to function, more attention and staff were given to internal communication and community relations.

The important conclusion that can be drawn from this discussion is that the scope of the public relations function can be influenced by the type of departmentalisation arrangements made by the organisation and by the public relations department. Alternatively, the scope of public relations may influence the choice of the type of departmentalisation.

Staff and line functions and authority

A distinction that may cause confusion, particularly in the case of public relations, is that of line and staff functions. **Line functions** are those activities essential for realising the organisation's objectives. They are those functions that are involved in the primary activities of producing and selling the organisation's products or services. They make a direct contribution to the organisation's bottom-line, such as the marketing and operations functions. Line managers have the authority and responsibility to see that work is tackled and completed. Line authority originates at top management and is delegated through the various hierarchical levels of the organisation to where the primary product- and profit-producing activities of the organisation are carried out.

Staff functions are those activities that directly influence the line functions by means of advice, recommendations, research, and technical knowledge and plans. In the case of staff functions, management must decide what type of authority will be granted to staff managers. Public relations and human resources are staff functions. Public relations practitioners are experts in communication and line managers, including the chief executive officer, rely on public relations staff to utilise their skills in preparing and processing data, making recommendations, and executing communications programmes to implement the organisation's policies. The public relations department may propose that an open day be held in order to inform the community of the organisation's operations. It will recommend this to top management, who will order the other departments to co-operate if the proposal is approved. The public relations department will then take responsibility for organising the event.

Public relations departments function with the approval of top management, but various placements of these departments have implications for the degree of influence and authority that each one can exert. We have already considered some of these placements and their implications for public relations. A further placement that can be distinguished is that of the public relations department as a service function, directly responsible to top management but also separate from the other major departments. Figure 2.6 illustrates this placement. In this type of placement, public relations is regarded as an advisory function with responsibility to top management. Where top management places public relations in a compulsory advisory position, organisational policy requires that top managers at least listen to the appropriate experts before deciding on a policy.

Figure 2.6 Public relations as a service function

Public relations can also be placed on another level in an advisory relationship, that of concurring authority (see figure 2.7 for a schematic representation). In this type of relationship, the line and staff manager must agree on a certain plan of action, for example if the purchasing department wishes to produce a brochure, the public relations department must approve the copy and layout. In this situation, the staff manager's authority is extended while the line manager's authority is limited.

A staff manager can also have command authority, whereby other departments are forced to accept his or her decision. For example, the public relations manager may have the authority to reject any publications or communication messages from other departments that do not conform to the organisational policies. This is particularly important when an organisation wishes to achieve a uniform corporate image in terms of all its material. However, this type of authority can also work against the public relations manager when, for example, the legal department has command authority to change a news release with or without his or her consent.

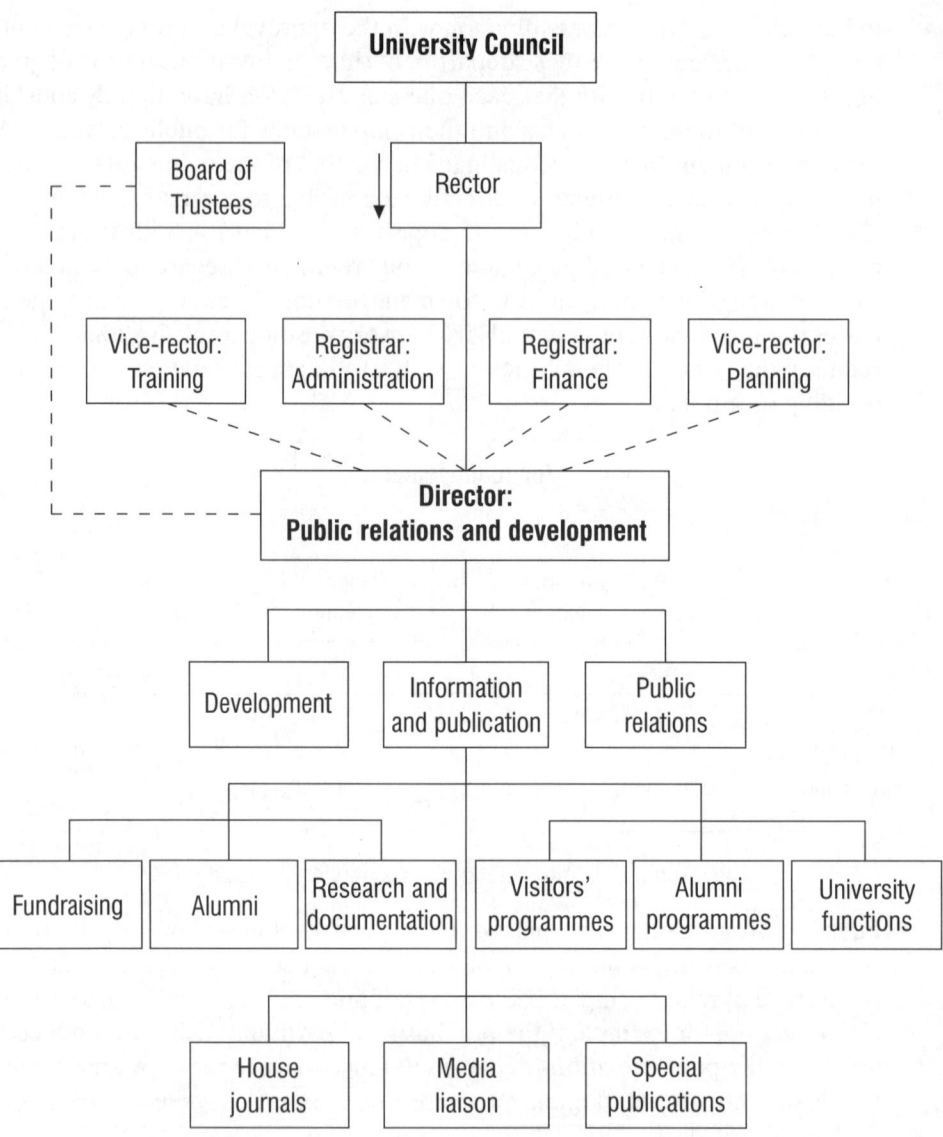

Figure 2.7 Public relations at a university

Conflict can arise between line and staff people. This problem may be the result of a variety of factors, for example personality clashes, orientation and place on the organisational chart. In public relations, where the publics that a function is concerned with overlap with the publics of each of the other functions, friction can occur because – unless the activities and responsibilities are clearly delineated – it may seem that public relations is intruding on the human resources, marketing or legal functions. An interesting argument which relates to the sources of friction between line and staff positions is that line people are generally orientated to the advancement of the organisation, and their future is heavily dependent on being loyal to the organisation. Staff people, however, are orientated towards the advancement of their profession, whether it be medical, scientific research, engineering, marketing or public relations. Staff people identify strongly with their profession rather than with the organisation.

Although the public relations function is essentially a staff function, the head of public relations has line authority within his or her own department. As a manager with line authority, the public relations chief can delegate authority, assign projects and supervise his or her staff.

The Public Relations Institute of Southern Africa has distinguished five clearly defined levels of public relations practice. These roles encompass both the management and technical functions of public relations, with the higher levels fulfilling the management functions to a greater degree than the lower levels:

1. **The public relations director** reports to the chief executive officer of the organisation and/or is a member of the board of directors. The responsibilities of this multidisciplinary post include the formulation of corporate policy, mission and culture, and the planning of the total communication strategy. This is a management position where public relations programmes are proactively conceptualised in support of the organisational mission. In this respect, the input of the public relations director in the formulation of the mission and long-term objectives of the organisation is essential as the publics' perceptions of the implications of organisational policies must be taken into account.

2. **The public relations or communications manager** is responsible for providing input for an organisation's strategic planning, formulation of public relations and communication strategies, interpretation of corporate and communication goals and programmes, initiating research, and externally contributing to the development of the public relations profession. This position is also primarily involved in the management sphere, but requires the ability to envisage the implementation requirements of the decisions.

3. **The public relations practitioner** exercises a large measure of creative and inventive decision making and initiative in the implementation of communication projects, the supervision of specific activities, and the compilation and control of project budgets. The role of the practitioner is dependent on the nature of his or her involvement with the organisation. On the one hand, a practitioner can act as a consultant to the management of one or more organisations, thus contributing to management decisions regarding the communications strategy of the organisation. On the other hand, the

practitioner can be appointed to implement public relations programmes, thus becoming a technical back-up to management.

4. **Public relations assistants** are at the entry level to public relations, and execute basic public relations assignments under instruction and supervision. This position is that of a public relations technician.

5. **Secretaries** are seen as having a 'frontline' function in influencing an organisation's image, as they are the first point of contact with the organisation and play an interactive role. The secretary fulfils neither a management nor a technician's role but, as a result of his or her influence in terms of initial contact with the public/s, a certain public relations role does exist, albeit an indirect one. The public relations manager does not have line authority over secretaries in all departments, but only over the secretaries in the public relations department.

Public relations departments in organisations are called by a variety of names, such as corporate communications, public affairs or external relations, in an attempt to capture the essence of the concerns of these departments. The important point to note, however, is that while certain organisations concentrate on specialised areas of public relations such as public affairs, *public relations* is the most acceptable term since it encompasses all the communication activities with which organisations are normally involved.

Conclusion

Public relations does not exist as a function on its own. It is an integral part of the marketing function of an organisation. Public relations affects almost everyone and all of us practise public relations in one way or another.

During the past few decades, public relations has increased in prominence as well as professional stature. While marketing and sales have as their primary objective the selling of an organisation's products, the aim of public relations is to sell the organisation itself. Good public relations cannot be bought, it must be earned. Public relations is not a once-off phenomenon but an ongoing process, which may take years to bear fruit.

Public relations came into being in South Africa only after World War II, and today is a major force in corporate life. Internationally, various factors led to public relations coming of age. These factors included the growth of large institutions; the increased changes, conflicts, and confrontations among groups in society; the heightened awareness of people in society; and the spread of global democracy.

The relationships between public relations and the other functions in an organisation were discussed in this chapter, as well as the maintenance of good relationships, which is crucial to the make-up of an organisation. In addition, the public relations process – consisting of four steps, namely, defining public relations problems, planning and programming, action and communicating, and the evaluation of the programme – was considered.

Questions for self-evaluation

1. Define public relations.
2. Explain the role and function of public relations.
3. Give a brief overview of the evolution of public relations with specific reference to South Africa.
4. Discuss the public relations process.

Endnotes

1 Cutlip, SM; Center, AH and Broom, SM 1994. *Effective Public Relations.* *(*7 Ed.) New Jersey: Prentice Hall:1.

2 Seitel, FP 2001. *The Practice of Public Relations*. (8 Ed.) New Jersey: Prentice Hall:4.

3 Belch, GE and Belch, MA 2001. *Advertising and Promotion: An Integrated Marketing Communication Perspective*. Boston: Irwin:57.

4 Skinner, C and Van Essen, L 1998. *The Handbook of Public Relations.* (4 Ed.) Johannesburg: ITP:4–6.

5 Seitel, op. cit.:25–28.

6 Scitcl, op. cit.:18.

7 Taken from Skinner and Von Essen, op. cit.:18–22.

8 Taken from Lubbe, BA and Puth, G 1994. *Public Relations in South Africa: A Management Reader*. Sandton: Heinemann:20–23.

9 Taken from Seitel, op. cit.:9.

10 Lubbe and Puth, op. cit.:9–13.

11 Lubbe and Puth, op. cit.:11–13.

12 Seitel, op. cit:9–11.

13 Seitel, op. cit.:10.

14 Taken from Lubbe and Puth, op. cit.:26–35.

Section 2

The Performance Dimensions
of Public Relations

Section 2 deals with the performance dimensions – the practical implementation – of public relations.

Strategic planning and management are extremely important in the arena of public relations, and although this book vehemently emphasises that public relations practitioners should be strategically-oriented, the actual implementation of strategies is equally important.

The chapters in this section describe the implementation or the performance dimensions of public relations. Chapter 3 discusses public relations campaign planning and management, whereas Chapter 4 investigates the interrelationship of marketing, public relations and relationship management. Chapter 5 provides insight into marketing, public relations and the media. Chapter 6 gives an overview of the importance of internal branding and its role in creating and sustaining business performance. In view of the fact that electronic communication is already a crucial variable in the business environment and for the survival of organisations, Chapter 7 looks at the Internet and public relations. Chapter 8 deals with a highly important ingredient in the practice of public relations, namely public relations research.

Chapter 3

The Performance Dimensions of Public Relations: Campaign Planning and Management

LEARNING OUTCOMES

After studying this chapter, you should be able to:

▲ contextualise public relations planning and management

▲ describe and use the various elements of public relations planning and management

▲ discuss the differences between campaigns, programmes and social movements

▲ distinguish between various models of public relations campaign planning

▲ plan a public relations campaign on your own.

Introduction

This chapter investigates a particular sphere of the performance dimensions of public relations, namely the planning and management of communication and public relations campaigns or programmes. The interaction of organisations with their various publics creates the setting for the planning, management and implementation of a public relations campaign as one of the most important functions of the public relations practitioner, because it combines strategic planning and input with technical know-how.

Public relations planning and management

Public relations or communication planning entails planning for unstructured, informal communication. This means initiating communication for the sake of starting a communication process (Windahl, Signitzer & Olson, 1993). Public relations or communication management is the process of monitoring the planned communication from its *initiation* (the pre-implementation phase), through the *implementation* phase, up to the post-implementation or *evaluation* phase (Rensburg, 1996:41).

Public relations management should always include both systematic elements and creative elements. Public relations planning may be viewed as predominantly strategic and creative in finding new ideas to relay a message; finding new solutions to corporate communication problems; searching for and using new and novel communication media; and defining and segmenting publics in interesting new ways.

The elements of public relations planning and management

There are certain important elements that underlie the processes of public relations planning and management. These elements are pivotal in any communication process and can also be utilised in public relations planning and management. They include the following:

The environment

The environment is made up of the circumstances surrounding the publics of public relations – it is the background or 'setting' in which communication takes place. It can also be referred to as the *situation* in which public relations planning and management occurs. The environment can change rapidly. The South African environment (political, social and economic) has changed notably since the first democratic elections in 1994. The environment in general, and environmental changes specifically, play important roles in public relations planning. The role of *environmental scanning* has become increasingly popular as a means of 'scanning the corporate environment' before planning public relations messages. In this process, the public relations practitioner becomes the nexus between society and the organisation he or she represents. In a country like South Africa, the public relations practitioner should also be reminded of the importance of planning public relations messages for a multicultural or intercultural environment. One of the great opportunities and challenges of practising public relations in South Africa is the rich cultural environment in which public relations operates.

The organisation

The communicator or initiator of the public relations message is usually the organisation, person, group or institution that the public relations practitioner or consultant represents. This organisation usually wishes to express some meaningful idea to its publics by utilising communication. Here the organisation can fulfil a variety of roles (Westley & MacLean, 1957; Rensburg, 1996). The organisation can have an *advocacy role* by striving to influence publics in the environment, directly or indirectly. A *channel role* has a less purposive character. Its objective is to provide the public with information and to act as an intermediary between the organisation and the public. A *behavioural role* is held by the publics, for example readers, listeners, viewers and the public in general, who can become active communicators by acting on the information that they receive.

To illustrate these roles: The Department of Health launches an HIV/AIDS communication effort involving the mass media, government and other channels of communication. Clearly, in this case, the Department of Health plays an advocacy role. Using the mass media (a channel role), the Department of Health also transmits the information. The publics (target audiences) who receive the communication assume a behavioural role.

The communication planner

This is an important role and is usually played by the public relations practitioner, consultant or corporate communication manager on behalf of the organisation. In an initiating role, the public relations practitioner is usually working for the organisation – formulating the organisation's messages. In this role, the public relations practitioner is regarded as a communication planner and is seen by publics as the real source of what is being expressed by the organisation. In an affirmative action drive in an organisation, for example, the public relations practitioner or corporate communication manager will put the organisational message together and convey it to all relevant publics of the organisation – both internal and external.

The message

The communication content that is transmitted in the communication process is called the message. This message can be overtly expressed or it can have an underlying meaning – the covert meaning. The message of any communication or public relations effort embodies the meaning attributed to the content by those publics who receive the message. The message then, while existing on its own, may be the property of the organisation, the public relations practitioner and the publics it intends to reach.

The medium

The media are the channels through which the communication messages of the organisation reach the publics. *Medium* and *channel* are often used interchangeably in communication, although there is a technical distinction between the two concepts. Channel, in this context, denotes the physical means of carrying a signal (O'Sullivan et al., 1983:31–32). It therefore has little to do with meaning, but rather refers to the capacity to carry information. A medium, in the public relations planning and management context, is an intermediate agency that enables communication to take place through the use of one or more channels (O'Sullivan et al., 1983:134). Usually the term is used synonymously with mass media, but people may also take on the role of medium.

In the South African context there is a distinction between mainstream conventional mass media (film, radio, television, outdoor, print, electronic and transportation), and unconventional media (including group communication such as rural television, roadshows, industrial and community theatre, and the like). In South Africa there are also traditional media, folk media or 'oramedia' (Jefkins & Ugboajah, 1986), which are based on the indigenous culture produced and consumed by members of a group. Unlike the mass media, which reaches many publics at a time but mainly has cognitive influence (knowledge, awareness and interest), oramedia reaches only a few people at a time, but can be an effective relay chain to the mass media.

Oramedia has visible cultural features by which social relationships and a world view are defined and maintained. It takes on many forms and is rich in symbolism. Oramedia includes ceremonial socialising, rumours, oratory, poetry, music, singing and dancing, charms and insignia, marketplace gossip, praise singing, and many others. It is of particular importance for the professional public relations practitioner, as communication planner, to realise that – in the South African environment – there are more media of communication to choose from than only the conventional media.

The target audience or publics

The target audience or publics may be defined in this context in terms of people who attend to the particular prepared message content. The public relations practitioner, as communication planner, must realise when planning communication material that the publics may often be a heterogeneous audience – from different ethnic, subcultural and cultural settings. In the national and global context of communication, the communication environment is usually made up of publics that are largely heterogeneous and geographically dispersed. These may cause difficulties in public relations planning, management and implementation (Rensburg, 1996:44).

Effects and effectiveness

When dealing with communication content and public relations efforts, it is necessary to distinguish between campaign *effects* and *effectiveness*. Public relations effects can be described as consequences of a communication process – circumstances that would not have occurred without the presence or intervention of some other circumstances (Anderson & Meyer, 1988:161). Public relations effectiveness is an outcome of objectives fulfilment. A public relations practitioner, finding that a communication action has generated only meagre results, might argue that it was not 'effective'.

Feedback and feedforward

There is no doubt that *feedback* is an important element in any communication process. Feedback is a response on the part of the publics or target audience to a public relations practitioner's communication. Feedback is reactions that are transmitted back to, and actually reach, the organisation. For the public relations practitioner, feedback on his or her communication efforts is important, providing a tool to better understand the outcome of these efforts.

Feedforward, however, is information about publics and their possible reaction that is gathered by a public relations practitioner prior to initiating communication with them (Rogers, 1973). It is true in planned communication that the more one knows beforehand about the target audience or public, the greater the chances are for effective communication. Hornik (1988) has indicated the need for feedforward in developing countries' agriculture development work, where government agents acting as communication planners are often insensitive to the needs of farmers. Feedforward may also encompass active public relations campaigns by giving hints as to the messages that will follow. For example, the flying of a trial balloon before an official announcement of a drastic reduction in the general speed limit could provide a measure of the strength of the opposition to such a measure. Feedforward can therefore be viewed as an activity that enables a public relations practitioner, as communication planner, to formulate a comprehensive background on which to plan and design a public relations strategy (Rensburg, 1996:45).

The above are essential elements in communication planning and management, and are concepts that will occur throughout the discussion of the performance dimensions of public relations.

The campaign, programme and social movement

Before the public relations campaign can be described in more detail, it is necessary to distinguish between campaigns, programmes and social movements since, although they may have many similarities, there are degrees of difference between them.

The public relations practitioner or consultant should ideally have an ongoing relationship with organisations, clients and publics. There should be continuous *programmes* for stakeholders. A *campaign* that continues over a long period of time, therefore, is called a public relations programme.

A *social movement* can be defined as an ideological, issue- or cause-oriented campaign or movement (Larson, 1986:201). The African National Congress (ANC) was an ideological movement before it became a political party. Many activist activities are organised in ideological or social movements rather than programmes or campaigns.

Organisations can have a variety of campaigns – from marketing campaigns, advertising campaigns and corporate identity campaigns to public relations campaigns. Planning, implementing and managing the public relations campaign is one of the public relations practitioner's most important strategic as well as technical functions.

Most changes in attitude, behaviour, belief or action are not the result of a single communication message. In many instances, where people or institutions change their attitudes or behaviour, the change is the result of their being exposed to many data, or a series of messages, or the effect of combined messages. This is called a campaign.

Objectives of campaigns

According to Rensburg (1996:55), campaigns may have different general objectives (outcomes or effects) in mind. A campaign can be planned that merely wants to *inform* target publics about an issue or to *create awareness* about an issue or cause, for example to inform voters about the venues in their areas where they should register as voters for the local elections. This would also create awareness about the upcoming elections. In addition, a campaign can seek to *persuade* publics to change their attitudes, for example a campaign may seek to persuade voters that the local elections 'are even more important than the national elections'. Campaigns can also urge publics to act – their objective is to make publics *behave* in certain ways. For example, a campaign could say: 'Take action against AIDS now!' A campaign's objective may also be to *educate*, for example a voter education campaign before the actual elections. It is also possible, according to Rensburg (1996:55), for a campaign to include all these objectives – to inform, to create awareness, to persuade, to urge publics to act and to educate – presenting them in various phases over a period of time.

The above are *general objectives.* Individual campaigns may also have *specific objectives* – objectives set out by communication planners for a particular situation or campaign.

Types of campaign

According to Larson (1986:201), there are three kinds of movement, programme or campaign. They are:

1. the politically oriented campaign

2. the product- or service-oriented campaign

3. the ideological, issue- or cause-oriented campaign.

Newsom et al. (1993:474–475) add to the above and differentiate between six types of public relations campaign:

1. The **public awareness campaign** that makes people aware of something.

2. The **information along with awareness campaign** that includes not only awareness, but also information about something.

3. The **public education campaign** that educates or 'teaches' the publics about something.

4. **Campaigns** that **reinforce the attitudes and behaviour** of those who are in agreement with the organisation's position. All these publics may need is a reminder of shared values.

5. **Campaigns** that **have to change or attempt to change the attitudes** of those who do not agree with the organisation's position, for example activist groups that disagree with how the organisation conducts its business in the environment.

6. **Behaviour modification campaigns** which convince publics, for example, that they ought to wear their seatbelts or that drunk driving is not in their or society's best interests.

Each of these campaigns attempts to motivate different levels of behaviour, which is the sole reason for conducting campaigns. Behaviour is the outcome that campaigns seek – not necessarily the thinking or feeling or even social interaction that precedes the behaviour. These are merely the means to an end. (See also the discussion on pages 72 and 73 regarding objectives of campaigns; the types of campaign align perfectly with those objectives.)

Stages of effective campaigns

A campaign is not just a series of messages, all dealing with the same issue. Nor is it a debate over an issue. Campaigns are developmental in nature. They move from stage to stage. They have a beginning, a middle and an end. They neither run on the same level and at the same pitch from beginning to end, nor do they always have the same strategy. Instead, campaigns grow and change and adapt to the response by the publics and the emergence of new issues. They use different methods and lures. If one method does not succeed after a period of time, another is developed and tried. As the mood of the publics develops, the mood of the message of the campaign also develops and changes. If campaigns are to succeed, they must create a sense of the dramatic in their publics. Campaigns need to depict their cause as one of historic magnitude. Then they need to invite publics to join and share in the great cause in some real or symbolic way. Campaigns also need to convince publics to align or identify themselves with the organisation, cause or idea being promoted.

There are, according to Larson (1986), five functional stages of development in all campaigns. They are now discussed.

Identification

An organisation, product, service, or idea must develop identification. It must design identifying symbols (for example logos, emblems, corporate colours, insignia) to encourage public buy-in and recognition. Slogans also assist identification and frequently become a corporate heritage if they are catchy enough. In addition, jingles, uniforms, salutes and all sorts of campaign paraphernalia (for example corporate gifts) assist in establishing name and purpose identification.

Legitimacy

The second functional stage is to establish legitimacy. Organisations can demonstrate legitimacy in several ways. They can show they care about the environment, for example, by communicating their intention to take care of the surrounding environment and the community. In idea campaigns, large numbers of participants or amounts of money are frequently used to demonstrate the legitimacy of a particular idea or cause. The participants are usually known supporters.

Participation

In the participation stage, the communication planners seek to involve previously uncommitted persons. There are many techniques for doing this. Some include effort by participants, while others involve minimal or only symbolic involvement. The wearing or display of a red bow on a jacket lapel illustrates 'symbolic' support for the fight against HIV/AIDS. Requesting motorists to switch on their lights at a particular time to show solidarity in welcoming delegates to the World Summit for Sustainable Development in Johannesburg in August 2002 was a symbolic gesture. The effects of these gestures are to increase commitment to a cause.

Penetration

This stage can be described as having 'made it' in the market. The organisation, idea, cause, product or service has been successful enough to establish a meaningful share of the market or constituency, or a meaningful 'presence' in the environment. In idea- or cause-oriented campaigns, penetration is achieved when those in power find that they are hearing about the campaign frequently enough that they must do something about it. A recent example in South Africa has been the Treatment Action Campaign (TAC) and the debate surrounding the anti-AIDS drug Nevirapine. Politicians and supporters of the dissident view that HIV does not cause AIDS were compelled to pay attention to those campaigners who felt strongly that Nevirapine had to be given to pregnant women with AIDS. Another example is the launch of a counter campaign, as attempted recently by President Robert Mugabe of Zimbabwe. At the beginning if 2002, during the general elections in Zimbabwe, President Mugabe's objective was to fight the imposition of possible sanctions against Zimbabwe by the international community, which doubted that the elections were conducted in a free and fair manner. He lobbied the international community against the sanctions, and appointed a public relations company, Cohen & Woods International, to assist him in fighting against the imposition of sanctions.

Distribution

In the final stage of development – distribution – the campaign or movement succeeds and becomes institutionalised. The communication planners of the campaign, programme or movement, having eventually achieved the control that they sought, must now live up to their promises in some way. They must show the target publics that some action or change will occur. Implementation

of the campaign ideas must take place and plans of action are usually suggested. These plans of action must align with the promises made in the campaign
and with the objectives spelled out in the campaign. A serious problem is that
campaign planners do not always live up to their promises, for example, land
is not distributed, or drugs cannot be supplied, or legislation cannot be passed
in the promised format. The targeted publics then usually become cynical about
the campaign, and about the organisations and communicators involved.

Defining the public relations campaign

It has already been stated that there are many types of campaign and, although
all campaigns have some similarities in their definitions, there are important
differences. The purpose of this chapter is to concentrate on the public relations campaign, which is the initial tangible product of the public relations
planning process. The term communication campaign is also often used. Of
course, there are many different definitions for a communication or public
relations campaign. Generally the term campaign means 'a connected series
of operations designed to bring about a particular result' (Kendall, 1992). For
the purposes of this chapter, we borrow from the definition devised by Rogers
and Storey (1987:817):

> [Public relations] campaigns are purposive attempts to inform, persuade or
> motivate behaviour changes in a relatively well-defined and large audience,
> generally for benefits to the individual and/or society at large, typically within
> a given time period, by means of organised communication activities in-
> volving mass media and often complemented by interpersonal support.

If we examine the above definition of a public relations campaign more closely,
we can see that it contains *four basic elements*:

1. A public relations campaign is *purposive* – general and specific outcomes
   are intended.

2. It is aimed at *various diverse publics* that usually make up a large audience.

3. It occurs during a *given time period*, which may range from a few weeks (for
   example, it involves traffic information concerning an upcoming long week-
   end) to many years (for example, it deals with the fight against breast cancer).

4. A public relations campaign involves an *organised set of communication
   activities*, for example, environmental scanning or research, message production, distribution and evaluation.

Public relations campaigns may include support communication that deals with
family planning, AIDS prevention, general primary health care, nature conservation, voter registration and education, organisational diversity and
employment equity, etc. The target publics of the public relations campaign

may be urban or rural, from the developed or developing world, the whole population, employees in an organisation, etc. The effects or outcomes sought for the public relations campaign may range from increasing literacy to acquiring votes; from preventing drug abuse to promoting road safety; from changing eating habits to transforming a social or political structure.

The criteria for campaign effectiveness

The following are criteria that might contribute to communication campaign effectiveness or success. They have been drawn from various literature reviews on campaigns (Rogers & Storey, 1987; Rice & Atkin, 1989).

The role of the mass media

The mass media are important for creating awareness and knowledge and for stimulating publics to participate in the campaign process. However, it is unlikely that more ambitious effects such as behavioural change might occur by using the mass media as a message vehicle on its own.

The role of interpersonal communication

Interpersonal communication, particularly through peer groups and social networks, is instrumental in attitude and behaviour change and in the maintenance of such change.

Characteristics of communicator and medium

The *credibility, reliability* and *believability* of the communicator and medium are extremely important and can influence the outcome of a public relations campaign. The more credible, reliable, believable and legitimate the communicator, and the more believable the medium, the more effective the campaign will be.

Formative evaluation

Both public relations campaigns and messages need to be evaluated to make sure they fit media habits, public dispositions and the availability of resources. For example, if bicycle riding in a particular area is promoted as a viable exercise option, then communication planners must ensure that the supply of bicycles is capable of handling increased demand, and that the public relations effort is promoted through all possible communication channels available.

Campaign appeals

Public relations campaigns must be specific rather than general in order to appeal to the values of publics. Campaign appeals or campaign approaches are the ways in which a campaign decides to communicate about a certain organisation, product, service, cause or issue. For example, message appeals in an HIV/AIDS campaign could emphasise the danger to the individual rather than referring to abstract national health standards.

Preventive behaviour

Long-term prevention goals are difficult to achieve because rewards are often delayed and uncertain (for example, wearing safety belts in a vehicle). As a result, delayed benefits must be related to immediate ones as far as possible.

Timeliness, comparability and accessibility

Public relations campaign messages must be timely and culturally acceptable, and the channels through which they are transmitted must be accessible to all the target publics. Rogers (1973) refers to cues to action as critical events that may spur a change in attitude or even behavioural change. For example, after an accident, a person might be more disposed to adopt the practice of wearing safety belts.

Public relations campaign effectiveness is a key factor in planned communication. It is measured in relation to the objectives for the campaign, set out by the public relations practitioner as communication planner. These objectives should be in line with established norms and values (McQuail, 1987). However, these norms and values might not be universally accepted. If the norms on which a campaign is based reflect the communicator's or communication planner's point of view rather than the target public's point of view, the campaign is not likely to be effective. An example is family planning, which is a positive value in the developed world but, in many developing countries, birth control campaigns encounter considerable opposition from religious, social and cultural groups.

The communicator or organisation in a campaign is usually a collective, striving to appear as sympathetic, as authoritative and as credible as possible to the target publics. The nature of the relationship between communicator and publics is crucial in a public relations campaign. If the organisation as communicator ignores the needs, values, interests and communication potential of the receiving target publics, or if the receiving publics do not attend to and understand the message of the organisation, it is likely that the public relations campaign will fail.

Case study 1 illustrates the difficulties experienced when the content of communication or public relations campaigns or programmes enters the realm of religious and cultural beliefs.

Case study 1

The last rites

For centuries women have suffered in traditional African circumcision rituals. Now women's movements are trying to stop these dangerous ceremonies.

Massita, 61, takes a piece of old cloth from her battered white purse, unfolds it and gingerly lays out seven miniature knives. The crude blades are nicked, the wooden handles worn. An older woman, sitting next to her, leans over and taps the knives twice with the fingers of her right hand, then touches her forehead. This is to avoid eye problems after looking at the knives, she says. Massita picks up one knife and explains how it is used to remove the clitoris of young women. Her mother did the same job before her, she says, and her grandmother. 'These are the very knives they used.'

The World Health Organization estimates that more than 100 million women worldwide have been circumcised, that is, had part or their entire clitoris, labia or vulva cut out. The practice, now commonly called female genital mutilation (FGM), is most widespread in sub-Saharan Africa, especially in the Horn of Africa, where up to 98% of girls are circumcised, and in Islamic populations in the continent's west. It is also found in Christian countries such as Ethiopia and Kenya. 'It doesn't matter whether it's Christian, Muslim or whatever,' says Zipporah Kittony, a Kenyan MP and chairperson of the Kenyan women's lobby group *Maendeleo Ya Wanawake* (Progress for Women). 'It's cultural and it's commonplace.'

But attitudes toward FGM are slowly changing. In a quiet revolution, African women are beginning to speak out against the practice. Media campaigns linking such rituals to difficulties in pregnancy and to HIV/AIDS have slowed the custom, especially in urban areas. The growing number of educated women has also assisted. In the countryside, success is emerging not by abolishing coming-of-age rites altogether, but by recognising their importance and replacing the cutting with alternative rituals. 'In some tribes you cannot become a mature woman unless you have come through the ritual,' says Kittony, whose group has used alternative rites to reduce the incidence of FGM in some parts of Kenya by up to 15%. 'So we teach these women to be role models rather than circumcisers. They teach the girls maturity; they counsel them.'

An alternative rite of passage, which in one Kenyan language is known as circumcision through words, commonly involves a period of seclusion for the girls. Elder women teach them health issues, including the dangers of AIDS and other sexually transmitted diseases. Sometimes a group of girls is taken to a local school or hall and shown films about the dangers of FGM. The week often ends with a party. 'We are not against people's customs, we are against the cutting,' says Traore Dosso Mariam, secretary-general of the Ivorian Association for the Defence of Women's Rights, which encourages alternative rituals.

The idea is spreading. In 2000, more than 100 former circumcisers from across Africa grouped together and agreed to put down their knives and razor blades for good. Now they instruct rural women on health and childbirth. 'We teach [the circumcisers] a trade that responds to their economic needs,' Gambian Fatou Waggeh, an anti-FGM campaigner who was circumcised at 15 and is now 32, told a Rome conference in March. '[We] recognise that we must provide them with alternatives for training and [keeping their] power within the community.'

Pressure for change is also coming from governments. At least eight sub-Saharan African nations, including Ghana, Ivory Coast, Kenya and Senegal have passed legislation or announced presidential decrees banning FGM. Africa's courts are also becoming tougher. In a historic ruling, a Kenyan court issued an order preventing a father from forcing his daughters, aged 15 and 17, to undergo circumcision. Women's groups across Africa applauded the ruling. 'You can talk to these women all you want about the human rights side of it, or the danger to the girls. But it's the threat of being arrested that has an effect,' says Drissa Kone, a 29-year-old community health worker in northern Ivory Coast. 'Let one woman in this region be arrested for performing excisions, and watch how fast they stop doing it.'

Still, prosecutions remain rare. And, unless laws are strictly enforced, they may even do more harm than good. In some places, the threat of punishment has pushed the practice underground, leading to an increased possibility of botched operations. In Odienne, north-western Ivory Coast, festivities surrounding the excision ritual are now modest affairs. 'People used to hold great fetes,' says Mabana Toure, 37. 'Streets were blocked off, there was music and the girls would run around town all made-up and dressed in special clothes. Now, we might have a special meal together in the house – something much more discreet, because people are scared.'

Elsewhere, elders continue to encourage circumcisions because the custom provides an important social and economic role. Families in the Sabaot tribe in Kenya, for instance, receive cows on the circumcision of their first girl. And alternative ceremonies can cause problems of their own. Julie Maranya, co-ordinator of a Kenyan anti-FGM group, says that because young girls are being taught sex education as part of their alternative initiation, 'they think they are now free to engage in pre-marital sex. That's why we have made many tiny mothers.'

But, as it slowly becomes more common for young women to shun circumcision, the heavy stigma of being 'uncut' is fading. Ivorian Banassiri Sylla, 34, recalls the day 26 years ago when she was to be circumcised. 'I remember the blade. How it shone! There was a woman kneeling over me with the knife. I bit her; it was all I could do. Then three women came to hold me down. One of them sat on my chest. I bit her with all my might.' The women finally let Sylla go, but her uncut status was a mark of shame for her family. 'Never, ever would I do this to my daughters,' she says. 'It strips a woman of her very womanhood.'

Even circumciser Massita realises the changing times. None of her daughters has shown an interest in taking up the family trade. When she dies, she says, she will have her knives buried with her.

(*Source:* Adapted from Robinson et al., 2001)

Planning the public relations campaign: A selection of models

Based on broad steps or phases in communication or public relations planning, there are various campaign models that the public relations practitioner as communication planner can select from when planning a campaign. These models offer practical frameworks for how public relations or communication campaigns may be planned and managed.

Each of the campaign models is briefly discussed and illustrated by means of examples. It must be kept in mind that, although these models may sound similar and might have similar stages, they differ in respect of certain important aspects. It must also be noted that the different campaign models sometimes make use of different terminology to explain similar campaign activities.

Earlier in this chapter the importance of communication planning and management were discussed. The key to effectiveness in public relations essentially concerns its contribution to the problem-solving process within an organisation, and whether it leads to attitude and behavioural change in the target publics. Systematic planning of the public relations campaign is vital.

Different authors and scholars conceptualise the steps or phases in the planning of a campaign (Van der Meiden & Fauconnier, 1982:157). Although there are a variety of other campaign models, the following ones are selected for the purposes of this chapter. They are similar in many areas, but also different in others.

The four-step public relations campaign of Cutlip, Center and Broom

The Cutlip, Center and Broom model (1985) places emphasis on the broad phases in the public relations process (called the four-step public relations process).

The four-step public relations process

1. **Defining the problem.** This involves probing and monitoring the knowledge, opinions, attitudes and behaviours of those concerned with, and affected by, the acts and policies of the organisation. It therefore involves research and fact-finding. In essence, this is an organisation's intelligence function as it requires determining: 'What is happening now?'

2. **Planning and programming.** This phase involves assessing and determining the policies and programmes of the organisation. It results in decisions affecting publics, objectives, procedures, and strategies, in the interests of all concerned. This phase in the process answers the question: 'What should be done and why?'

3. **Taking action and communicating.** In this phase the plans and programmes are implemented through both action and communication, designed to achieve the specific objectives related to the campaign goal. With respect to each of the publics, the question is: 'How do we do it and say it?'

4. **Evaluating the campaign.** This phase involves the results of the campaign, as well as assessing the effectiveness of the campaign preparation and implementation. Adjustments can be made in the continuing campaign, or the campaign can cease after learning: 'How did we do?'

The communication by objectives (CBO) model

One model to plan and manage a communication or public relations campaign was developed by Fourie (1982). His system can be viewed as communication by objectives – communication actions that are planned and purposive. This model consists of 21 steps, which are combined to form four stages: planning (steps 1–15), encoding (steps 16–17), delivery (step 18), and feedback (steps 19–21). The CBO model refers to the target publics as the destination, and to the communicator as the initiator of the communication action. This model is summarised below.

The CBO model

Planning stage

Step 1: Identify the communication needs of both the communicator and destination. These could include general or specific communication needs.

Step 2: Formulate the message. More than one message can be communicated in a single campaign. Some messages may be explicit (the overt message) and others may be implicit (the covert message).

Step 3: Formulate the objectives. The objectives of the communication are set down and are directly related to the needs and messages, as already determined.

Step 4: Determine the profitability. Campaigns can be costly. The communicator should clearly determine the communication expenditure and profit received (in terms of reaching the objectives set) as a result of the communication campaign. Resources, cost of equipment, time and effort should all be considered.

Step 5: Gather the communication elements. This step is usually known as 'gather the data' or 'find the information' or 'get the facts'. It means gathering all possible information about the campaign topic at hand.

Step 6: Analyse the destination. One of the most important steps in the planning of *any* communication or public relations campaign is the analysis of the destination (target publics or audiences). Four main areas of information can be identified when analysing the destination: their *demographic characteristics* (including gender, age, living area, and social, political and religious affiliation); their *comprehension capacity* (their level of understanding, education and knowledge of the topic); their *communication disposition* (their beliefs, attitudes and stereotypes, and their opinions of the communicator and communication campaign); and their *communication habits* (their code preferences, media preferences, and the time they have available).

Step 7: Analyse the communicator. The communicator should also determine his or her own capabilities to communicate the campaign. Own attitudes and credibility should be taken into consideration.

Step 8: Determine the circumstances. Since the circumstances in which the destination receives the communication are of pivotal importance, the communicator should try to gain as much control as possible over the delivery of the campaign.

Step 9: Timing the communication. Determining the ideal time to deliver the communication is important. The right time is when the destination is most receptive to the campaign.

Step 10: Determine the approach. A communicator should study the destination carefully to determine the approach best suited to the particular communication campaign envisaged. A choice can be made out of a serious, humorous, rational, or emotional approach. There are few communication situations in which only one approach is relied on. Usually a combination approach is used, with the emphasis on one or more of the four basic approaches as the campaign develops.

Step 11: Choose the format. There is a large variety of communication formats from which to choose. Selecting the correct format for a particular communication topic is a matter requiring careful consideration. Some of the formats in which the message can be engaged are pictorial, vocal, article, narrative, three-dimensional and musical formats. Communication campaign messages usually make use of a combination of formats as well.

Step 12: Determine the tempo. A communicator may vary the tempo of the messages in the communication campaign, either by changing the rate of presentation or by changing the structural composition of the campaign. The tempo in which campaign messages are delivered will rely on the topic of the campaign and the comprehension capacity of the destination.

Step 13: Structure the communication. Structuring the communication campaign may be effected in various ways. There are different structures that a communicator can employ: problem solution (where the emphasis is on the development of a problem and a possible solution to that problem); climax (where the communicator places the most important arguments or communication elements at the end of the communication); anticlimax (where the communicator places the most important arguments or communication elements at the beginning of the communication). There are many more structures to choose from.

Step 14: Select the codes. There are various codes that a communicator can select. In this step a distinction is made between linguistic codes (written and spoken words) and non-verbal or semiological codes (signs).

Step 15: Select the media. In this step the ideal is to combine mass media, group and interpersonal communication. The media selection will be determined by the type of communication campaign, the accessibility to media of the destination, and the available budget for the campaign.

Encoding stage

Step 16: Encode the communication. The communication campaign is shaped during this step and comes to life.

Step 17: Test the communication. Before the communication campaign is presented, it should be tested. Testing of the campaign (sample testing by experts, researchers or the communicator) is essential to ensure that the encoding is correct.

Delivery stage

Step 18: Deliver the communication. This is the last stage of the campaign that a communicator can control before the destination receives the communication and starts the decoding process. It is important, therefore, that communicators know as much as possible about the different presentation techniques and are able to make use of them as and when they are needed. These techniques may include speech or personal presentation; written communication through the printed media; audiovisual and electronic communication; or a combination of all of these.

Feedback stage

Step 19: Arrange for feedback. Feedback is the information that the communicator acquires from the destination once they have received the communication campaign, and from which the communicator can determine the measure of success (the eventual attitudinal or behavioural change of the destination) that has been achieved in terms of the objectives set. There are a number of ways to receive feedback: by means of direct observation; through research – for example the use of questionnaires; through marked changes in attitude and behaviour; through voluntary comments; through support for the campaign; and through expert evaluation.

Step 20: Evaluate effectiveness. After receiving feedback from the destination, the communicator is now in a position to evaluate his or her campaign efforts.

Step 21: Stop or repeat. After evaluating the success (or lack thereof) of the campaign, the communicator must decide on future action, that is, whether to stop or repeat the campaign.

(*Source:* Adapted from Fourie, 1982)

The CBO model is one of the many models that can be used in the planning of a communication campaign. Although it is a detailed model, it might be criticised for being too elaborate and lengthy.

The Public Relations Institute of Southern Africa (PRISA) model

Jefkins (1982) identified the following basic key steps in the planning of a campaign:

▲ appreciation of the situation

▲ definition of objectives

▲ definition of publics

▲ selection of media and techniques

▲ budget

▲ assessment of results.

Using the Jefkins model, the Public Relations Institute of Southern Africa (PRISA) identified seven key stages in planning a public relations programme or campaign. The importance of each stage is now reviewed.

The PRISA model

1. **Defining the situation (situation analysis).** The situation analysis and techniques that are used in a campaign are determined by the motivation for the planning and implementing of the campaign. Should the public relations campaign be implemented in order to solve a problem, the SWOT analysis (determining the *strengths*, *weaknesses*, *opportunities* and *threats*) will identify what the problems are and how they can be solved. Examples of these kinds of problems are poor organisational image, poor product recall, or a major disaster or crisis. However, should the public relations campaign be implemented in order to establish and develop regular, ongoing communication, the emphasis will be more on the organisation: how it functions and its role within society. It will also be important to identify and develop close and harmonious relations with the organisation's target publics or stakeholders. This stage of the campaign is perhaps the most crucial. Without an understanding of the strengths and weaknesses of the organisation in question, the public's perception towards it, its performance and – above all – its managers, no real progress is likely to occur. Putting out fires is one thing, but building trust, confidence and commitment are at the heart of effective public relations (Skinner & Von Essen, 1995:129).

2. **Formulating objectives.** The objectives of a campaign are formulated in accordance with the situation analysis, and should be specific and measurable. For example, in the development field, the overall,

---

long-term objective could be 'black empowerment'. More specific, short-term objectives will flow from this overall mission statement, which could assist in informing, motivating and educating specific target publics about the organisation and what it stands for. It is pivotal to be aware of the difference between *motivational objectives* (to achieve action) and *informational objectives* (to spread information). The effectiveness of the campaign will eventually be evaluated in terms of these objectives.

3. **Identifying target publics.** The target publics may be divided into internal and external, or primary and secondary target publics. According to Jefkins (1982:19–25), an organisation's publics may be categorised in the following groups, depending on the type of organisation:

   ▲ the community

   ▲ opinion leaders

   ▲ employees

   ▲ shareholders

   ▲ suppliers and services

   ▲ distributors/dealers

   ▲ competitors

   ▲ consumers and users

   ▲ the financial environment

   ▲ government or government-related bodies or authorities

   ▲ the media.

   The above constitute a broad definition of an organisation's target publics. In order to formulate a message in the campaign targeted at each public in particular, one may need to break down these publics even further.

4. **Formulating messages.** The essence of the public relations campaign is the basic message transmitted to the organisation's publics. The concept *message* in public relations should be interpreted in a broader sense. It has to do with the communication content that needs to be communicated through the public relations campaign. Often an overall theme is designed to convey a message (Skinner & Von Essen, 1995:129).

5. **Implementing actions.** This step refers to the broad range of public relations strategies and techniques that can be implemented to communicate a specific message to the targeted publics in order to meet a number of specified objectives. It is important that each of these strategies and techniques be properly researched, costed, and prioritised. This will allow for careful and considered assessment of each one in the final analysis. The overall public relations activities must be related to the problem, the objectives, the target publics and the message.

6. **Drawing up a budget.** In drawing up a budget, a clear distinction must be made between administrative and campaign budgets. The administrative budget comprises the running costs of a public relations department or consultancy and includes staff salaries, office equipment, stationery, postage and other operational costs. The campaign budget comprises costs related to the execution of the public relations campaign and to the techniques employed in the action plan, including exhibitions, conferences, seminars, catering, printing, publicity and photography. It is important that correct budgeting and careful monitoring be undertaken with variances noted and reported on (Skinner & Von Essen, 1995:131).

7. **Conducting an evaluation.** This is a vital step in the planning of any campaign. It is important to determine the effectiveness of each and every campaign. This can be achieved by using a selection of formal and informal research techniques, for example interviews, focus groups and questionnaires. At the end of a comprehensive campaign, the management of the particular organisation should be informed of its success in tangible terms, measured against specific, measurable objectives.

The PRISA model is concise and provides the opportunity to collect essential information to put together a substantial campaign. Perhaps one criticism is that it might be more effective in the planning and management of actual public relations campaigns as a supportive communication function, rather than in communication campaigns on a more strategic, concentrated and wider scale. However, it is a tried and tested mechanism.

Case study 2 makes use of some of the basic steps in the PRISA model.

Case study 2

A non-profit public relations campaign – Sefin Marketing Communications Consultants

Synopsis

The Foundation for Human Rights is a non-profit, independent South African body that funds non-government organisations (NGOs) active in the field of human rights. The Foundation was established four years ago under an agreement between the European Union and the South African government. It focuses on making human rights a practical, daily reality for those communities that have been – and in many cases still are – the most disadvantaged, the most vulnerable and the most marginalised.

Sefin Marketing's campaign ran from December 1999 to September 2000, with two primary objectives:

1. to create awareness of the Foundation and its work among the general public

2. to make South Africans at all levels of society aware of their human rights under South Africa's new constitution, and also of the redress mechanisms available to those who had suffered human rights abuses. The general public was a primary audience of the campaign. NGOs and the Chapter Nine institutions – such as the Public Protector, the Commission on Gender Equality and the Human Rights Commission – were secondary audiences.

Media liaison

The best means of reaching all the audiences was through the printed and electronic media (including mainstream news media and community radio stations and newspapers). Sefin's major challenge was to persuade journalists that human rights are not dry, legalistic and constitutional issues. To do this, Sefin used human interest stories illustrating human rights principles. Also, as most human rights issues are controversial, Sefin triggered public debate by linking Foundation information to topical issues. It also needed to ensure mention of the Foundation in stories that would otherwise be dominated by the NGOs running the projects. To achieve this, Sefin got Foundation spokespeople to explain the human rights principles that caused them to fund the project.

Prior to Sefin's involvement, the Foundation had received virtually no publicity. In the ten months of the campaign, Sefin achieved coverage worth more than R4,7 million, a 2 000% return on the client's investment. A notable measurement of success was the fact that a Foundation story titled 'Government housing creates more problems than it solves' influenced a change in government housing policy. The story triggered the Minister of Housing to ask for Foundation recommendations for adequate housing to be presented to a parliamentary portfolio committee tasked with revising government housing policy and procedures.

The entire Sefin campaign was founded on pure public and media relations. At no stage was there any advertising or paid advertorial support.

Other activities

To reflect the fact that the Foundation is an independent South African organisation, a decision was taken to change its name from the European Union for Human Rights in South Africa to the Foundation for Human Rights. A new visual identity was created for the Foundation, moving the logo away from a classical European style to a more African look and feel. A community event was held at Makhulong Stadium, Tembisa, near Kempton Park on Human Rights Day (21 March 2000) to celebrate the progress made in realising human rights for all South Africans since the country's first democratic elections, and to increase awareness of human rights at grassroots level.

To mark the Foundation's achievements during its first four years, Sefin produced a 20-page review that was distributed throughout European Union embassies, local and international academic institutions, South African national government departments, and mainstream news media. Sefin also produced an eight-page bulletin covering human rights issues for the use of 25 nationwide advice offices that the Foundation funds, and whose contact with grassroots communities is close and direct.

Statement of problem/opportunity

Background

With the writing of the new constitution and the adoption of a Bill of Rights, South Africa became one of only a quarter of the world's nations to entrench human rights in the constitution, and one of only three countries to establish a national plan of action. The world then looked to South Africa to demonstrate how a country might be taken from a zero base to a full human rights culture – at all levels of society. The government took only five years to put the necessary legislative framework in place to enable the enforcement and practical implementation of human rights through the national plan of action. What remained to be done was to make the general public aware of their human rights, to let them know where to get help in cases of human rights abuses, and for government to deliver on socio-economic rights (jobs, adequate housing, access to energy sources, clean water, etc.) at grassroots level.

Foundation for Human Rights

The Foundation for Human Rights was founded in October 1996, by agreement between the European Union (EU) and the South African government, to fund projects undertaken by NGOs working in the human rights field in South Africa. The Foundation is a non-profit body funded by the EU. Its objectives are to promote the cause of human rights in South Africa through four main pillars of funding activity:

1. promotion of socio-economic rights

2. support for substantive equality

3. emphasis on access to justice

4. support for victims of human rights abuse.

The Foundation's work is aimed at creating a national human rights ethos.

Problems at media level

The media's approach to human rights was to regard them as constitutional and legalistic issues and to relegate them to parliamentary and court reporters who, by the nature of their work, focused on news rather than background issues. Also, parliamentary and legal coverage can be abstract and complex, and somewhat inaccessible to the ordinary reader. As a result, the considerable work the Foundation was doing to restore the dignity of – particularly – poor, rural and marginalised people was going unnoticed by the media and therefore by the public.

Research

During 1999, the Foundation had instituted a grassroots awareness campaign co-ordinated by the NGO Rights Africa. It was based on free concerts in townships and therefore limited in reach. The campaign provided some statistics regarding levels of awareness of human rights at grassroots level – as at the middle of 1999. These showed that at least half of all South Africans did not know about their rights under the new constitution and Bill of Rights. There was awareness of the existence of the Bill of Rights, but understanding of its contents and ramifications was low. Awareness of institutions of redress such as the Public Protector, the Commission on Gender Equality, and the Human Rights Commission was non-existent. Where there was knowledge, it was highest among teenage girls and boys, and lowest among older men and women. There was low awareness of issues relating to disability, refugees and immigrants, as well as the rights of people living with HIV/AIDS, although there was high awareness of AIDS itself. From these findings, it was clear that Sefin would be working from a zero base and that any publicity would result in a gain in awareness.

Strategic planning

Sefin was appointed in December 1999 to work with the Foundation during the closing ten months of its initial four-year programme. Sefin began the assignment with a series of brainstorming workshops with the entire Foundation staff team, headed by the director and including its four project officers. During these sessions, the Foundation's visual identity, objectives, target audiences and messaging evolved in a highly participative way, through the use of an inclusive democratic process.

Objectives

The communication campaign had two primary objectives:

1. to create awareness of the Foundation and its work among the general public

2. to make South Africans at all levels of society aware of their human rights under South Africa's new constitution, and also of the redress mechanisms available to those who had suffered human rights abuses.

Given the short (ten-month) timespan of the project, the media objective was to obtain as much news coverage of Foundation-funded projects as possible for the full duration of the campaign.

Establishment of measurable criteria for success

In view of the broad scope of the campaign, and in the absence of a budget for formal market research, it was agreed that evaluation would be based on coverage received in the media and through other platforms.

Identification of publics

The Foundation's audiences were comprehensive, and included:

Primary audiences:

▲ the general public

▲ South Africans at all levels of society.

Secondary audiences:

▲ non-government organisations (NGOs)

▲ government departments

▲ Chapter Nine institutions such as the Public Protector, the Commission on Gender Equality and the Human Rights Commission

▲ European Union officials and embassies

▲ local and international academic institutions

▲ the legal profession.

Formulation of messages

The basic messages agreed upon during the workshop sessions were that:

▲ the Foundation for Human Rights promotes the cause of human rights in South Africa

▲ the human rights of each and every South African are entrenched under the constitution

▲ all South Africans have the right of redress if they suffer human rights abuses.

Selection of communication channels

Media liaison

The best means of reaching all audiences ranging from NGOs and government departments to the general public in a short space of time were the printed and electronic media (including mainstream news media and community radio stations and newspapers). Sefin gave the media liaison campaign a formal structure by focusing on official recognition of human rights days such as Women's Day and International Human Rights Day, and features planned by mainstream publications such as Water Month (*The Star*) and Corporate Social Responsibility (*Business Day*). A database of all features for the period January to September 2000 was compiled at the outset of the programme, and updated regularly. Sefin also focused on planned Foundation or NGO project events such as a public event on South African Human Rights Day, the publication of a resource manual on women's rights, a national conference on language rights, and the publication of research on the right to adequate housing.

Corporate identity

It was agreed that the Foundation's original name – the European Union Foundation for Human Rights in South Africa – was limiting and should be changed to reflect the fact that the body is an independent South African organisation. This would pave the way for a change in directorship – from a French national, employed on assignment from the European Union, to a South African citizen – and could prove useful in the future, should the Foundation need to rely on local resources for funding.

Human Rights celebratory event

The Foundation wished to make Human Rights day on 21 March 2000 a day of celebration of South Africa's progress thus far towards a human rights culture. It also wished to make this a day for making South

Africans aware of what lay ahead in delivering human rights to each citizen. For this reason, it was agreed to hold an event on Human Rights Day to celebrate and increase awareness of human rights. A human rights concert was held in Tembisa.

Four-year review

It was agreed that a review of the Foundation's activities from October 1996 to September 2000 should be produced so as to account to all those involved in human rights issues in South Africa for what it had done. The review would be distributed chiefly to European Union embassies, local and international academic institutions, South African national government departments, and mainstream news publications.

Execution: A description of implementation (activities deployed)

Media liaison

The Sefin team working on the Foundation account comprised an account director, an account manager, an account executive and a writer. Story research was an essential platform for all the media material that the team generated. Sefin's writer and account manager sourced background information on the general field of human rights. They researched the legal human rights principles involved in specific projects funded by the Foundation and discussed them with the Foundation's project officers. Sefin's writer also conducted interviews with the NGOs running the projects. In all the stories, however, the focus was not on the human rights principles but on human interest angles which would illustrate relevant principles to South Africans. Also, since most human rights issues are controversial, Sefin wrote stories that would trigger public debate by linking Foundation and NGO project information to topical issues. Sefin sourced special interest publications whose audiences matched their secondary target audiences (NGOs and government departments). They then built relationships with, and created specially targeted material, for such publications as *Reconstruct* (*Sunday Independent*), *De Rebus* and various government digests. In addition, they established relationships with a selection of community radio stations and newspapers in order to address the special language needs of remote communities in putting the message across.

In all cases, Sefin sold the concepts to editors and journalists before submitting written material for publication. It also arranged interviews for Foundation and project spokespeople with journalists. This was particularly successful with the electronic media. Sefin found that print journalists preferred to receive – and use verbatim – material they had written.

Corporate identity

Following several brainstorming sessions with the client and some informal research, the name of the organisation was changed from the European Union Foundation for Human Rights in South Africa to the shorter, more relevant Foundation for Human Rights. At the same time, the visual identity of the Foundation was revamped, moving the logo away from the classical style of a European (Greek) temple to a looser, more African interpretation. The Foundation's colours of red, green, blue, yellow and black were retained, because of their vibrancy as primary colours and their association with the colours of the South African flag. The new identity was implemented across basic stationery items ranging from folders to letterheads, compliment slips and business cards.

Human rights concert at Tembisa

A community event was held at Makhulong Stadium, Tembisa, near Kempton Park, on Human Rights Day (21 March 2000) to celebrate the progress made in realising human rights for all South Africans since the country's first democratic elections in 1994. The event was organised by the Foundation for Human Rights together with the Human Rights Commission, the Public Protector and the Commission on Gender Equality, in partnership with the NGO Rights Africa – the first time ever that these bodies had collaborated on a project.

The celebration got off to a flying start with a five-kilometre fun run organised by the Rainbow Athletic Club and Youth for Aids and sponsored by the Foundation. The home soccer side, Classic FC, got the upperhand in a soccer match against a Celebrity Eleven including Bafana Bafana player Daniel Mudau, Sundowns player Isaac Shai, and former Chiefs player Marks Maponyane. More than 15 000 people braved pouring rain to enjoy the day's highlight, a high-energy concert featuring Kwaito stars Arthur and Aba Shante. Some 20 NGOs involved in human rights activities staffed stalls to inform members of the public about their rights and the mechanism of redress open to them in the case of rights abuses. The large turnout was catered for by community vendors. Addressing the crowd, Louise Asmal, chairperson of the Foundation for Human Rights, said: 'The world can still look to South Africa to solve seemingly intransigent human rights problems.' Foundation director, Nicolas Marcoux, added: 'This event has demonstrated that it is possible to create awareness about human rights by involving the community at grassroots level.' The Public Protector, advocate Selby Baqwa, and Dr Barney Pityana, chairperson of the Human Rights Commission, reinforced this message by outlining the critical role their organisations play in the promotion and protection of citizens' human rights.

Four-year review

The intention of the four-year review was to provide an overview of the 309 projects the Foundation funded from October 1996 to September 2000, disbursing more than R80 million to the NGOs involved. The review posed a considerable challenge to the Sefin team in terms of covering the full range and scope of Foundation activities, while working within a limited budget. In all its work, the Foundation focused on making human rights a practical, daily reality for those communities that were – and in many cases still are – the most disadvantaged, the most vulnerable and the most marginalised. This work was to form the major content of the review. Again, following brainstorming sessions with the Foundation's team, it was agreed to manage the huge amount of material by dividing it into four sections, each concentrating on one of the main pillars of funding activity:

1. socio-economic rights

2. human rights abuses

3. access to justice

4. equality.

Adjustments to plan

Media liaison

There was an *ad hoc*, news element to the campaign: precedent-setting litigation funded by the Foundation could arise suddenly and could not be planned for. An example was the urgent interdict brought by Live Africa Network against the King Commission of Inquiry into cricket match-fixing. In support of the right of individuals to receive information, Live Africa applied to be allowed to transmit Hansie Cronje's cross-examination live on national radio.

Paralegal bulletin

During the course of the campaign, the project officers identified a need on the part of paralegal advice officers for specific information on legal aspects of human rights. As a result, Sefin produced an eight-page bulletin for the use of 25 Foundation-funded advice offices nationwide, whose contact with grassroots communities was close and direct.

Difficulties encountered

Challenges and obstacles overcome

The challenge identified at the outset was to have the media focus on human rights issues, and to persuade them that these were not dry, academic constitutional matters. Sefin achieved this by focusing on human interest angles and making human rights real to South Africans. Once journalists understood that they were not going to foist legalese and complex human rights theory on them, they became eager for Sefin's stories. Another challenge was to achieve mention of the Foundation in the stories, when these more often than not focused on an NGO project. Sefin did this by having the Foundation's project officers explain the human rights principles that had prompted it to fund the featured project. Sefin also briefed all NGO project spokespeople to mention the Foundation in interviews they had with the media. *Ad hoc* news items presented the challenge of turning the stories around quickly enough to meet media deadlines. Obviously, this happens with all news items. However, the Foundation's news stories presented three additional complications: first, the Foundation project officers needed for comment were often present at court proceedings and therefore inaccessible to Sefin; second, it took considerable time to reduce to layperson's terms the legal intricacies involved in judgements; third, judgements are seldom clear-cut and, therefore, are lengthy and difficult to summarise accurately to acceptable press release length – in time to make the evening's major bulletins.

Evaluation: Identification, analysis and quantification of results

As had been established at the beginning of the campaign, Sefin was working from a zero base of human rights awareness among the general public and government officials, and a limited base of awareness among NGOs. Thus, any publicity constituted a gain. In fact, Sefin achieved some remarkable results, measured not only in financial terms, but also in terms of influencing attitudes and policies.

Impact on government policy

In one landmark case, the publicity arranged by Sefin positively changed government housing policy. A Sefin story entitled 'Government housing creates more problems than it solves' received rolling national coverage, creating heated debate and occasional critical comment by various stakeholders and opinion influencers. It triggered the Minister of Housing to ask for Foundation recommendations for adequate housing to be presented to a parliamentary portfolio committee tasked with revising government housing policy and procedures.

Return on investment

In terms of a return on the Foundation's investment in a public relations campaign, Sefin achieved a 2 000% return by receiving coverage of 108 stories in the print media and 25 in the electronic media, achieving publicity worth more than R4.7 million (using the standard formula of 6x advertising rates based on single column centimetres). Sefin's fee for the campaign was R21 500 per month. Several notable successes were achieved as a result of the media liaison campaign. For example, at the time of Human Rights Day in March 2000, *The Sowetan*, in its four-page feature on the day, carried four articles submitted by Sefin. The next day, *The Citizen* carried five photographs of the Human Rights concert at Tembisa. The event also attracted widespread television and radio coverage.

Reach

Moving from a zero base, Sefin's Foundation messages and information broke the silence on human rights for the first time for millions of people – via ongoing national television, radio and print media coverage, as well as community radio and print coverage. Also, coverage encompassed all official language groupings and all strata of society – a rare achievement in as diverse a society as ours.

Budget details (investment)

A full 100% of the programme budget was spent on public relations activities. There was no advertising or paid advertorial support.

(*Source:* Adapted from the PRISM entry proposal; Sefin was the winner of a Silver PRISM Award in 2000)

The interactive model of campaign planning

This is a two-way, interactive model of public relations planning in which the targeted publics yield information to the organisation through its research efforts, and the publics participate in the public relations programming or campaigning itself. In the best of these interactive examples, the publics actually become the programming. The interactive model is best suited for persuasive communication situations (Hendrix, 1992:3).

A simple way of defining public relations has been to invert the term so that it becomes 'relations with publics'. The interactive model suggests a further modification so that the definition becomes 'interrelationships with publics'. This interactive or mutual dimension of public relations planning is seen in the comprehensive description by the Public Relations Society of America (PRSA), made in 1982.

This model involves four procedures. A brief discussion of this campaign model follows.

The interactive model

Research

Research consists of investigating three aspects of the overall public relations procedure:

1. *client research* (researching the client or organisation for whom the campaign is being prepared)

2. *opportunity* or *problem research* (researching the problem or opportunity that accounts for the campaign)

3. *audience research* (researching all publics targeted for the public relations campaign).

In the research effort, a number of research methods can be used, including quantitative and qualitative research techniques.

Objectives

Objectives are the single most important elements in this public relations campaign-planning model. They represent the public relations practitioner's desired outcomes in communicating with the targeted publics. Some scholars and practitioners draw a distinction between *goals* as more general outcomes and *objectives* as specific, immediate results (Hendrix, 1992:19). Two basic types of objective are used in public relations campaigns according to this model: impact objectives and output objectives.

Output objectives represent the work to be produced – the distribution or execution of campaign materials. These objectives refer to stated intentions regarding campaign production and effort (or output). They describe a type of desired outcome often stated in public relations campaigns. Some practitioners use only output objectives in their public relations campaigns. The advantage of this is that output objectives set definite, specific and attainable goals, which can be measured quantitatively. Once these goals have been met, the practitioner can claim success. Unfortunately, output objectives are unrelated to the actual impact the campaign may have on its internal publics.

Impact objectives measure the impact the planned campaign will have. There are three kinds of impact objectives:

1. *Informational objectives* include message exposure to, message comprehension by, or message retention by the target public. Such objectives are appropriate when the practitioner wishes to publicise

an action or event; seeks to communicate instructions or any other form of information; or wants to educate publics about a topic that is non-controversial.

2. *Attitudinal objectives* aim at modifying the way a target public feels about the client or organisation and its activities, products or services. These objectives can have as their goal the reinforcement, enhancement or intensification of existing attitudes, or the changing or reversing of – usually negative – existing attitudes. Attitudinal objectives, then, may attempt the formation of new attitudes where none exist; the reinforcement of existing attitudes; or change in existing attitudes.

3. *Behavioural objectives* involve the modification of behaviour towards the client or organisation. Like attitude modification, behaviour modification may consist of the creation or stimulation of new behaviour; the enhancement or intensification of existing favourable behaviour; or the reversal of negative behaviour on the part of a public towards the practitioner's client or organisation.

Programming

Public relations programming (or campaigning), as presented in this model, includes the following elements of planning and execution:

▲ statement of a theme, if applicable, and messages to be communicated to the publics

▲ determining the available budget

▲ planning the action or special event(s) sponsored by the client or organisation

▲ planning the use of media, either controlled or uncontrolled

▲ effective communication of the campaign or programme.

The use of *uncontrolled media* involves the communication of news about the client or organisation to the mass media and to specialised media outlets. The objective is favourable news coverage of the organisation's actions and events. The media are uncontrolled because the practitioner loses control of them at the media outlet itself. The use of *controlled media*, however, involves communication about the organisation that is paid for by the organisation. The wording of the material, its format, and its placement in the media are at the discretion of the organisation. The formats of controlled media include printed materials such as brochures, newsletters, annual reports, and interpersonal communication such as speeches, meetings and interviews.

Evaluation

Evaluation is an ongoing process of monitoring and, when appropriate, final assessment of the stated objectives of the public relations campaign. In this process, the following need to be evaluated:

▲ **informational objectives** – measured by publicity placement, surveys, etc.

▲ **attitudinal objectives** – measured by attitude and opinion surveys

▲ **behavioural objectives** – measured by surveys and observation of behaviour

▲ **output objectives** – measured quantitatively by counting the actual output.

This model has fewer steps than other models and is easier to implement.

Steyn and Puth's model for developing a communication plan

Based on various steps in the communication planning process, a working model for developing a communication plan is provided by Steyn and Puth (2000). This model provides new insights in the strategic planning of a public relations campaign.

Steyn and Puth's communication plan model

Research
▲ Problem or opportunity statement
▲ Situation analysis

Planning
▲ Communication goals (overall, long term)
▲ Communication objectives (specific, short term)
▲ Management liaison

Adaptation phase
▲ Specific target groups
▲ Statement of limitations

Message

▲ Central message derived from goals

▲ Message for each target group

▲ Theme or slogan

Implementation strategy and activities

▲ Implementation strategy (what needs to be communicated)

▲ Activities (how they will be communicated)

▲ Central action of special event

▲ Media for each activity

Scheduling

▲ Which day, week or month?

Budget

▲ Cost for each activity must be determined

Evaluation research

▲ Process/impact research

▲ In-process/internal/external evaluation research

▲ Formative/summative evaluation research

Selling the plan to top management

(*Source:* Adapted from Steyn and Puth, 2000:82)

This model is useful because it pays deliberate attention to the strategic role of public relations practitioners in planning campaigns. It also emphasises the importance of management 'buy-in' on a campaign effort. Selling the plan to top management is often downplayed or ignored in other models of campaign planning.

This section of the chapter provided a summary of various communication and public relations models for campaign or programme planning. All of these models can be utilised effectively in campaign planning, depending on the situation and variables to which they are most suited.

Case study 3

Pampers provides pregnancy education for all – Meropa Communications

Synopsis

Meropa Communications first introduced the concept of Pregnancy Education Week (PEW) to Pampers, the disposable nappy brand, in 1999. As both a social responsibility project and a business building exercise, the first PEW was so successful that Pampers briefed Meropa to launch the week on an annual basis.

The brief

▲ The overall objective of PEW is to communicate to all expectant mothers the importance of attending antenatal classes for a happy and healthy pregnancy. By attending classes, Pampers aims to assist in reducing South Africa's high maternal mortality rate, as well as to introduce parents to the Pampers nappy brand in the classes.

▲ As a result of South Africa's high maternal death rate, the primary PR challenge for Pregnancy Education Week 2000 was to communicate the key message of the importance of attending pregnancy education classes to moms-to-be, and to subsequently increase the number of pregnant woman attending antenatal classes by 5%.

The strategy

In response to the brief, Meropa developed a two-pronged strategy:

1. **Ambassadors of PEW** – Meropa recommended linking with strategic partners to profile the need for pregnant women to attend antenatal classes. Meropa and Pampers approached the Department of Health to work closely with Pampers to highlight South Africa's high maternal mortality rate and, therefore, the need for all women to attend antenatal classes. Meropa also recommended working with the Childbirth Educators' Resource Group (CBERG) to create partnerships with childbirth educators and to utilise this national network to create awareness and excitement about Pregnancy Education Week. Pampers and Meropa created PEW kits for the childbirth educators, containing posters, PEW ribbons and information leaflets, which were distributed to the childbirth educators to enable these ambassadors to organise regional events during PEW. By organising local activities, Meropa ensured that the PEW message also reached rural areas.

2. **Media strategy** – In tandem with this ambassador programme, Meropa developed an extensive media strategy. Individual angles

were brainstormed to ensure the media had relevant and targeted stories. For example, Meropa produced a chromalin with the PEW story, complete with pictures, and syndicated it to all the Caxton newspapers. In addition, it drafted a sample press release and issued it to regional childbirth educators in order to reach the regional press effectively. Meropa also took journalists from *The Sowetan* to visit an antenatal ward at a rural hospital to ensure that the PEW message reached women where maternal mortality is highest. As a result of specific targeting, Meropa was successful in securing editorial coverage of PEW and its core messages across parenting, consumer, electronic, national and regional media.

The results

Meropa Communications believes that PEW 2000 stands as an excellent PR case study. First, Meropa was successful in creating generic awareness of PEW and why pregnancy education is so important for all women. Second, the Childbirth Educators' Resource Group reported a direct increase in the number of pregnant women attending antenatal classes:

▲ Meropa secured 123 editorial stories, with a media coverage value of R1 231 203 (based on a straight advertising rate).

▲ CBERG reported that it witnessed a 10% increase in the number of pregnant women attending antenatal classes following PEW 2000.

The client

Procter & Gamble (the client) believes PEW is an excellent PR achievement. Alex Cowie, Pampers Brand Manager adds: 'Meropa Communications developed a concept that makes Pampers a socially responsible brand, as well as placing us in a business-building position. The media coverage that was achieved was phenomenal and PEW 2000 is a case study we use at P&G to demonstrate the power of PR.'

The problem

South African women are twelve times more likely to die from pregnancy or pregnancy-related complications than their American or European counterparts.

The opportunity

The World Health Organisation's 'Saving Mothers' report shows that obstetric complications and maternal deaths are highest in Africa. After a national campaign in England to improve antenatal care, the maternal death rate dropped from 54 deaths per 100 000 births to 12,2 deaths per 100 000 births.

The answer

Pampers, the disposable nappy brand, launched Pregnancy Education Week as an annual event to demonstrate the importance of antenatal classes, and offered Pampers' starter kits to mothers at these classes. The week became a social responsibility project as well as a business-building exercise for Pampers.

Challenges and obstacles overcome

The main challenge was the short time allocation to implement the strategy. Meropa experienced several time delays in securing the Department of Health as a partner and, as a result, its implementation time was significantly reduced.

Strategy

Objectives

▲ To promote awareness of Pregnancy Education Week.

▲ To create awareness of the importance of attending childbirth education classes for a happy and health pregnancy.

▲ To promote awareness of Pampers' link with Pregnancy Education Week.

▲ To increase the number of pregnant women who attend antenatal classes and thereby assist in reducing South Africa's high maternal mortality rate, as well as to build Pampers' business by exposing the brand to pregnant women at antenatal classes.

Communication messages

Core:

▲ All pregnant South African women should attend antenatal classes for a happy and healthy pregnancy.

Secondary:

▲ To find an antenatal class in your area, call the CBERG hotline at 0800 18 18 18.

▲ Pampers supports pregnancy education for all.

Target audiences

▲ Meropa recommended using the Childbirth Educators' Resource Group and the media as the correct communication channels to reach all women aged 18–34 years.

Measurable criteria

▲ To achieve R1 million worth of editorial coverage in communicating Pregnancy Education Week's key messages.

▲ To increase the number of women currently attending antenatal classes by 5%.

The way forward: PEW PR strategy

Meropa recommended a two-pronged approach:

▲ Create pregnancy education ambassadors to spread the word among the target market.

▲ Communicate PEW's message via an extensive but highly targeted media strategy.

Programme execution

Ambassadors

▲ **Department of Health:** Meropa approached the Department of Health to work together as a strategic partner for Pregnancy Education Week and to add credibility to the campaign. As a result, it was able to utilise the Minister of Health, Dr Manto Tshabalala-Msimang, as a spokesperson at both the PEW press conference and in all the press material.

▲ **Childbirth Educators' Resource Group (CBERG):** Similarly, Meropa approached CBERG, the national network of childbirth educators, to become ambassadors for Pregnancy Education Week. Meropa staged three roadshows in Durban, Cape Town and Johannesburg, where it introduced PEW to over 330 childbirth educators. At the roadshows, Meropa presented the educators with PEW kits containing posters, PEW ribbons, event posters, etc. and encouraged the educators to organise regional events to raise awareness of antenatal classes. Meropa developed a starter kit containing ideas on events, how to organise an event, how to secure publicity for an event, etc. In addition, Meropa provided each educator with sample press releases to send to their local newspapers to publicise their activities, as well as contact details for local media to ensure the educators had relevant resources with which to maximise awareness of the week. To assist the educators with profiling their regional events, Meropa approached *Your Baby* and *Ons Baba* magazines and, together, they produced a PEW events directory which detailed activities across South Africa. The events directory was attached to the front cover of each magazine and was banded with a PEW yellow ribbon.

Media strategy

▲ Meropa developed an extensive media strategy, which targeted electronic, national, consumer and regional media. It worked closely with the Department of Health to develop a PEW media pack, including a media release, a pregnancy fact sheet and information on the Childbirth Educators' Resource Group (CBERG).

▲ **PEW media launch:** To launch PEW 2000, Meropa co-ordinated a press conference with the Minister of Health and the Director of Women's and Maternal Health as spokespeople. Meropa launched PEW to 80 guests including media, key health professionals and Department of Health personnel.

▲ **Media plan:** Meropa segmented the media and approached each individually:

△ *Television* – Meropa invited SABC News to attend the media launch, and offered footage of antenatal classes in action. It secured an insert on the evening news reiterating the importance of pregnancy education for all South Africans. In addition, it approached the SABC continuity presenters and invited them to wear a Pregnancy Education bow to show their support of the week, as well as to introduce PEW to their viewers. Meropa secured television coverage on SABC 3 news, *Morning Live* and SABC 2.

△ *Radio* – Meropa approached specific radio programmes, for example *Women's Hour*, and offered a relevant spokesperson to talk about PEW. It secured a one-hour slot on SAFM to discuss pregnancy issues, antenatal classes, etc. Meropa also received editorial exposure on Highveld, Kaya FM, Radio 786 and Voice.

△ *Internet* – Meropa submitted press material to various health and parenting websites, resulting in stories on Iclinic, Netparent and Woza.

△ *Parenting press* – Meropa worked closely with the various parenting magazines to provide each publication with an individual angle. For example, it took *Your Baby* magazine to an antenatal ward in a rural area to demonstrate the impact of adequate antenatal care for all. Each parenting title, including *Living & Loving, Your Baby, Ons Baba* and *Clicks Club Card Baby Magazine* covered PEW and its key messages.

△ *National media* – Each national newspaper was contacted with the PEW story, resulting in features in *The Saturday Star, Independent on Saturday, The Citizen, The Mail & Guardian* and *Beeld*. Meropa also invited *The Sowetan* to visit an antenatal ward in a rural area to ensure the PEW message reached all pregnant women.

△ **Regional media** – Meropa approached the regional media in two ways: first, it negotiated with the Caxton newspaper group to circulate a chromalin with the PEW story and pictures. The PEW story was subsequently syndicated to all the Caxton newspapers. In addition, Meropa offered the leading Caxton newspapers the opportunity to run PEW-related competitions in their papers. Second, utilising the network of childbirth educators, Meropa developed localised press releases to discuss PEW and the events taking place in a specific region. This ensured extensive coverage in all areas.

△ **Health press** – The health magazines were offered access to health professionals and childbirth educators, which resulted in relevant and interesting information for their publications. Most major titles attended the PEW press conference.

Budget

▲ As a result of the social responsibility nature of PEW, the total PR budget was R80 000. This included Meropa Communications' PR fee and expenses, for example the press conference launch.

▲ On a PR budget of R80 000, Meropa secured editorial coverage valued at R1 231 203. The return on investment for PEW 2000 was therefore 1 538%.

Evaluation

▲ Meropa secured PR coverage that communicated the PEW message in 118 different media titles. This achieved a total editorial value of R1 231 203, with a reach of over 9 499 223 people.

▲ CBERG reported a 10% increase in the number of pregnant women attending antenatal classes.

(*Source:* Adapted from Meropa's entry proposal for the PRISM Awards)

Conclusion

This chapter provided a description of the following:

▲ the context of communication planning and management

▲ the different elements of communication planning and management

▲ the degrees of difference among campaigns, programmes and social movements

▲ various models for the planning of public relations campaigns

▲ a variety of case studies to illustrate how public relations campaigns are planned, executed and evaluated.

Questions for self-evaluation

1. You are a public relations practitioner in a large organisation. Your organisation decides to launch a campaign to illustrate its social responsibility towards South African society. In so doing, the organisation asks you and your department to assist in a countrywide 'South African business campaign against indiscipline'.

   (a) Plan such a campaign for your organisation, using any one of the campaign planning models described in this chapter.

   (b) Substantiate why you have used a particular model.

References

Anderson, JA and Meyer, TP 1988. *Mediated Communication: A Social Action Perspective.* Newbury Park, California: Sage.

Backer, TE; Rogers, EM and Sopory, P 1992. *Designing Health Communication Campaigns*: *What Works?* Newbury Park, California: Sage.

Cutlip, SM; Center, AH and Broom, GM 1985. *Effective Public Relations.* (6 Ed.) Englewood Cliffs, New Jersey: Prentice-Hall.

Fourie, HP 1982. *Communication by Objectives.* (2 Ed.) Johannesburg: McGraw-Hill.

Hendrix, JA 1992. *Public Relations Cases.* (2 Ed.) Belmont, California: Wadsworth.

Hornik, RC 1988. *Development Communication: Information, Agriculture and Nutrition in the Third World.* New York: Longman.

Jefkins, F 1982. *Public Relations.* Estover, Plymouth: MacDonald.

Jefkins, F and Ugboajah, F 1986. *Communication in Industrialising Countries.* Hong Kong: Macmillan.

Kendall, R 1992. *Public Relations Campaign Strategies: Planning for Implementation.* New York: HarperCollins Publishers.

Larson, CU 1986. *Persuasion: Reception and Responsibility.* Belmont, California: Wadsworth.

McQuail, D 1987. *Mass Communication Theory: An Introduction.* Beverly Hills, California: Sage.

Mersham, GM; Rensburg, RS and Skinner, JC 1995. *Public Relations, Development and Social Investment: A Southern African Perspective.* Pretoria: Van Schaik.

Newsom, D; Scott, A and Van Slyke Turk, J 1993. *This is PR. The Realities of Public Relations.* (5 Ed.) Belmont, California: Wadsworth.

O'Sullivan, T; Hartley, J; Saunders, D and Fiske, J 1983. *Key Concepts in Communication.* London: Methuen.

Rensburg, RS (Ed.) 1996. *Introduction to Communication: Communication Planning and Management.* Course Book 4. Cape Town: Juta.

Rensburg, RS and Angelopulo, GC 1995. *Effective Communication Campaigns.* Johannesburg: Southern.

Rice, RE and Atkin, C (Eds.) 1989. *Public Communication Campaigns.* (2 Ed.) Newbury Park, California: Sage.

Robinson, S; Githing, W and Paulus, N 2001. The last rites. In *Time Atlantic,* 158(23):70–72.

Rogers, EM 1973. *Communication Strategies for Family Planning.* New York: Free.

Rogers, EM and Storey, JD 1987. Communication campaigns. In *Handbook of Communication Science,* Berger, CR and Chaffee, CH (Eds.) Newbury Park, California: Sage.

Skinner, C and Von Essen, L 1995. *Handbook of Public Relations.* (4 Ed.) Johannesburg: Southern.

Van der Meiden, A and Fauconnier, G 1982. *Profiel en Professie: Inleiding in de Theorievorming van Public Relations.* Leiden: Stenfert Kroese.

Westley, B and MacLean, M 1957. A conceptual model for mass communication research. In *Journalism Quarterly,* 27:383–390.

Windahl, S; Signitzer, B and Olson, JT 1993. *Using Communication Theory. An Introduction to Planned Communication.* London: Sage.

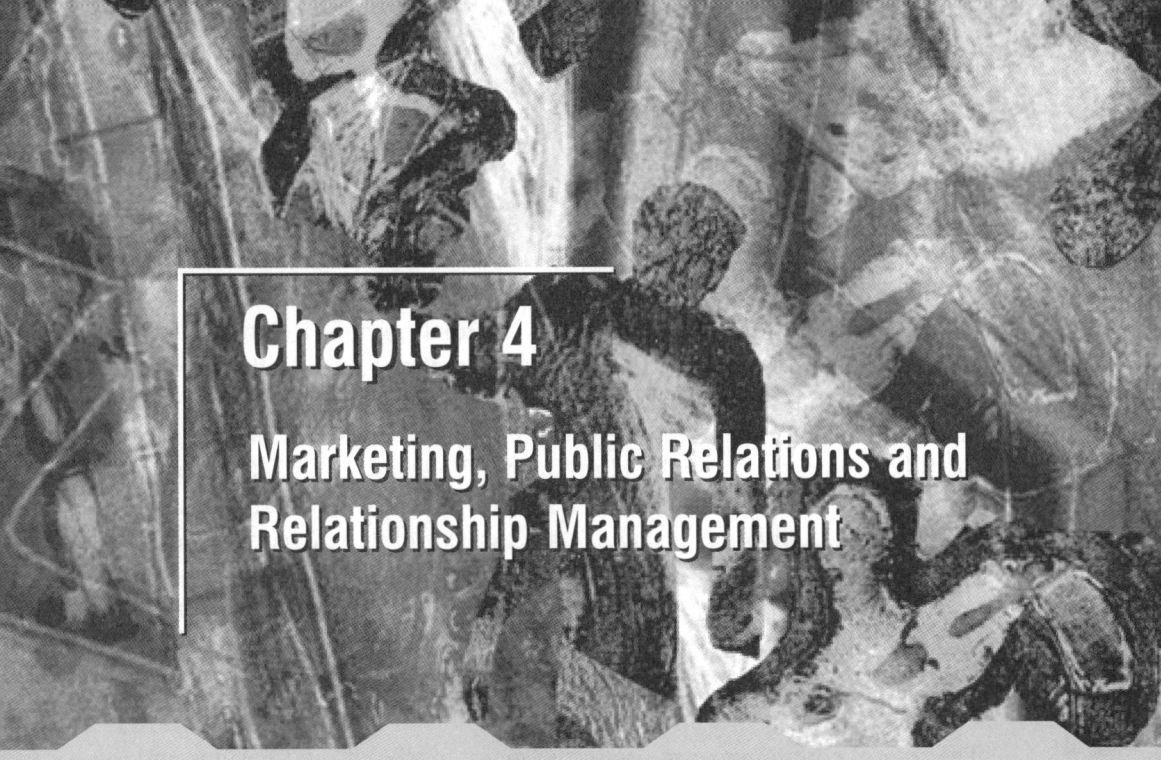

Chapter 4

Marketing, Public Relations and Relationship Management

LEARNING OUTCOMES

After studying this chapter, you should be able to:

▲ discuss the present dynamic nature of the business environment and explain the renewed focus on communication

▲ discuss the paradigm known as 'relationship marketing' and explain its implications for marketing and public relations as organisational activities

▲ describe the role of relationship building and management in an integrated communication approach

▲ outline the role of communication in relationship building and management

▲ identify various relationship networks and discuss the key elements of a relationship

▲ outline the importance and value of relationship management in gaining a competitive edge, and formulate useful guidelines for relationship management.

Introduction

People's lives are profoundly influenced by relationships. Relationships form such an integral part of our lives that we can assume that everything we do has some connection to the outside world. Relationships are seen as the key asset of an organisation and it can be accepted that all efforts by an organisation should be geared towards building them. The trend towards close relationships between organisations and all stakeholders (employees, customers, shareholders, suppliers, the media, etc.) has accelerated in many business sectors, resulting in an 'outward-inward' approach in terms of customer or shareholder orientation. Relationships are the business of the entire organisation and the objective should be to enhance the value of these relationships. Central to this is the need for organisations to change from a 'need to know' to a 'need to share' approach.

The role of communication – with the maintenance of relationships and the facilitation of interaction as its core responsibility – has become pivotal in an increasingly competitive and global business environment. This shift to becoming more customer/stakeholder-orientated points to the realignment of all communication activities between the organisation and its publics, and has proved to be crucial for the building of beneficial personalised relationships.

Conceptualising the challenges posed by the information age and relationship age

It is anticipated that globalisation, increased competition, and technology will affect every facet of business in the world marketplace, with organisations facing new challenges in terms of social, political and economic conditions, thus forcing them to adopt new models of business. Historically, challenges to the existence of organisations determined the dominant business approaches, which were mainly mechanistic. It is accepted that the different management eras within these approaches were responses by organisations in order to survive.[1] As a result, organisations have opted to reposition themselves by adopting an organic view of business. The emergence of new models of business is indicative of the changes in the context within which public relations and marketing function.

A combination of the above-mentioned factors and the increasing complexity of relationships between organisations and their stakeholders have resulted in the disintegration of the traditionally stable environment within which organisations used to function. As a result, organisations are faced with the following challenges:

▲ fundamental shifts in the relationships of corporations with individuals and with society

▲ increasing competition and changes in key elements of market relationships

▲ an increasing need for communication.[2]

Organisations are finding themselves in an age of chaos as a result of the impact of these factors and, once again, are finding their existence being challenged. In an attempt to adapt to an environment that is changing at an ever-increasing pace, with the emphasis on survival, organisations have adopted new approaches. The 'information revolution', also referred to as the 'communication revolution', forms the basis of a new model of business which has interconnectivity as its ultimate objective and is characterised by an organic view of business.[3] This points to the paradigm shift by organisations towards a more 'humanistic' and 'holistic' approach in an attempt, through acknowledgement of the worker as a valuable resource in the organisation and the interrelationship of components within and outside the organisation, to meet the challenges posed to organisational functioning. The next transition can rightly be termed the 'relationship age', where intentional efforts are made to engage individuals in building beneficial relationships. Characteristics of the 'communication age' and 'relationship age' are compared in table 4.1. The emphasis on aspects such as knowledge, the need to invest in people, knowledge tools, and relationship assets as strategic resources, is evident.

Issue	Information age	Relationship age
Basis of value creation	Better information	Better knowledge
Strategic plan	Three years	Perpetual
Management structure	Decentralised	Virtual
Key investment	IT and IT networks	People and knowledge tools
Strategic resources	Information	Relationship assets
Nature of production	Specialisation	Customisation and personalisation
Economic output	Services	Experiences
Marketing, sales and service	Segmentation	One-to-one

Price	Flexible	Dynamic
Nature of competition	Co-operation, loose affiliation	Collaboration, trust

Table 4.1 Characteristics of the different economic ages

(*Source:* Adapted from Galbreath, 2002)[4]

This chapter focuses on the increased emphasis on the co-ordination of all communication activities of the organisation and on the growing importance of building and managing relationships, representing a move from a traditional relationship between public relations and marketing towards closer convergence. For the organisation to achieve its ultimate objective, namely to build and maintain beneficial relationships in an effort to achieve organisational goals, it is pivotal to explore the emergence of this era of relationship building and the opportunities it holds.

In this chapter, the shift to a more customised approach by the 'total' organisation and the pivotal role of relationship building is highlighted, including the role of communication, key elements, the value of relationships, different types of relationships, and the importance of relationship management.

A renewed focus on communication

The increasing interdependency between the organisation, the environment and stakeholders has placed renewed emphasis on the vital role of communication for organisational survival. The emergence of new technology, in particular, has proven valuable here because it provides new systems of linking for business, information, knowledge and communications. In fact, this has 'empowered' the way communication takes place and has impacted on the consumer decision-making process. In addition, in terms of quality, it is believed that the relationship age will also impact on the way goods and services are produced, sold and delivered, hence impacting on all levels of organisational functioning.

Communication in and by the organisation is used to create mutual understanding and is aimed at maintaining balanced relationships between the organisation and its publics. In this process, management uses all organisation activities to formulate communication strategies, maintain effective two-way communication channels, and determine prevailing attitudes and opinions, in an attempt to build beneficial relationships. This implies a constant demand for effective communication between organisations and their publics.

Organisational communication is defined by Andrews and Herschel[5] as a process 'wherein mutually interdependent human beings create and exchange messages, and interpret and negotiate meanings, while striving to articulate and realize mutually held visions, purposes, and goals'. Owing to technological advances, organisations presently face the challenge of disseminating large volumes of information at an ever-increasing speed. The increasing need for information, the desire for effective information management and the challenges and opportunities offered by technology are influencing the structures of organisations, the way people manage and share power and, in particular, the nature of organisations and the way they communicate.

By acknowledging the crucial role of communication as a prerequisite for its functioning and survival, the organisation in turn acknowledges the importance of *relationship building*. As maintained earlier, organisations have become more aware of the interrelationship of various internal and external components, highlighting the existence of individual relationships between these components and organisations. These relationships are dependent on the nature of the link between the environment (comprising so-called publics, stakeholders, or audiences) and the organisation, with all organisational activities fulfilling a vital role, namely to build ongoing relationships through communication.[6] It can be concluded that communication is an important concern of the organisation, with its ultimate objective being the building and maintaining of beneficial relationships between the organisation and its stakeholders. This chapter holds the view that the terms 'stakeholder' and 'public' refer to all those individuals or groups (internally and externally) who are affected by decisions of the organisation, or who affect decisions taken by the organisation.[7] These terms are used interchangeably throughout this chapter. Stakeholders or publics, for the purpose of this chapter, include employees, shareholders, suppliers, the media, and customers.

A new paradigm: Towards relationship building and management

Within the 'relationship age', as briefly highlighted in the introduction, relationship building in particular has received renewed attention in an 'outward-inward' approach in terms of client orientation. The increasing realisation of the importance of merging all organisational activities has led to a paradigm shift by organisations as regards their approach to communication. Underlying this shift is the idea that the communication approach should comprise customised and personalised communication efforts. This has forced organisations to adopt an integrated communication approach, which contributes to the realignment of all communication activities in general, and to customer-orientated communication in particular. The need for organisations to adopt an integrated communication approach has already been substantiated in chapter 1. However, to contextualise the increased focus on relationship building and management, it is necessary to review the terms 'integrated marketing communication' and 'integrated communication' briefly.

An *integrated communication approach* (IC), also referred to as an *integrated marketing communication approach* (IMC), encompasses the integration of all communication activities. It is believed that the goals and objectives of an organisation can be best accomplished through such an approach.[8] The role of all organisational activities in such an approach is to contribute to the communication objectives at a strategic level. This approach has the main objectives of achieving success through personalised (also referred to as customised) communication, one-to-one communication, managing communication and accountability for realigning communication, and facilitating continuous interactive, dialogic communication in an effort to build and maintain long-term customer relationships.

Integrated communication (IC) can be regarded as an integrated, uniform and comprehensive communications programme in organisational functioning, with the emphasis on evaluation of results and the competitive advantages for the organisation.[9] The American Association of Advertising Agencies defines integrated marketing communication (IMC) as 'a concept of marketing communications planning that recognises the added value of a comprehensive plan that evaluates the strategic roles of a variety of communications disciplines and combines them to provide clarity, consistency and maximum communications impact through the seamless integration of discrete messages'.[10] Fundamental to this approach is the need to create synergy and cohesion among the different communication efforts and to co-ordinate all the communication activities of an organisation. It is maintained that there is greater value for the organisation when strategic messages are co-ordinated than when activities are planned and executed independently by the different organisational disciplines/functions. The concepts 'integrated communication' and 'integrated marketing communication' have been equated, calling for the co-ordination of all communication activities or efforts, with the ultimate aim to build relationships. Accordingly, these concepts are used interchangeably in this chapter.

It is believed that the shift towards integrated communication is driven by the following factors:

▲ downsizing and re-engineering through the consolidation of departments and staff reductions

▲ the increased use of product publicity, direct mail, and sales promotions as a result of budget constraints

▲ the realisation that public and social policy issues affect the marketing function through the empowerment of activist groups

▲ the rise of relationship marketing and the shift from the four Ps (product, price, place, promotion) to the four Cs (customer needs, cost to meet those needs, convenience to purchase, communication).[11]

When compared to more traditional, function-oriented activities, this era holds the promise of planned, developed, executed and evaluated customised communication,[12] and represents a move from transaction-based marketing (finalising the exchange or sale) to relationship-based marketing (creating lifetime customers). This can also be explained or understood as a shift from selling and telling to communicating and trading knowledge.[13]

The following differences between traditional marketing and one-to-one marketing (in other words a holistic or integrated approach), as formulated, highlight this focus on relationship building and management:

▲ Rather than measuring success by market share, one-to-one marketing measures success by share of customer, measuring one customer at a time.

▲ Instead of finding customers for a product, this new theory tries to find more products and services for a customer.

▲ While traditional marketing is being held accountable for product sales, one-to-one marketing focuses on the management of customers and growing the expected values of these customers (reverse marketing).

▲ Rather than promoting functioning in isolation or independently, this theory promotes continuous contact with the customer by means of tracking, a series of interactions, and the measurement of the customer's business.[14]

Perspectives of an integrated approach

An integrated approach consists of four main perspectives, namely total quality management (TQM), the spin doctor, an interactive perspective, and integrated marketing communication. These perspectives are now explored briefly.

▲ *Total quality management (TQM)* points to a continuous process with the following objectives:

△ to improve product and service quality through feedback

△ to examine quality leaders through benchmarking

△ to use teams

△ to achieve total employee involvement.[15]

The TQM movement requires constant improvement of organisational approaches, the development of internal communication programmes, and the monitoring of customer perception.[16]

▲ Characteristics of the *spin doctor* approach are that it is reactive, uses new technology, applies direct public relations techniques, and emphasises customer interpretation and the effect of media events.[17]

▲ The *interactive approach* emphasises the importance of service in the organisation, especially the quality of service from the continuous interaction and information exchange between the organisation and its publics.[18]

▲ *Integrated marketing communication* is a fourth perspective of an integrated communication approach. Compared to the traditional marketing communication approach, the focus is now placed on the customer and not solely on sales and profit goals.[19]

Implications for marketing and public relations

The relationship between public relations and marketing, as organisational activities, has traditionally been somewhat controversial. Historic 'turf battles' have centred on the delineation of the respective roles of these functions, often resulting in the relegation of public relations to a technical support function *vis-à-vis* marketing. However, as early as 1978, Kotler and Mindak envisaged a breakdown of the divisions separating public relations and marketing. The relationship marketing era has contributed to the increasing recognition of a common responsibility within the organisation, namely to build and maintain relationships between the organisation and its publics. The implication for public relations is a renewed focus on relationship building as its basic premise, and for marketing an increased realisation of the importance of two-way interactive communication in relationship building.[20]

Within an integrated communication approach, existing commonalities in public relations and marketing serve to support the assumption of a breakdown of the divisions separating these functions, and the recognition of a common responsibility. It is clear that both functions:

▲ talk in terms of publics and markets

▲ realise the need for market segmentation

▲ acknowledge the importance of market attitudes, perceptions and images in formulating programmes

▲ acknowledge the primary tenets of a management process, namely analysis, planning, implementation and control.[21]

The growing focus on integrated communication is indicative of an increased focus on service as an issue separate from products, with the focus on individual customer interaction pointing inevitably to the increasing importance of, and emphasis on, relationship building.[22] It represents a move towards the building

of personal consumer relationships and stresses the importance of public relations and marketing in integrated programmes.[23]

Such an integrated approach represents moves in marketing from customer to
individual, and in public relations from publics to people. The focus in marketing is placed on building customer share rather than market share, and it is
actually regarded as fashionable to talk of becoming 'customer-oriented' or
'customer-driven'.[24] Kotler admits that, from a relationship-building point of
view, marketing needs to view its interactions with customers in a more serious light. He states that these interactions should be regarded as ongoing
relationships that need to be managed.[25]

This approach, inter alia, requires public relations to understand 'the role of
communication in the initiation, development, and maintenance of organisational public relationships',[26] and to recognise that key publics are 'active,
interactive and equal partners of an ongoing communication process'.[27] Challenges posed by this approach include a recognition of the need for user-friendly
information and to support ongoing relationships, as opposed to merely transferring information. It represents a move from the traditional above-the-line
(all commercial advertising and short-term objectives) and below-the-line (any
alternative communication tools other than the sales force, and long-term
objectives) approaches towards a through-the-line approach.[28]

Relationship building and management as dominant driving factors in an integrated communication approach

As pointed out earlier, organisations are facing fierce competition from global
markets, forcing them to restructure in an attempt to enhance survival and
growth. Restructuring efforts include, *inter alia*, the emergence of relationship
marketing that requires organisations to view their interactions with customers in a more serious light. As pointed out earlier, relationship marketing is
regarded as a driving factor towards communication integration.

Presently, the term 'relationship marketing' is used in many ways, most often
being associated with the marketing function of an organisation. This chapter
focuses on investigating *relationship management* in both marketing and public relations; hence, for the purposes of this chapter, the terms 'relationship
management' and 'relationship marketing' are used interchangeably.

Relationship marketing (equated to relationship management) is defined as
'the process of establishing and maintaining mutually beneficial long-term relationships among organisations and their customers, employees, and other
stakeholders'.[29] The shift to building relationships is offered as a solution to
organisations for coping in this era of ever-increasing competition, but should

not be confused with marketing as it involves entire enterprises with the focus of treating customers individually.[30] Based on the fundamental premise of an integrated communication approach, namely, a concern only with communication activities and involving entire enterprises, it can be assumed that such a focus includes *all stakeholders* of the organisation (including employees). The building of long-term relationships with strategic publics is regarded as crucial to achieve organisational goals.

In an effort to make the move from a traditional, product-focused enterprise to a customer-focused, customer-driven enterprise, the organisation will have to make definite changes that will require significant adaptation by the organisation and its employees. These changes are believed to pose the following challenges:

▲ allowing decision making by the entire organisation

▲ encouraging teamwork, communication and utilisation of information tools in the organisation through the training of employees

▲ acquiring the necessary technology.[31]

The role of communication in relationship building

Communication is believed to affect directly the building of long-term relationships with the stakeholders of an organisation. Stakeholders can be described as individuals or groups who are linked to the organisation, and who are in the position to affect or be affected by the activities of the organisation. It is therefore necessary to acknowledge the role of communication in building relationships between the various activities in the organisation, and between the organisation and its stakeholders. A relationship begins with conversation that is maintained and sustained by frequent communication.[32] The importance of communication in an integrated communication approach has already been substantiated earlier in this chapter and should be regarded as a prerequisite for organisational survival.

Dialogic communication encourages the process of feedback, which implies that communication *with* the stakeholder takes place. It has been suggested that the successful building of relationships takes place only when communication occurs in the form of dialogue. A discussion of the concept of 'dialogue' reveals the following:

▲ A dialogue perspective focuses on the attitudes of the participants towards each other.

▲ Human communication is viewed as an intersubjective process in which parties come to a relationship with openness and respect.

▲ Dialogue is the basis for a relationship such as the one mentioned above.

▲ In a dialogue relationship, communication between parties should be the ultimate goal.

▲ Dialogue takes place when parties agree to co-ordinate their plans of action in *good faith*, implying a co-operative, communicative relationship.[33]

Communication is identified as the common denominator in public relations and marketing activities. An integrated communication approach means that communication will be looked at by the organisation from the stakeholder's point of view, thus from an 'outward-inward' perspective.[34] It can be deduced that this will promote a stakeholder orientation in terms of communication, with an increasing emphasis on one-to-one communication, the use of electronic communication systems, receiver (customer) and client needs, the use of visual communication, symbols, pictures and sound, and the replacement of a traditional functional media-specific approach with an integrated approach. This chapter argues that communication and interaction form the essence of any relationship, with communication providing linkages between people and/ or organisations.

Relationships contextualised

Forms of relationships or relationship networks

The objective here is not to develop a universal set of relationships for any given business context, but to explore existing views on the classification of relationships. It should be accepted that key relationships are currently difficult to pinpoint, since the environment of every organisation comprises unique stakeholders or publics. Three different views are now presented.

Supplier partnerships, lateral partnerships, buyer partnerships and internal partnerships[35]

This view maintains that ten forms of relationship exist in any organisation. These relationships can be grouped into supplier partnerships, lateral partnerships or organisations, buyer partnerships or customers, and internal partnerships or employees (see figure 4.1 on the next page).

It is evident from figure 4.1 that these forms of relationship marketing are particularly relevant to an integrated communication approach. Apart from the inward orientation (internal partnerships, including all employees) and outward orientation (supplier, lateral, and buyer partnerships) as portrayed, evidence is to be found of key aspects of the integrated approach such as 'just-in-time' procurement, 'total quality management', 'internal marketing', and 'within-firm relational exchange'.

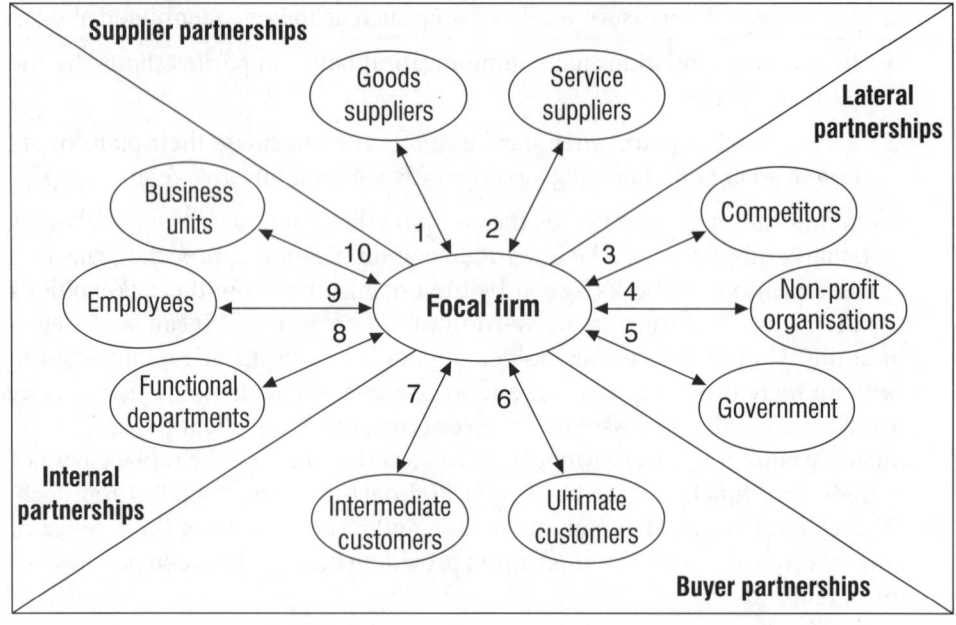

Figure 4.1 Forms of relationship marketing

(*Source:* Morgan and Hunt)[36]

Primary relationships and secondary relationships[37]

A second view attempts to determine the minimum number of relationships in any given business context, and it is proposed that a set of relationships mainly consists of a primary relationship and secondary relationships. A *primary relationship* (figure 4.2 on the next page) implies the organisation's relationship with the customer and is recognised as the ultimate objective of the organisation. This relationship is believed to offer long-term benefits in terms of loyalty, value to the customer, and retention. The role of employees in providing personalised and close relationships through human interaction is also acknowledged.

Secondary relationships (figure 4.3 on the next page) identify various stakeholders that the organisation must 'establish' and 'nurture', such as employees, suppliers, retailers and shareholders. It is maintained that the support of secondary relationships is founded on the fact that competitive advantage is dependent on the extent to which strategic alliances are forged with various stakeholders. This refers to the holistic 'competency' of the organisation and emphasises the importance of the development of relationships, but also of the marketing and management (nurturing) of these relationships.

**Firm
Customer/stakeholder**

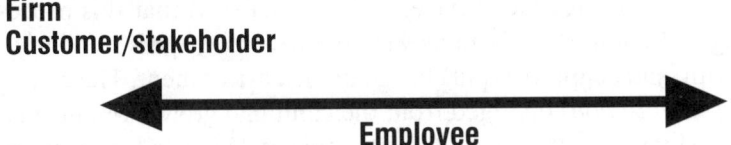

Employee

Figure 4.2 A primary relationship

(*Source:* Kandampully and Duddy, 1999)[38]

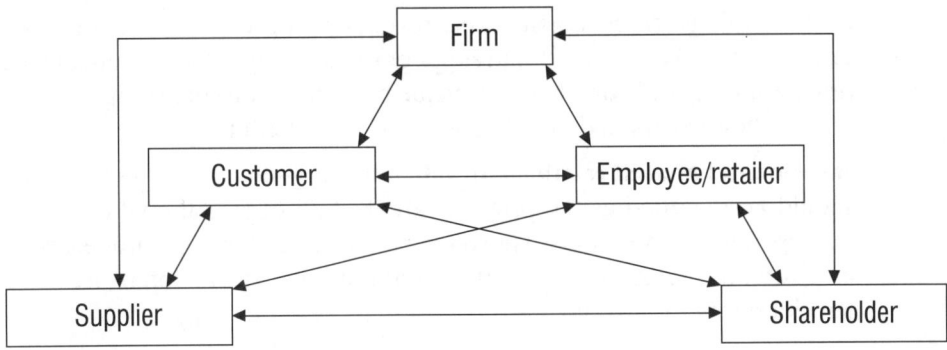

Figure 4.3 Secondary relationships

(*Source:* Kandampully and Duddy, 1999)[39]

The relationship network[40]

A third view on the different types of relationships has evolved around a more holistic approach, maintaining that key relationships go far beyond relationships with customers. Such an approach includes relationships with employees, suppliers and partners, investors and market analysts, government regulators, trade associations and 'other entities' that exert influence on the environment in which the organisation functions. This relationship network is depicted in figure 4.4 and consists of customer relationships, employee relationships, partner and supplier relationships, and investor and analyst relationships. It has as its objective the building of quality relationship assets for market value creation.

▲ **Customer relationship value:** This implies a shift in focus to creating loyalty and trust through beneficial long-term relationships. A combination of mutually beneficial relationships and customer knowledge forms the basis for building these relationships.

▲ **Employee relationship value:** This refers to an organisation's most valuable asset, namely its people. It also emphasises the importance for the organisation of adopting a learning approach to create opportunities to grow and increase its competitive advantage. This era of globalisation and competition forces organisations to learn from their own experience and that of others in order to survive, and it is believed that this process of learning will equip organisations with the necessary tools to align themselves with, and adapt to, rapid change in the environment. The concept of *learning organisations* emerged from the continual growth of information, and it is evident that the concepts of learning and knowledge are inseparable. Knowledge of the customer has already been identified as a primary contributor to customer relationship value.

▲ **Partner and supplier relationship value:** This points to the important role of these relationships in generating revenue and profits for the organisation. The essence of partner and supplier relationship value is to enable the organisation to do more, to create value by focusing on core competencies, and to allow others to do the things they can do better.

▲ **Investor and analyst relationship value:** It is argued that this relationship should be regarded as the primary target of all organisational efforts to harness relationship assets. Thorough planning and foresight are regarded as pivotal to the management of expectations and the maintenance of financial stability.

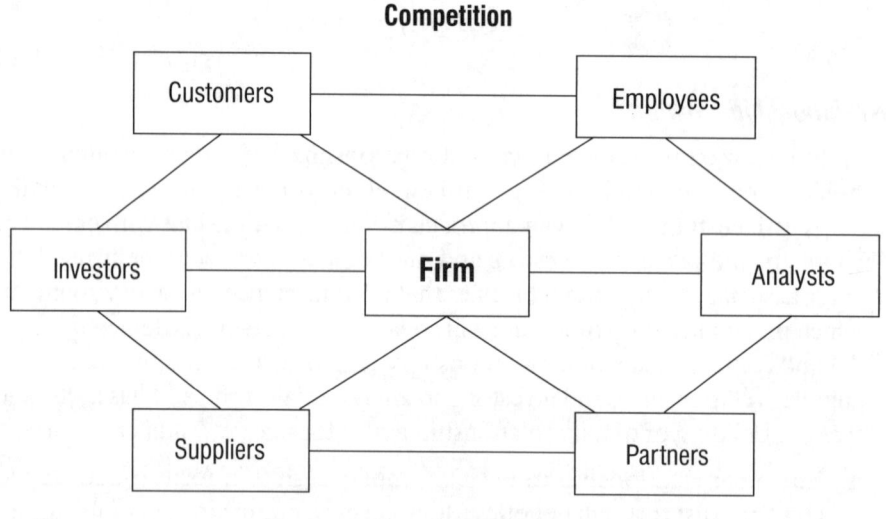

Competition

Business environment

Figure 4.4 The relationship network

(*Source:* Galbreath, 2002)[41]

It is believed that these main relationships all contribute to a cash flow and value output, which are dependent on how they are holistically understood, organised and leveraged by the organisation. The key defining attributes of each of the main relationships are portrayed in table 4.2 on the next page.

Key defining attributes	Customer relationships	Employee relationships	Partner and supplier relationships	Investor and analyst relationships
Goal	Loyalty	Personal growth	Increased business velocity and innovation	Full economic evaluation
Key value outcome	Lifetime revenue and profit	Improved value contribution and productivity	Increased customer share and revenue growth	Share price and investment capital
Key ingredient for success	Customer knowledge	Organisational leadership	Collaboration and communication	Continuous measurement, education, and relationship asset communication

Table 4.2 Key defining attributes

(*Source:* Galbreath, 2002)[42]

To conclude, it can be accepted that at present different types of relationships are found in any given business context, and the attributes or value of these relationships for the organisation depend on the environment of that particular organisation.

Relationship building

Relationship building refers to a continuous process of mutual adaptation and response that exists between the organisation and its strategic publics, while a *relationship* can be regarded as the desirable 'outcome' or 'product' of such a process, consisting of collaborative interactions that hold the promise of being mutually beneficial for both parties. Relationships can be regarded as a fundamental asset of an organisation.[43] They are all about the creation and sharing of new value, internally and externally. An overview of existing literature indicates that good relationships consist of effective communication, mutual adaptation, mutual dependency, shared values, understanding, credibility, behaviour, mutuality of control or conflict avoidance, and the maintenance of the relationship.[44]

Research undertaken has proved useful in identifying key relationship dimensions. The following indicators or relationship dimensions exist:

▲ the willingness of the organisation to engage in open communication with the public

▲ the level of trust expressed by the consumer that the organisation will keep its promises

▲ community involvement by the organisation

▲ the organisation's financial investment in the community

▲ the organisation's long-term commitment to the community. [45]

Planning for relationship building

It should be stated from the outset that relationship building and relationship management are interdependent. This means that the building of successful relationships is dependent on their strategic management and vice versa. The following principles contribute to the building of long-term relationships:

▲ Relationships are based on *open communication*. It is maintained that effective listening skills are crucial to the building of relationships.

▲ Relationships are built on *reliability*. This principle emphasises the importance of trust as a determining element in relationship building.

▲ Relationships are strengthened when the *parties stay in contact*.

▲ Relationships depend on *trust, honesty,* and *ethical behaviour.* This refers to a thorough understanding of the stakeholders. [46]

A relationship consists of a continuing series of collaborative interactions. It is further characterised by the fact that it is a continuous process which, as a result of interactions, develops a 'context' and, depending on its participants, is unique. [47] Relationships develop over time and can result in long-term, loyal attachments.

Evidence of a 'learning relationship' and a 'positive relationship' is found in literature. The 'learning relationship' [48] refers to constant interaction with, and customisation of, a product or service that in the end satisfies the specific need of the customer, while a 'positive relationship' [49] is defined as a relationship in which both or all parties perceive that they benefit. These two types of relationship may well form part of a two-step process to indicate the development of a successful relationship, where the learning relationship focuses on the individual needs of a customer (in marketing) or people (in public relations), and then develops into a positive relationship in which both parties benefit in terms of an integrated approach (individual customer/people and organisation). The emphasis in such a process is first on the individual customer/people and their needs, and second – as the relationship progresses or develops to the next step or stage – the promise of benefits for both parties (individual customer/people and organisation).

The keys to successful relationships

Trust and commitment

A relationship of trust is regarded as a prerequisite for the facilitation of two-way information flow in an organisation, and must be earned by the organisation by its following an integrated approach that refers to the way customers are treated throughout the organisation as a whole. The quality and sharing of information is believed to influence the success of relationships.

Various attempts have been made to pinpoint the dimensions or components of a relationship. The opinion exists that *trust* and *commitment* should be regarded not only as two essential variables in successful relationships, but also as important indicators as to whether or not relationships are successful.[50] Trust is defined as a belief that the 'provider' or organisation is reliable and committed to serving the long-term interests of the 'buyer' or client, and is regarded as a key construct of most business models and personal relationships. Apart from the fact that trust is a fundamental step in establishing long-term business and personal relationships, it is regarded as a prerequisite for the continuation of a relationship and the primary contributor to good relationships. Trust is measurable by *disclosure*. The willingness of target audiences to communicate or disclose their concerns can be a good indicator of whether communication is perceived by all as being open, adequate and responsive.[51] The absence of complaints or candour is a sure indication that there is a decline of trust and possibly a deterioration of the relationship.[52]

Relationship commitment, as the second variable, is regarded as a function of communication effectiveness, service quality and trust, as portrayed in figure 4.5 on the next page. It involves the belief by all stakeholders that an ongoing relationship is so important that it deserves the maximum input by all. As portrayed in figure 4.5, service quality comprises two components, namely a technical quality (the outcomes or the 'what' of the service, as perceived by the stakeholder) and a functional quality (the interaction between stakeholders or 'how' the service is delivered). It is evident that communication effectiveness can thus be regarded as 'instrumental' in building beneficial long-term relationships and critical in inter-organisational relationships.[53]

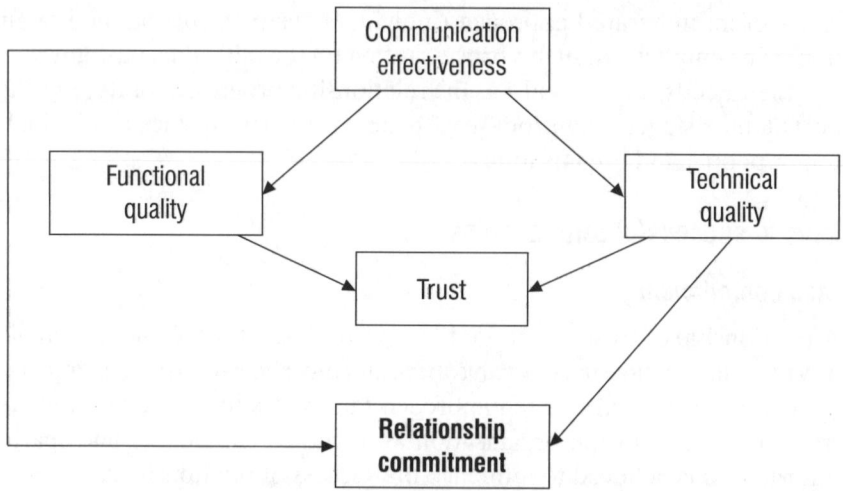

Figure 4.5 A conceptual model of the determinants of relationship commitment

(*Source:* Sharma and Patterson)[54]

Interpersonal communication, marketing and social psychology

The value of interpersonal communication, and of marketing and social psychology in relationship building has been well documented in literature. It is evident that interpersonal communication plays a significant role in relationships. The following four dimensions of successful interpersonal relationships exist:

1. **Investment** – time, energy, feelings, efforts and other resources given to build the relationship.
2. **Commitment** – the concerted decision to continue a relationship.
3. **Trust** – a feeling that the parties in the relationship can rely on each other.
4. **Comfort with relational dialectics** – the factors that can move a relationship in opposite directions.[55]

In the 'buyer-seller' relationship, as found in marketing, the dimensions of commitment, trust, co-operation, mutual goals, interdependence/power imbalance, performance satisfaction, comparison level of the alternatives, adaptation, non-retrieval investment, shared technology, summate constructs, structural bonds, and social bonds are identified. Social psychology contributes in terms of commitment, intimacy and passion.

Intra-organisational collaboration and internal marketing

An ongoing process of internal collaboration is regarded as of strategic importance to building and managing successful relationships. The objective is to promote collaboration among all people, functions and departments of the organisation that are responsible for the product itself, for advertising, delivery, handling complaints, billing, product documentation, etc.[56] Thus, it is evident that, within an integrated communication approach, collaboration efforts should incorporate all communication activities.

The concept *internal marketing*, Grönroos states that 'the internal market of employees is best motivated for service mindedness and customer-oriented performance by an active, marketing-like approach'.[57] Thorough and continuous internal marketing processes contribute to committed, loyal and motivated staff, who are pivotal to enduring internal and external relationships. Just as organisations view their customers as individuals, so too should employees be seen as individuals with whom new value will be developed. Hence, satisfying internal customers (or employees) is a prerequisite to satisfying external customers.

Shared values

Values can be regarded as the technical, economic, service, and social benefits an organisation receives in exchange for the price it pays. The building and maintenance of long-term relationships is also approached through creating and cultivating shared values[58] between buyer and seller or stakeholder and organisation. Furthermore, it is maintained that these values may occur in the form of shared goals.

Developing existing relationships

The shift in emphasis to customer/stakeholder relationship building and management brings with it the need to maintain and increase the motivation of existing stakeholders to invest in an ongoing relationship and to focus on the development of existing relationships. The implementation of these four phases is believed to contribute to the development of such relationships:

1. awareness, without interaction
2. exploration
3. expansion, marked by mutual satisfaction and patronage
4. commitment.[59]

Good communications and interaction

Communication and interaction form the essence of any relationship, a fact that has already been substantiated. Within an integrated communication approach, continuing communication aims at seeking a greater understanding of prospective and existing stakeholders, and at reducing uncertainty about the outcomes of future exchanges. The resulting objective is to change behaviour so that loyalty ensures stakeholder retention and a developed trust.

Given the importance of 'strategic' relationships for the holistic functioning of an organisation, it is necessary to explore the role of relationship management in an effort to create value for the organisation and its stakeholders.

Relationship management

The strategic management of organisations is increasingly regarded as being inseparable from the strategic management of relationships, with the role of strategic relationship management contributing to the 'balancing of internal processes of organisations with external factors'.[60] It is maintained that an important component of relationship management comprises the identification of mutual interest, values and benefit between a client organisation and its publics. The emphasis is on mutual trust, compromise, co-operation and, whenever possible, win-win situations (also referred to as positive relationships). It is argued that relationship commitment and trust, as desirable 'outcomes' of relationship development, are therefore also the results of effective relationship management.[61]

In contrast to the transactional approach that tends to overemphasise individual transactions rather than spend time on relationship building with stakeholders, and that ignores customer retention, a relationship management approach is based on:

▲ building and maintaining long-term relationships that are founded on trust and commitment

▲ the same elements as found in personal relationships, such as shared values

▲ trust, mutual respect, mutual benefit, flexibility, understanding, and relationship commitment

▲ partnerships between buyers and sellers in product development, etc. through information sharing and technology

▲ the retention of existing customers through long-term relationships.[62]

Relationship management actually requires an integrated communication approach to be adopted by the organisation, thus removing the boundaries of separate functions, focusing on the individual customer and building valuable relationships.[63]

In the relationship age, the emphasis has shifted to the management of 'intangible assets', namely the relationships with customers, employees, and suppliers and partners.[64] As pointed out by Galbreath (2002), relationship assets represent the value of these relationships. The organisation should regard relationship management as being just as important as its tangible assets (constituting book value), with an even broader role predicted, namely that it will become a necessity – in business and for global survival.[65]

The process of relationship management should start by determining the current state of the relationship (see figure 4.6), that is, identifying, classifying and assessing.[66] This will enable strategic planning in terms of enhancing, maintaining, and renewing existing relationship assets, and will contribute to the effective management of key relationships that will create value in the end.

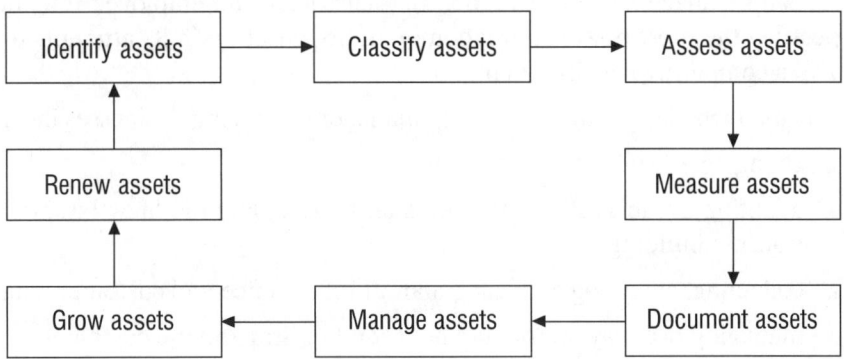

Figure 4.6 Assessing relationship assets

(*Source:* Galbreath, 2002)[67]

In the effective management of relationships, the following requirements should be met:

▲ **Awareness.** This entails an understanding of the problem as well as the opportunity.

▲ **Assessment.** This means continuous determination of the standing of the organisation, especially in terms of achieving the desired results.

▲ **Accountability.** This includes regular reporting on individual and group relationships so that these relationships can be weighed against other measures of performance.

▲ **Actions.** These include constantly making decisions and establishing routines and communications based on their possible impact on target relationships.[68]

Conversely, if the organisation fails to meet these requirements the results are bound to be disappointing. The process of implementing a relationship management programme includes the following:

▲ *Identify* the customer.

▲ *Differentiate* the customer by means of the levels of value and the different needs.

▲ *Interact* with the customer.

▲ *Customise* either products, services or (true to an integrated communication approach) communication, to meet the needs of the customer.[69]

The concept of relationship marketing is based on the assumption that it is more viable economically to concentrate on the maintenance and enhancement of existing customer relationships than constantly to seek new customers, thus posing the challenge to organisations to retain customers through relationship management. It is argued that customer and employee retention is possibly the most powerful weapon of an organisation in its attempts to survive a competitive environment.[70]

The main challenges in relationship management facing businesses include:

▲ changing attitudes to the customer

▲ adapting organisational structures and addressing the 'new task' of relationship building

▲ collecting, analysing and using market intelligence and customer data

▲ managing two-way interaction between the firm and the customer

▲ measuring customer satisfaction and service quality

▲ forming partnerships, and formulating positioning and sales strategies

▲ managing the functions of training, support and implementation.[71]

Relationship management guidelines

Research undertaken has identified the following eight key guidelines for strategic partnership management:

▲ **Realise the critical importance of planning.** The importance of specifying strategic objectives, evaluating alternative objectives and deciding on the structure and its management is emphasised.

▲ **Balance trust with self-interest.** As a result of the detrimental nature of confrontational relationships, prior information experience is regarded as valuable. The interdependency between trust and communication is acknowledged, thus emphasising its role in building and sustaining relationships.

▲ **Anticipate conflicts.** An important aspect of a relationship is the acknowledgement of the possibility of conflict occurrence. Conflict resolution should include, *inter alia*, personnel/employee training.

▲ **Establish strategic leadership.** The non-existence of an effective leadership structure is believed to impact seriously on the co-ordination and speed of development, and will erode the decision-making process.

▲ **Provide flexibility.** The dynamic nature of relationships is acknowledged, pointing to the importance of continuous adaptation.

▲ **Accommodate cultural differences.** It should be accepted that strategic relationships, within the organisation and with stakeholders, are influenced by cultural differences. Failure to accept these realities will affect the relationship adversely.

▲ **Orchestrate technology transfer.** In developing and transferring technology, implementation requires special attention.

▲ **Learn from partners' strengths.** This guideline refers to the exploitation of skills and experience by the organisation. It is maintained that the objective should be to acquire skills from the relationship.[72]

The value of relationship building and management

The role of relationship building is evident in the new drive towards profitability. Apart from providing a foundation for marketing initiatives and the drive towards profitability,[73] relationship building is valuable in creating a climate of, among other things, trust, understanding, and credibility, which is crucial for achieving long-term organisational goals.

Good relations hold the promise of exploiting economic opportunities and saving money by preventing, minimising or resolving conflict and crisis[74] that may impact negatively on employee satisfaction and productivity, customer satisfaction and loyalty and, in the long run, profitability. Consequently, the following two-step process is proposed in which organisations must:

▲ focus on building relationships with their key publics

▲ communicate their involvement in these activities to members of their publics.[75]

The value of relationships in an integrated mix is acknowledged, and certain commonalities in the public relations, marketing and advertising disciplines are identified, namely 'product characteristics, perceptions of quality, service, price, levels of technology, demographics, and predispositions that impact on the behaviour of members of an organisation's significant publics'.[76]

The development of successful relationships is dependent on the ability of the organisation to:

▲ track the customer across different business units, thereby integrating customer relationships into every aspect of the business process

▲ remember or track the needs and interests of the customer, in other words, to develop a long-term relationship

▲ regard the management of the relationship as an important prerequisite for successful relationships.[77]

It is posited that relationship management encompasses all organisational activities aimed at establishing, developing, and maintaining successful relational exchanges.[78] Prerequisites for successful relationship management are relationship commitment and trust, which need to be nurtured by the organisation through the offering of superior opportunities, high corporate values, timely and accurate communication, and not taking unfair advantage of exchange partners. Well-managed relationships, in turn, lead to value creation for the organisation and all stakeholders.[79] The value may be financial, economic or social, and will differ according to the different stakeholders of the organisation.[80] An integrated communication approach seems valuable in that it combines a variety of disciplines in the organisation to provide a comprehensive communications programme with the main aim of creating a competitive advantage for the organisation.

The role of database technology in relationship management

The value of new technologies for the long-existing relationship between marketing and public relations has been acknowledged.[81] Marketing was originally successful in building relationships with customers on an individual basis, but this method has become increasingly difficult to maintain and manage as a result of the industrial revolution and mass production, and the difficulty of monitoring sales on an individual basis. The role and importance of technology should not be underestimated and, combined with a focus on stakeholders, should be regarded as a prerequisite for relationship marketing. This interdependency is supported by the argument that, without the effective use of technology, relationship marketing cannot be regarded as an effective strategy.[82] Technology is believed to provide the required tools and is crucial for the management of strategic relationships.

It is widely accepted that the effects of public relations are not easily measurable, and the success of 'goodwill building' is therefore not easily determinable. Apart from the fact that this new approach implies the development of a long-term focus and the recognition of the value of public relations for the organisation, existing database technology may also successfully measure certain public relations efforts,[83] thereby offering a solution to the long-existing problem of determining the relation between goodwill-building activities and sales.

Organisations are increasingly moving away from mass marketing to relationship marketing and, in this regard, what is actually re-emerging in the marketing and public relations fields is so-called 'customised marketing' and 'customised

communication'. Of importance here is the increased realisation among public relations practitioners and marketers of the usefulness of existing technology
in effective relationship management. The role of technology in relationship
management is explored later in this book.

Case study

The Mount Nelson Hotel

Challenging colonial ideals

What do you do if your organisation was founded in the Boer War, and
was a pillar of the British Empire and the English establishment, and
you are expected to make it a leading player in a new, international
market? These are the problems facing Swiss-born Nick Seewer, brought
in by new owners – the Orient Express Group – to reform the Mount
Nelson, one of Cape Town's leading hotels. For Seewer (pronounced
'savour'), the challenge was to change the existing marketing strategy,
invent new traditions where necessary, and make the hotel the industry
leader again. Fundamentally, the hotel faced the challenge of repositioning itself in the minds of customers, both locally and abroad.

Vagrant VIPs

The hotel's dilemma is summed up by a story that has become part of
the hotel's legend. One day a formidable matron of the old guard, who
frequented the hotel in the 1970s and 1980s, summoned a staff member. She told him, in a tone of indignation, that a young man, 'probably
a vagrant', seemed to be in a disorderly state on the lawn, and could he
do something about it. Upon investigation, the young man turned out to
be a hotel guest, a 'Mr Greenwood' – in fact John Lennon on an incog-
nito visit to Cape Town, engaged in meditation in the hotel's gardens.
Mr Lennon was left to his inner thoughts, and so began the transition
from the Mount Nelson being thought of as a dowager palace, to a
place where the 'hip' and the famous feel comfortable.

Realising the changing market dynamics and the importance of creating a perception that befitted the hotel, the Mount Nelson was forced to
adapt and adjust its marketing strategy, resulting in the increased focus
on building and maintaining relationships.

Good relationships are paramount

When Nick Seewer joined the Mount Nelson Hotel, he made many adjustments to the hotel's image and styles of service to attract business
from a younger clientele, and also from the local and business sectors.

This 'outward-inward' approach in terms of stakeholder needs and pref-erences contributed to the decision to refurbish the bedrooms and public areas in more modern styles, to make the hotel children-friendly, and to change the menus and dress codes in the restaurants. Further, many Capetonians were scared off by the imposing and unfriendly nature of its pillared entrance. This was turned around by the introduction of monthly food promotions in the hotel's lounge and restaurants. As the hotel's afternoon teas were better known, promotions such as Herit-age, Botanical Teas and Death by Chocolate were introduced with great success as a vehicle to bring people to the hotel. Its centenary, which was a great excuse to celebrate during the whole of 1999, was also a wonderful means of communicating with the world at large.

The role of communication in building and maintaining relationships was regarded as crucial. The Mount Nelson introduced various means to communicate all these developments, such as writing and circulat-ing a series of press releases regularly (both locally and internationally), compiling pictorial newsletters, changing to more modern advertising techniques, and holding regular Food & Beverage promotions to at-tract 'locals' to the hotel. The hotel also started making use of its guest database, as well as the 'ACT' marketing database, to communicate with its regular guests and to keep in touch with the media, suppliers, travel agents, tour operators, etc. 'Keep in the Know' cards are pres-ently used to determine the needs of all stakeholders and to assess prevailing relationships.

In addition, the Mount Nelson Hotel joined local associations such as Cape Town Tourism, SATSA, and SAACI, so that positive networking could be done with similar organisations and the local community in an attempt to build beneficial relationships with all its stakeholders.

Success to date, and in the future?

Of course, it is tempting for Seewer and his team to rest on their laurels. The Mount Nelson has recently been voted best hotel in Africa by the Condé Nast *Traveller* magazine, and one of the eight best in the world by this influential journal. This certainly expresses the new spirit of the hotel and provides evidence of the hotel's commitment to building and maintaining relationships.

(*Source:* Adapted from Simpson, J and Dore, B 2001. *Marketing in South Africa: Cases and Concepts.* Pretoria: Van Schaik.)

Conclusion

The role of relationship building is evident in the drive towards profitability and value creation, and is crucial for achieving organisational goals. The move from mass marketing to relationship marketing holds specific benefits for the organisation, namely:

▲ The trend may lead to the development of a long-term focus, and to the recognition of the value of integrating all organisational communication activities.

▲ The use of database technology, where information is stored on individual customers, may prove useful in measuring the effectiveness of these communication activities.

An integrated communication approach seems valuable in that it combines a variety of disciplines in the organisation to provide a comprehensive communications programme, with the main aim of creating a competitive advantage for the organisation. In terms of the new market orientation (an externally focused business culture), an integrated approach is required to assist in upholding and promoting reputation, increasing customer satisfaction and support by focusing on customer preferences and needs, and improving communications with the customer.

To summarise, it is important to note that, although various terms are used to refer to relationship building and management, successful relationships may hold the following advantages for any organisation:

▲ They facilitate constant adjusting and restructuring within the organisation in an effort to respond to changing relationships.[84]

▲ They enable the organisation to follow a holistic approach by 'balancing the internal processes of organisations with external factors'.[85]

▲ They assist in identifying strategic relationships that the organisation wishes to enter into, and in building and maintaining these relationships.[86]

▲ They foster trust through meaningful and timely communication, in turn resulting in better communication.[87]

▲ As highlighted earlier, they prevent, minimise, and resolve conflict and crisis.[88]

▲ As pointed out, they assist in keeping up with reality 'because nothing exists independent of its relationship with the environment'.[89]

▲ The relationship between the organisation and the public places the organisation in a position to differentiate between the 'stayers' and 'leavers', and this relationship impacts on the level of consumer satisfaction.[90]

▲ 'Mutually productive relationships respond to the needs of both the organisation and its key publics'.[91]

Questions for self-evaluation

1. Discuss some of the important challenges facing organisations and the context within which marketing and public relations function, and highlight the significance of these functions in the shift to a 'shareholder orientation'.

2. By referring to the characteristics of the information age and relationship age, describe how you would distinguish between these eras.

3. Write your own definition of an integrated communication (IC) approach. Why is this approach different from a marketing approach?

4. Describe the implications of an integrated communication approach for marketing and public relations.

5. Working either on your own, or preferably with some of your fellow students in a group, develop an original 'relationship network' model for either the organisation you are employed at, or any other organisation. Clearly identify the 'partners' or 'stakeholders' important to your organisation and include them all in your model.

6. Identify the guidelines for relationship management. In view of these guidelines, and with reference to your organisation or any other organisation, critically evaluate the approach followed by your organisation in relationship management.

Endnotes

1 Du Plooy-Cilliers, F 2001. Paradigmaverskuiwing in veranderingsbestuur: 'n kommunikasiebenadering. Ongepubliseerde MA-graad. Johannesburg: RAU.

2 D'Aprix, R 1996. *Communicating for Change*. California: Jossey-Bass Publishers.

3 Verwey, S 1998. The Age of Communication: A new organisational paradigm for the new millenium. In *Communicare*, December 1998, 17(2):1–15.

4 Galbreath, J 2002. Success in the relationship age: Building quality relationship assets for market value creation. In *The TQM Magazine*,

14(1):8–24. Website: http://ninetta.emerald-library.co (Date of access 4 September 2002.)

5 Andrews, PH and Herschel, RT 1996. *Organizational Communication: Empowerment in a Technological Society*. Boston: Houghton Mifflin Company.

6 Lubbe, BA and Puth, G 1994. *Public Relations in South Africa: A Management Reader*. Durban: Butterworths.

7 Steyn, B and Puth, G 2000. *Corporate Communication Strategy*. Johannesburg: Heinemann.

8 Wilcox, DL; Ault, PBH; Agee, WKL and Cameron, GT 2000. *Public Relations: Strategies and Tactics*. New York: Addison-Wesley Educational Publishers Inc.

9 Duncan, T; Caywood, C and Newsom, D 1993. Preparing advertising and public relations students for the communications industry in the 21st century. A report of the task force on integrated communication. December.

10 Yeshin, T 1998. *Integrated Marketing Communications*. Oxford: Butterworths-Heinemann.

11 Wilcox et al., op. cit.

12 Schultz, DE; Tannenbaum, SI and Lauterborn, RF 1994. *Integrated Marketing Communications*. Illinois: NTC Publishing Group.

13 Harris, TL 1988. *Marketing Communications*. In Hiebert, RE (Ed.) *Precision Public Relations*. NY & London: Longman Inc.

14 Peppers, D and Roger, M 1999. *The One-to-one Manager: Real-world Lessons in Customer Relationship Management*. New York: Doubleday.

15 Berman, B 1996. *Marketing Channels*. New York: John Wiley & Sons.

16 Grunig, JE 1992. What is Excellence in Management? In *Excellence in Public Relations and Communication Management*. Grunig, JE (Ed.) Hillsdale, NJ: Lawrence Erlbaum:219–249.

17 Sumpter, R and Tunkard, JW Jr 1994. The spin doctor: An alternative model of public relations. In *Public Relations Review*, 20(1):19–27.

18 Serini, SA 1994. Power networks and surveillance: Viewing service as an interactive component of PR professionalism. In *Public Relations Review*, 20(1):43–54.

19 Schultz et al., op. cit.

20 Grayson, K and Berry, R 1999. The strategic advantages of direct selling. In *Mastering Marketing: The Complete MBA Companion in Marketing*. *Financial Times*. London: Pearson Education Limited.

21 Harris, op. cit.

22 Rudolph, H 1997. Database marketing and relationship management. In *Marketing Mix*. July 1997, 15(6).

23 Schultz et al., op. cit.

24 Kotler, P 1999. *Kotler on Marketing: How to Create, Win, and Dominate Markets*. NY: Free Press.

25 Kotter, op. cit.

26 Bruning, SD 2000. Examining the role that personal, professional, and community relationships play in respondent relationship perception recognition and intended behavior. In *Communication Quarterly*, 48(4):437–448.

27 Ibid.

28 Kruger-Barker, R 1995. Ontwikkeling van 'n geïntegreerde kommunikasie evalueringsmodel. Unpublished doctoral thesis. Johannesburg: RAU.

29 Nickels, WG and Wood, MB 1997. *Marketing: Relationships, Quality, Value*. NY: Worth.

30 Peppers and Roger, op. cit.

31 Ibid.

32 Cram, T 1994. *The Power of Relationship Marketing*. London: Pitman Publishing.

33 Kent, ML and Taylor, M 1998. Building dialogic relationships through the World Wide Web. In *Public Relations Review*, Fall, 24(3):321–334.

34 Schultz et al., op. cit.

35 Morgan, RM and Hunt, SD 1994. The commitment-trust theory of relationship marketing. In *Journal of Marketing*, July 1994, 58:20–38.

36 Ibid.

37 Kandampully, J and Duddy, R 1999. Relationship marketing: A concept beyond the primary relationship. In *Marketing Intelligence & Planning*, 17(7):315–323. Website: http://tamino.emerald-library.com (Date of access 4 September 2002.)

38 Ibid.

39 Ibid.

40 Galbreath, J 2002. Success in the relationship age: Building quality relationship assets for market value creation. In *The TQM Magazine*, 14(1):8–24.

41 Ibid.

42 Ibid.

43 Gordon, I 1998. *Relationship Marketing*. Ontario: John Wiley & Sons.

44 Hutton, JG 1999. The Definition, dimensions, and domain of public relations. In *Public Relations Review*, 25(2):199–214.

45 Bruning, SD and Ledingham, JA 1998. Organization-public relationships and consumer satisfaction: The role of relationships in the satisfaction mix. In *Communication Research Reports*. Spring, 15(2):198–208.

46 Gordon, I 1998. *Relationship Marketing*. Ontario: John Wiley & Sons.

47 Peppers and Roger, op. cit.

48 Ibid.

49 Lindenmann, WK 1998–99. Measuring relationships is key to successful public relations. In *Public Relations Quarterly*. Winter, 43(4):18–24.

50 Morgan and Hunt, op. cit.

51 Lindenmann, op. cit.:18–24.

52 Sviokla, JJ and Shapiro, BP (Eds.) 1993. *Keeping Customers. A Harvard Business Review Book*. USA: Harvard Business School Publishing Corporation.

53 Sharma, N and Patterson, PG 2000. The impact of communication effectiveness and service quality on relationship commitment in consumer, professional services. In *The Journal of Services Marketing*, 13(2):151–170.

54 Ibid.

55 Ledingham, JA and Bruning, SD 1998. Relationship management in public relations: Dimensions of an organization-public relationship. In *Communication Research Reports*, Spring, 24(1):55–63.

56 Gronroos, C 1996. Relationship marketing: Strategic and tactical implications. In *Management Decision*, 34(3):5–14. Website: http://haly.emerald-library.com/v (Date of access 4 September 2002.)

57 Ibid.

58 Voss, GB and Voss, ZG 1997. Implementing a relationship marketing program: A case study and managerial implications. In *Journal of Services Marketing*, 11(4):278–298. Website: http://haly.emerald-library.com/v (Date of access 4 September 2002.)

59 Ibid.

60 Ledingham and Bruning, op. cit:55–63.

61 Morgan and Hunt, op. cit.

62 Berman, B 1996. *Marketing Channels*. NY: John Wiley & Sons.

63 Petrison, LA and Wang, P 1993. From relationships to relationship marketing: Applying database technology to public relations. In *Public Relations Review,* 19(3):235–245.

64 Galbreath, op. cit.:8–24.

65 Youngblood, MD 1997. *Life at the Edge of Chaos: Creating the Quantum Organization.* Dallas: Perceval Publishing.

66 Galbreath, op. cit.:8–24.

67 Ibid.

68 Sviokla and Shapiro, op. cit.

69 Peppers, D and Roger, M 1999. *The One-to-one manager: Real-world Lessons in Customer Relationship Management*. New York: Doubleday.

70 Lindenmann, WK 1998–99. Measuring relationships is key to successful public relations. In *Public Relations Quarterly,* Winter, 43(4):18–24.

71 Rich, MK 2000. The direction of marketing relationships. In *The Journal of Business and Industrial Marketing*, 15(2/3):170–191.

72 Collins, TM and Doorley, TL 1991. *Teaming Up for the 90s*. Burr Ridge, IL: Irwin Professional Publishing.

73 Jobber, D and Lancaster, G 1997. *Selling and Sales Management*. (4 Ed.) Pitman Publishing: London.

74 Lindenmann, op. cit.:18–24.

75 Ledingham and Bruning, op. cit.:55–63.

76 Ibid.

77 Peppers and Roger, op. cit.

78 Morgan and Hunt, op. cit.

79 Shani, D and Sujana, C 1992. Exploiting niches using relationship marketing. In *Journal of Services Marketing*, 6:43–52.

80 Cram, T 1994. *The Power of Relationship Marketing*. London: Pitman Publishing.

81 Petrison, LA and Wang, P 1993. From relationships to relationship marketing: Applying database technology to public relations. In *Public Relations Review,* 19(3):235–245.

82   Zineldin, M 2000. Beyond relationship marketing: Technologicalship mar-
     keting. In *Marketing Intelligence & Planning*, 18(1). Website: http://antonio.
     mcb-jonline.com/vl.../cw/mcb/02634503/v18nl/52/p9.html (Date of access
     6 January 2001.)

83   Petrison and Wang, op. cit.:235–245.

84   Dozier, DM with Grunig, LA and Grunig, JE 1995. *Manager's Guide to
     Excellence in Public Relations and Communication Management.* Lawrence
     Associates: New Jersey.

85   Ibid.

86   Ibid.

87   Morgan and Hunt, op. cit.:20–38.

88   Lindenmann, WK 1998–99. Measuring relationships is key to successful
     public relations. In *Public Relations Quarterly,* Winter, 43(4):18–24.

89   McDaniels, RRJ 1997. Strategic leadership: A view from quantum and
     chaos theories. In *Health Care Management Review*, 22(1):21–37.

90   Ledingham and Bruning, op. cit.

91   Bruning, SD and Ledingham, JA 1998. Organization-public relationships
     and consumer satisfaction: The role of relationships in the satisfaction
     mix. In *Communication Research Reports,* Spring, 15(2):198–208.

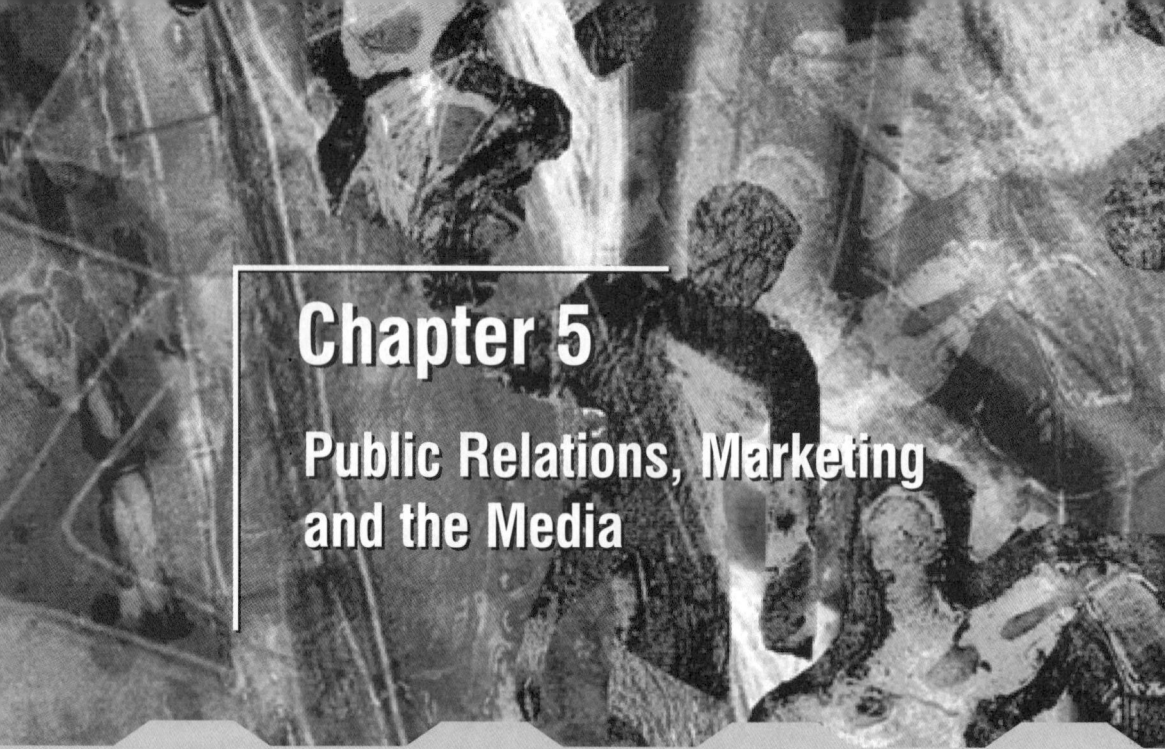

Chapter 5

Public Relations, Marketing and the Media

LEARNING OUTCOMES

After studying this chapter, you should be able to:

- ▲ explain the difference between controlled and uncontrolled media
- ▲ discuss the different communication media options available to a marketer/public relations practitioner
- ▲ identify the characteristics of each of the main media types
- ▲ discuss examples of specific media tools within each of the major media vehicles.

Introduction

The basic communications model shows that a transmitter encodes a message which is directed to the receiver or audience through a communication medium. In public relations the media are important because there is no guarantee that they will actually allow the public relations communication attempt to go through their media channels. In other words, just because we as practitioners choose a specific medium, this does not mean that the media will participate. In order to increase the likelihood of success, it is important to understand the media fully and to be able to distinguish between what makes a certain media type different from another. We need to be able to decide what media would be most appropriate to use for the objectives of the communication effort and in light of the target audiences. In this chapter we look specifically at media and how they can be used effectively to aid in the public relations communication effort.

Controlled and uncontrolled media

One way of characterising the type of media that a public relations practitioner could use is through the use of the 'control' variable.[1] Media that are controlled include those media where the public relations practitioner has a say over the content of the message, how it is said and even when it is said. This is usually because controlled media contains communication that it is generally paid for, so the client will have choice about the format of the message, the copy itself and even the placement of the communication.[2] Examples of controlled media include corporate print material such as pamphlets and annual reports, company-sponsored audio-visual material, and corporate speeches.

The term uncontrolled media, however, means that the practitioner does not have any direct influence over media content. In other words, the media manager (an editor, for example) has free rein over whether or not to use the media communication or even to write his or her own stories about the organisation. Examples of communications efforts in uncontrolled media are public relations releases, publicity efforts, new stories or photographs with a caption, and conferences. The main factor in the case of uncontrolled media is that they are not paid to run the story or to publicise an event. The media decides on all the aspects related to the communications effort. Examples of communication efforts aimed at both controlled and uncontrolled media are shown in table 5.1 on the next page.[3]

Print media – controlled
House journals; information brochures; handbooks and manuals; newsletters; bulletins; bulletin boards; posters; periodicals; annual reports; commemorative stamps; exhibits and displays; mobile displays; suggestion boxes; instructions; orders; pay inserts; flyers; written reports; financial statements; training kits; consumer information kits; teacher and student kits; student games; specific window displays

Print media – uncontrolled
News releases; feature stories; photographs with captions; media kits; business feature articles; pictorial publicity; letters to the editor; background editorial material

Audio-visual media – controlled
Transparencies for overhead projectors; telephone calls and recorded messages; multimedia exhibits and displays; audiotapes and cassettes; video-tapes and cassettes; visual multimedia window displays and training aids; oral presentations with visuals; slide shows; corporate film and video tapes

Audio-visual media – uncontrolled
Broadcast news releases; photo opportunities; radio and television public service announcements; broadcast interviews; news videotapes for television; news or media conferences; special programmes for radio or television; pictorial publicity; recorded telephone news capsules and updates from an organisation; informing and influencing editors and media gatekeepers such as news directors, public service directors, financial editors, columnists and reporters

Interpersonal media – controlled
Formal speeches; lectures; seminars; conferences; panel discussions; question and answer sessions; oral testimonies; employee counselling; committee meetings; legal, medical or miscellaneous counselling; staff meetings; demonstration and training programmes; interviews; personal instructions; the grapevine

Interpersonal media – uncontrolled
Interviews; personal appearances; news conferences; informing and influenc-ing editors and media gatekeepers through personal visits, appearances and testimony; committee meeting or government commission question-and-answer sessions with press

Private or folk media – controlled
Documentary films; private collections; ornaments or charms; puppet shows; village theatre; improvisational theatre; insignias; gossip; oratory; poetry; music; drama, mime and dance; marketplaces; festivals; storytelling; political rallies; community group meetings; weddings or funerals; sangomas; stokvels

Table 5.1 Controlled and uncontrolled media and corresponding communications efforts

It is clear that there are numerous media and communication vehicle choices available to the practitioner. Which one is most effective? The public relations practitioner must consider the target audience and the communication objectives, and then choose from the available options the media that will optimise the likelihood of the objectives being achieved. Of course, the available budget assists the practitioner in deciding on the best mix of options. To be successful in this effort, the practitioner must understand the type of media (controlled vs. uncontrolled), the dynamics involved, and the media gatekeepers and their values, to be able to design an optimal public relations effort. Let us consider the different media types.

Media for internal publics

It is necessary, from the outset, to clearly understand what is meant by internal publics. Internal publics, quite simply, are inside the organisation, and include supervisors, employees, clerks, managers, stockholders and directors.[4] Since many organisations consider employees to be one of the top two assets of any business (customers being the other asset), then the relationship with employees is extremely important. The results of an organisation will not be optimal unless the whole organisation understands what is needed for success in the marketplace, and aligns its effort and values to achieve those goals. The importance of internal publics in terms of the performance of an organisation has been highlighted by well-known marketing guru Philip Kotler. Kotler emphasises that, for most organisations with a service component to their product, there are three types of marketing that can occur.[5] For effective marketing, the organisation requires not only external marketing (organisation to customers), but also interactive marketing (employees to customers), and internal marketing (company to employees). This is illustrated in figure 5.1.

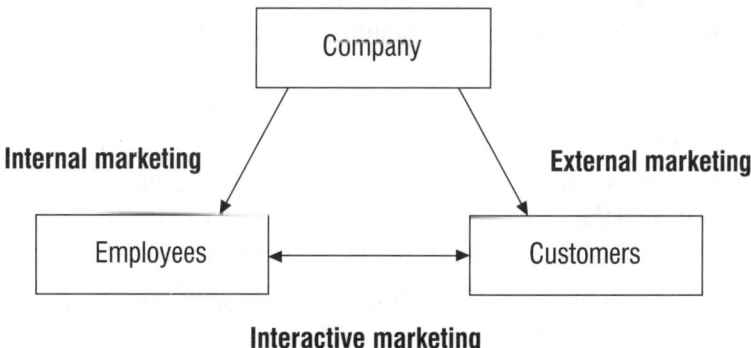

Figure 5.1 Three types of marketing

The usual view of what marketing entails is the view of *external marketing*, that is to design and implement a marketing mix to customers. The view shown in figure 5.1 expands on this, and brings in interactive and internal marketing. *Interactive marketing* describes the employees' ability to serve customers, that is, they should be ready, willing and able to meet customer expectations. *Internal marketing* involves the work done by an organisation to train and motivate employees to serve customers well and to understand their roles in the organisation. It should be clear that external marketing cannot occur without first considering internal marketing, that is ensuring the organisation is fully aligned to meet the needs of customers through interactive marketing.

The goals of internal communication can thus be described as communication to assist in establishing and maintaining mutually beneficial relationships between an organisation and its employees, who are so important to the achievement of organisation goals.[6]

Public relations practitioners should consider the following internal media in their communication efforts (note that these are controlled media).

Internal communication media

The public relations practitioner needs information on employee attitudes before deciding what media vehicle to use. This information could be the result of an internal communication audit to find out staff attitudes about their jobs, management, the organisation, and existing communication efforts. This could be obtained through research. The media vehicles that could be used include:

▲ **On-line communications:** This includes vehicle choices such as e-mail, voice mail and tailored intranets.[8] These allow the employees to receive news and information almost on a real-time basis at their desks. They can also be used to generate interactive communication with employees. This type of media is putting pressure on traditional internal print media vehicles. The increasing pace of change in terms of technology and its diffusion throughout organisations means that many organisations now rely more and more on intranets to disseminate information to interact with employees.

▲ **Print publications:** Although under pressure from the new options available through the evolution of technology, there are still many internal print media vehicles available to the public relations practitioner.[9] These include:

    △ *Bulletins* – these are short documents designed to convey information with a sense of urgency.

    △ *Newsletters* – these are popular tools used to inform employees about current and future events.

△ *News tabloids* – these communicate a much broader range of information than newsletters, and often contain features, photographs and a variety of information about the organisation and its employees.

△ *Magazines* – these are news tabloids produced in magazine format. Many large South African companies, such as Toyota and SA Breweries, utilise the magazine format for internal communication.

△ *Annual reports* – there are three types of annual reports. One type is the annual report aimed at stockholders, which reports on a company's financial position. This is often seen as a corporate showpiece, and there are even awards for the best annual report. The second type is an employee annual report, aimed at employees, which is factual, informational and motivational.[10] The performance of the company is highlighted, important financial and other performance measures are explained and important employee achievements are recognised. The third type is a summary annual report that streamlines information and presents it in a simple but colourful manner. This may even be available in video form.

△ *Specialty publications* – these are special purpose communication packages that highlight specific issues and provide detailed information.

△ *Outside publications that can be used internally* – these are special publications by organisations that allow the public relations practitioners of a company to overlay their company logo and name, showing them to be company sponsored.

△ *Underground publications* – these are usually produced by employees in an informal and non-company supervised method. They are useful because they represent the views of the 'grapevine'. An example could be an 'unauthorised newsletter' that appears on company noticeboards highlighting certain issues.

△ *Bargaining unit publications* – these are published by the bargaining units of organisations or labour unions to keep their members informed of important developments.

△ *Bulletin boards* – although tools used for many years, they have received new life as a news centre using enlarged pictures and text, motivational messages and other company announcements.[11] Many organisations now have electronic bulletin boards that can be accessed through the intranet.

△ *Electronic publications* – these are electronic media that employees can access through electronic means. They allow an organisation to communicate with its employees quickly, inexpensively and in a manner that can be quickly adjusted.

▲ **Audiovisual media:** These are used to communicate with specific employee groups. Traditional audiovisual media in organisations include flip charts and overhead transparencies. Technology has improved to such an extent that presentations to employees can be made through computer presentation programmes such as PowerPoint. Video is still popular, and is often used when presentations are done by regional offices and the organisation wants to control the video content. Nowadays, many organisations use multimedia presentations that include many audiovisual formats. Another increasingly popular form is using private media such as satellite television, closed circuit television or cable television to communicate with all members of an organisation, no matter how widespread the employees are in terms of geography.

▲ **Interpersonal communication media:** The most used and foremost communication medium is still personal interaction. One source states that supervisors are the preferred source for 90 per cent of employees – the top choice by far.[12] Organisations should create opportunities to communicate person to person or person to group, and use newsletters and video as support media. Often, however, this is not the case and other media – rather than interpersonal communication – are used. Examples of interpersonal communication include small group meetings, interviews, briefings, speeches or presentations, and conversation. The idea is to be consistent in the tone and content of the message delivered, so as to ensure effective communication.

The organisational grapevine or informal communication is also a tool or medium which should be harnessed for positive use and not only for rumour spreading. It is valuable because it is believed by employees, and it is effective in disseminating information quickly throughout the organisation. Any internal communication programme should include plans on how the grapevine can be used positively to disseminate information.

Mass communication media[13]

This type of media is used by marketers and public relations practitioners to reach mass audiences. Since an organisation does not usually control mass media, it is generally referred to as uncontrolled. Some controversy over impartiality often exists, however, when an organisation does control or own a media organisation, such as the SABC and the government; Multichoice, M-Net and DSTV; or a media mogul such as Rupert Murdoch and the specific print and visual media under his control. The bias or objectivity of the media is often questioned. A classic case is Zimbabwe and its government's control of most of the mass media available in the country. The independence of such media is often in question and anything broadcast over the airwaves is usually received with doubt and a clear understanding of who actually controls the media.

Let us now consider the major mass communication media.

The press

The press is the most versatile and resilient of all mass communication media and includes regional, national and international newspapers and magazines. Sophisticated electronic media have not destroyed the press in industrial countries and, as literacy grows in developing countries, so the press develops to satisfy the demand for knowledge, news and entertainment.

▲ **Newspapers.** When people think of advertising and publicity, they almost immediately think of newspapers. Examples of popular newspapers in South Africa are the dailies (e.g. *Cape Times, Beeld, The Star, Sowetan*) and the weeklies (e.g. *Argus, Rapport, Sunday Times*). These newspapers are read by many literate people. There are also regional newspapers in most cities and towns, and even in the suburbs of large cities, for example *Pretoria News* (daily) and *Benoni City Times* (weekly). There are also freesheets (knock-and-drop) newspapers that are delivered door-to-door, free of charge. Their circulations are large and there is saturation coverage of residential areas, making them increasingly valuable vehicles for public relations stories. Although no longer the dominant medium, newspapers are still a powerful force in shaping the public agenda and influencing the outcome of debate.

▲ **Magazines.** Magazines offer effective channels of communication to specialised publics. Research indicates that magazines are especially effective in providing information to younger, well-educated and more affluent adults. Research also indicates that magazine content is perceived, assimilated and reacted to by each individual consumer within a personal framework.[14] Magazines can be divided into many categories and, in industrialised countries, there are hundreds of titles. In developing countries there may be few magazines of any kind, while some of those on sale are imported (e.g. *Time, Newsweek*), or published abroad and sold locally. The main magazine categories are:

△ *consumer magazines*, which can be sold weekly (e.g. *Huisgenoot, Keur, Farmer's Weekly*); fortnightly (e.g. *Fair Lady, Sarie*); or monthly (e.g. *Bona, Cosmopolitan, Living & Loving, Thandi*)

△ *trade, technical* and *professional magazines* such as *Financial Mail, Finance Week* or *Finansies en Tegniek*, as well as miscellaneous publications which may include gay publications (such as *Link*) and those from various minority groups and causes. They meet needs not catered for by commercially published newspapers or magazines.

Circulation figures (averages based on audited net sales) and readership figures (estimates based on monthly research techniques) are available to public relations practitioners from the ABC (Audit Bureau of Circulations of South Africa) – a six-monthly detailed audit and overall summary of reading claims.

There are special advantages of the press as a medium. It can provide information in greater depth than transient broadcast media. It can be read anywhere, in the home or office, while commuting, during a meal – at times and in places where electronic media may be inconvenient or unavailable. The press is a portable medium that can be taken almost anywhere. In fact, in developing countries such as South Africa, educated members of a family may take newspapers to their dwellings and read them to illiterate relations. Newspapers and magazines often have an extended life because they are kept – binders are supplied for some magazines or back numbers may be found in libraries – or because they are passed on to other interested readers. Items can be cut out and sorted, either personally or by libraries, which maintain files on many subjects. Press cuttings are kept by many institutions on numerous subjects.

The press is therefore a living medium. But the public relations practitioner should also consider the disadvantages of the press as a medium. Newspapers in particular can have short lives and people should be wary of the large circulation and readership figures claimed for them. Some copies may never reach the home. Other copies may be discarded on a short commuter journey to or from the office. Not every section of a paper is read by all readers, and readerships have to be reduced to likely readership of certain stories. For example, research showed that the most read feature in the *Financial Times* was not the financial news but the digest of general news on the front page.[15] Some newspapers and magazines may be biased; thus, they either do not print certain stories or they distort them. There is seldom truly objective reporting by the press, and it is often true that a good, factual publicity release from a public relations source is more impartial than the average newspaper story. Newspapers in particular can be unreliable in their reporting, mainly because they are produced quickly and it is difficult to be editorially accurate.

Behind all the above, however, lies the freedom of the press and the fact that – where they are not state controlled – newspapers and magazines are published in order to make money. Consequently, they print what is most likely to sell copies. In public relations terms, this means that stories which editors consider to be of interest and of value to their particular readers are most likely to be printed. This is influenced by the fact that, in some cases, readers dislike multinational corporations, certain organisations or industrial disputes. Public relations practitioners, in submitting press material, have to reconcile themselves to the facts about the press and the peculiarities of democracy in a free enterprise society, which may not always have been part of their training.

Broadcast media

Broadcast media are quite different from the press, and television and radio have special advantages, but they are transient unless recorded on video or tape. Unlike printed messages, it is difficult to retain broadcast messages. They usually must be absorbed at the exact time of transmission. Yet these media can be extremely valuable in public relations programmes if they are understood and used properly, especially as broadcast media publics may well exceed the readerships of newspapers and magazines.

▲ **Television.** In South Africa there are the national networks of the SABC, namely SABC 1, 2 and 3, as well as the independent stations, e-TV and M-Net. Television in South Africa is no longer an elitist medium; not only has it become popular in urban areas, but – by means of community viewing in public halls – it has also been brought within reach of those who cannot afford sets of their own, for example RTV or rural television. Many taverns and sports bars provide free broadcasts of popular sports programmes.

Some advantages of television as a medium are that programmes are watched mostly in the home or in social settings, but may also be seen in schools and workplaces such as offices. While not as captive as a cinema audience, the television audience has to view the programmes in a particular place, and remain seated. The viewer cannot be mobile like a radio listener. Perhaps the greatest merit is the blend of sounds, movement and colour, which provides realism. This applies to people, places and objects. A special advantage of television is that it is a visual medium. Viewers tend to watch rather than listen to television. An important aspect of television has been its ability to introduce new interests to viewers who take them up and want to learn more about them. This leads to a demand for information in a more detailed and permanent form, such as new magazines, newspaper features and books. Recent innovations have made it possible to record and play back programmes, to show one's own programmes using films and cassettes, and to call up required information by means of teletext systems.

The major disadvantages of television as a medium are that it can be time-consuming, both in the negotiation of material and in the actual production of programmes. The message is limited to restricted time segments, there is no possibility for consumer referral to messages, and available time is sometimes difficult to arrange. High time and production costs and sometimes poor colour transmission are further disadvantages.

Taking these advantages and disadvantages into consideration, however, the public relations practitioner can make use of the following on television: news bulletins; discussion programmes (e.g. chat shows, discussion panels, debates and interviews); series and serials; give-away programmes (e.g. game shows and contests); and magazine programmes (e.g. *Special Assignment* and *Carte Blanche*, which provide many public relations opportunities).

▲ **Radio.** Radio broadcasting, once thought to be on the decline because of television, today plays a useful and pervasive role in South Africa's public information system. Radio is a highly underestimated medium in South Africa. Perhaps the feature that makes radio different from all other mass communication media, and of special interest to the public relations practitioner, is that it can often be an instantaneous medium. Immediate announcements can be made on the radio.[16] There are numerous radio stations in South Africa: international and national stations such as *Radio RSA* and *5FM,* and regional stations such as *Radio Jacaranda*, as well as the independent stations such as *Radio 702* and *YFM.*

Radio has various advantages as a medium. In contrast to the visual nature of television, radio has the intimacy of the human voice. Not unlike the newspaper, radio can be a portable medium. Many sets may exist in one household, or a set can be carried from room to room. A person can be listening to the radio while doing other things. A variety of listeners may tune in at different times of the day. Radio has long been an effective way of reaching people of different ethnic groups and languages in developing countries, including large numbers of people who cannot read, through either personal or public radios. Radio provides companionship, whether by means of the human voice or music. Radio has good saturation of local audiences at a relatively low cost.

There are also certain disadvantages to radio of which the public relations practitioner should be aware. Messages are limited by restricted time segments and there is no possibility for consumer referral to messages. Radio has no visual appeal.

Radio offers a wide variety of public relations possibilities. It is a mobile medium suited to mobile people (such as rural audiences). Public relations practitioners can use the radio for news programmes, live studio interviews, taped interviews, phone-ins and talk radio, and tie-ins with series and serials.

From the above discussion, it must be noted that television and radio are entirely different media with entirely different public relations opportunities. Each medium needs to be studied carefully to see how public relations coverage can be achieved. These opportunities vary from situation to situation and country to country.

There are various publications that the public relations practitioner should be aware of when selecting mass communication media. The *SARAD* is a bi-monthly directory that coves all media available in South Africa. *AMPS* (All Media and Product Survey) is an annual survey undertaken by the SAARF (South African Research Foundation) into readership, listenership and viewership of media, and usage of certain products. AMPS provides the basic data upon which most media planning in South Africa is based.

Public and trade exhibitions

Exhibitions, shows, displays and trade fairs represent a spectrum of communication media that have wider applications in industrial communication programmes. Exhibitions take many forms: they may be indoor or outdoor, portable or permanent, and can also be mobile, using specially designed road vehicles such as trailers, caravans or buses. There are also exhibition trains and ships. Exhibitions are unique in many ways: they provide better opportunities for two-way contacts than most other communication methods; they can be adapted for large-scale, impressive presentations or for highly specialised purposes; they can be vehicles for product selling or for corporate policy information, and they can be geared to practically any of an organisation's publics.[17]

The increasing number of exhibitions now being held in South Africa is a sure sign of the growing importance of this medium as a means of presenting new products and services.[18] Organisations use exhibitions to inform employees, stockholders and the general public about a variety of topics, from product information to local community relations programmes.

The public relations opportunities for exhibitions are numerous. Exhibitions, displays and trade fairs have a large public relations content. It is not uncommon for exhibitions of all kinds to be the responsibility of the public relations practitioner. Common exhibitions include Decorex, *Getaway* and Computer Faire.

Privately created media and folk media or 'oramedia'

These media are controlled media and can be specially created for the use of the public relations practitioner to support existing mass communication media.

Privately created media

Some of the most commonly used privately created media for public relations purposes are the following:

▲ **Documentary films.** Documentary films are also known as sponsored or industrial films, and are usually 10 to 20 minutes in length. They can be used to demonstrate the use of products, describe tourist attractions, show how products are made, or explain the purpose and policy of an organisation.

▲ **Videotapes.** These can be used in place of documentary films, or the films can be transferred to video.

▲ **Private and mobile exhibitions.** Exhibitions are mounted by one sponsor and can be housed permanently on company premises, or tour on special vehicles such as caravans or trailers, larger specially designed vehicles or converted buses.

▲ **Educational literature.** Not to be confused with sales literature, educational print media may consist of explanatory leaflets, folders, brochures, books or posters, which explain how a product or service works, or perhaps tell the story of an organisation or industry.

▲ **Seminars and conferences.** These are various invited assemblies for the purpose of making presentations, using speakers, slides, films, videos, displays and demonstrations.

Privately created media are especially useful when communicating with special interest groups or publics. In the South African context, and for public relations purposes, they should be functional, informative and educational.

Folk media or 'oramedia'

There are various ways of communicating public relations messages to specifically rural publics, some of which are useful when the publics are local or mixed ethnic groups with different languages and dialects. Some of these publics might live in remote places and may be beyond the reach of the main mass communication media. They may pay little attention to radio, beyond listening to music. They may also be uninterested in the affairs of the cities and show little interest in news bulletins.

'Oramedia' (also called folk or traditional media) are based on indigenous culture that is produced and consumed by members of a group. Unlike the mass communication media, which reach many people at a time but only have cognitive influence (knowledge, awareness and interest), oramedia only reach a few people at a time, but can be an effective relay chain to the mass communication media. These media have visible cultural features, often quite conventional, by which social relationships and a world view are maintained and defined. They take many forms and are rich in symbolism. Oramedia must be seen as interpersonal media that speak to common people in their language and idiom, and deal with problems of direct relevance to their situation.[19]

In South Africa, this device has not yet been adequately utilised. It can be used to promote all kinds of public relations programmes, from family planning to efficient farming, primary health care, adult literacy and the fight against AIDS. There is a wide variety of these media, some of which include:

▲ **Puppet shows.** These are used in many parts of South Africa and the message is communicated by a playlet, acted out and mimed by puppets.

▲ **Village theatre.** The public relations message can be presented in the form of a short play.

▲ **Improvisational theatre.** An issue can be communicated by actors who improvise – the play is not rehearsed and the audience determines the direction and outcome of the play. There is a great deal of audience participation.

▲ **Gossip.** In many industrialising communities, gossip is important where people congregate. It may be the gossip that takes place in markets and bazaars where people meet regularly, or which occurs in restaurants, or when friends gather at home. Public relations messages can be communicated by feeding these systems of gossip.

▲ **Oratory, poetry and music.** These media infuse all the activities of people in developing countries, from the cradle to the grave, and are a synthesis of artistic experience, creativity, expression, spiritualism and function. Music can be successfully utilised by public relations practitioners to communicate all kinds of messages. Drums, ornaments, charms and insignia are also important oramedia that can be used.

▲ **Market places.** These are diffuse communication forums where people go both to purchase or sell and for social interaction and exchange. As a news centre, the market place attracts personal as well as public information on subjects such as public and family affairs, educational and political matters, and religious concerns at the rural or village level.

▲ **Festivals.** These are reminders of the past, which therefore serve historical and solidarity purposes. They can be used effectively by the public relations practitioner.

▲ **Weddings, funerals and political rallies.** These can be and have been used by various political and ideological groups as occasions for public relations communication.

Contexts of public relations communication

The range of communication media that can be used for public relations purposes has been discussed briefly. It may seem a formidable list but, of course,
selections must be made according to the public relations objectives, the publics to be reached, and the available budget. We now turn to the various *contexts*
within which these communication media can be utilised for public relations
purposes.

Sponsorships

Sponsorship is a development of patronage.[20] It consists of giving monetary or
other support to a beneficiary in order to make it financially viable, sometimes
for altruistic reasons, but usually to gain some advertising, public relations or
general marketing advantage. The main categories of sponsorship are:

▲ **books and publications** such as maps

▲ **exhibitions**, which may be sponsored by trade associations and professional
societies, or by newspapers and magazines, or by company-sponsored private exhibitions

▲ **education** in the form of grants, bursaries and fellowships

▲ **expeditions**, such as mountaineering, explorations, round-the-world
voyages, and other adventures; *Getaway* magazine, for example, has sponsored a number of expeditions which generate publicity and provide material
for the magazine

▲ **sports events** (a popular area of sponsorship)

▲ **the arts**, such as music, painting and the theatre, for example the
Grahamstown Arts Festival and Nedbank's sponsorship of the arts

▲ **causes and charities**, especially by assisting in the promotion of their activities, for example pharmaceutical companies produce videos to explain
the causes, nature and treatment of illnesses

▲ **local events** that can be supported with prizes, such as gymkhanas and flower
shows

▲ **professional awards** for people associated with the sponsor's industry, such
as photographers, journalists, architects and others

▲ **public service and civic sponsorships** for the public interest contributed by
local authorities or businesses, for example socially responsible sponsorship for the care of street children.

The principle that people like what they know, that 'familiarity breeds *content*' – to reword the phrase in a public relations sense – is often applied to sponsorships.

There are various public relations opportunities in sponsorships:

▲ **Goodwill.** An important public relations objective may be to create goodwill towards the organisation – locally, nationally or internationally. A large organisation, making large profits, may adopt a social conscience by donating funds or gifts to society. It may give financial aid to a library, college theatre, hospital or medical research fund. By sponsoring sports or the arts, it may be seen to be acting in the public interest.

▲ **Corporate image and corporate identity.** Allied to what has been said above about goodwill, there may be a need to create understanding of the character of the organisation. Sponsorship can assist in identifying an organisation by making its logo and colour scheme familiar to publics. This has been successfully achieved by organisations such as Coca-Cola, which sponsors athletics and swimming worldwide.

▲ **Familiarising the name.** This is explicit in the discussion of corporate image and identity, but sponsorship usually involves continuous repetition of the name, especially in media coverage when reporters and commentators describe the event (or the prize or competition) by using the sponsor's name. When calculating the results of a sponsorship, these references can be monitored and assessments can be made. For example, during the rugby season, references are made in every match to the sponsor, Bankfin.

▲ **Hospitality.** Although not to be disregarded when considering the costs of sponsorship, hospitality can provide numerous opportunities for socialising. The managing director can invite a party of business friends or important customers to a sponsored event such as a cricket or rugby match, a golf tournament, etc. In fact, the *ability* to offer such hospitality may be a major reason for sponsoring.

▲ **Encouraging the interest of journalists.** A popular method is the presentation of awards to journalists for their skill and knowledge in writing about the sponsor's subject or industry.[21] An example is the annual awards for enterprising journalism presented by the Department of National Health and Population Development. The aim of the award is to promote enterprising reportage in the fields of health, welfare and population development.

Sponsorship is clearly an important local, national and international activity that contains a large element of public relations. It signifies that an organisation is successful and has a sound reputation, since no person or organisation wants to be associated with a benefactor of ill repute. To be able to sponsor is therefore a sign of acceptance, which in itself is good public relations.

Promotions

This is a context and function of public relations that involves special activities, such as events designed to create and stimulate interest in a person, product, organisation or cause. When a manufacturer puts special effort behind the sale of a product, it is called a promotion. When a store is geared up for the back-to-school buying time, it is called a promotion. When a soap manufacturer puts a free hand towel in every box, it is a promotion. And when you find a coupon worth R10 in your carton of breakfast food, that is also a promotion. Moreover, there are many types of *promotional items*:

▲ **Image marketing.** An image is the impression of a person, organisation or institution that is held by one or more publics. These images should be marketed to the various publics.

▲ **Publicity spin-offs.** Television audiences frequently see newsmakers and celebrities on talk shows. The whole purpose is to create spin-off publicity.

▲ **Celebrity spin-offs.** Promotion planners often look for a 'big name' to attract media attention. Celebrities' names and pictures are often used in the pre-promotion of a special event. Nelson Mandela is an example of a world figure who often lends his presence to humanitarian causes, such as the recent World AIDS Summit.

It is in promotion that one sees public relations' closest ties to marketing. These are so close, in fact, that some have called promotion 'marketing public relations'. Selling an image along with a product does not work, however, when the product is not there to sell. A co-ordinated effort works best and often involves advertising, as well as publicity and promotion. Promotional activities are the glamorous side of public relations but, for the public relations practitioner, they are a risky business.[22] An efficient promotion needs planning, measurement and specification.

Special events

A special event may be any newsmaking situation – from a corporate open house or a freeway ribbon-cutting ceremony to the preview of an exhibition of rare paintings. Special events create excitement among consumers, as well as among dealers, sales staff, stockholders and other publics involved in merchandising the organisation's product or service. Special events such as grand openings, recognition programmes, celebrity appearances and stunts of one kind or another demand a lot of planning, both for participants and for media coverage. The more unusual the special event, the more likely it is that it will be considered newsworthy and therefore merit media coverage.

Preparation for the *mechanics of a special event* include a timetable, which contains the dates of the special event; a mailing list for special activities and news media; and the planning of a promotional programme with a theme that will carry through to all advertising, publicity, letterheads, invitations and posters. A *media kit* should be prepared for the media with the following contents: a basic fact sheet that details newsmaking events; a historical fact sheet of background information on the event; a programme of events or schedule of activities; a straight news story; a complete list of all participants; visual material; a longer general news story; two or more feature stories of varying length for print media; brochures; a list of useful additional information and a newsroom for the use of members of the media.

To best advance the public image of an organisation, this special event should be substantive, usually serious, and in the public interest. It will be most effective if the event involves large numbers of people and includes the presence of at least one celebrity. Shallow 'pseudo-events' should be avoided; they sometimes do more harm than good by damaging the organisation's credibility.

Corporate advertising

Corporate advertising focuses on the reputation of an organisation or institution. It is advertising on the organisation's behalf to promote the business or financial interest of the organisation. Corporate advertising is one area where the professional concerns of public relations and advertising overlap. The corporate image is usually the concern of the public relations practitioner. Advertising, however, which is specifically orientated towards corporate image, is usually prepared by the advertising staff or agency. Obviously there is a need for maximum co-ordination.[23]

Most corporate advertising is geared toward ideas, images and attitudes rather than towards the sale of specific products. There are various types of corporate advertising:

▲ **Identity advertising.** This is used where an organisation is trying to define its identity and activities. An organisation may elect to change its name, which necessitates a new identity campaign. An example is the corporate identity advertising used by SASOL after it changed its corporate logo.

▲ **Image advertising.** Closely related to identity advertising is image advertising, which attempts to develop a personality for an organisation, such as a good neighbour, a leader in technology, or an innovator. Mazda, for example, has long been associated with the sponsorship of nature conservation projects.

▲ **Crisis advertising.** Advertising must sometimes deal with the unexpected, such as oil spills, pollution of rivers, mining accidents and strikes. Organisations must therefore have a crisis or disaster plan, and advertising ready to re-establish goodwill.

▲ **Service advertising.** Advertisements that teach or inform people about something provide a service to consumers. People feel more positively about an organisation that provides them with useful information, for example the health tips offered by a pharmacy chain, and Pick 'n Pay's successful campaign of providing safety driving tips to assist in reducing traffic deaths.

▲ **Financial advertising.** Many organisations undertake corporate advertising in order to make themselves more attractive to stock analysts and potential investors. These advertisements need to be built on facts and solid information – not on fluff or vague copy extolling technological breakthroughs and bottom lines. What the publics most often want is not figures and detailed data, but interpretation of the figures and the story behind the data.

▲ **Advocacy advertising.** This is sometimes called issue advertising and is used when an organisation wants to take a public stand on an issue. Recently, various South African organisations took a stand for the Proudly South African campaign. This type of advertising is used when an issue surfaces that is critical to the well-being of an organisation.

Corporate advertising should meet the public relations objectives of the organisation, and be creative as well as effective.

Publicity

Publicity is unpaid and either controlled or uncontrolled mass communication. The mass communication media carry the information without cost because they view it as socially responsible or newsworthy.[24] Publicity could involve, among other things, a column item in a local newspaper, a cover story in a national magazine, 30 seconds on the News at 8, a bit of chatter by a radio talk show host, the mention of an organisation's name once or twice in a story about the industry, a single photograph in a newspaper or magazine, an annual report, a house journal, or a film.

The terms 'public relations' and 'publicity' are sometimes mistakenly viewed as interchangeable.[25] While public relations can be briefly defined as two-way communication to promote mutual understanding, publicity is only one way of achieving this end. Publicity is a clear responsibility of the public relations practitioner, both as public relations practitioner and publicist (media representative for his or her client or organisation). It involves attracting media attention on behalf of a person, product, service, cause or organisation in the form of news coverage in the mass communication media, and announcements and articles in the trade press.[26]

There are two main categories of publicity that the public relations practitioner should be aware of. While *marketing publicity* aims to persuade publics to buy a product or service, *public relations publicity* aims to convince publics that an organisation or cause is worthy of their support and approval. These two are related in that both types are aligned to achieve an integrated publicity campaign.

Two important aspects of publicity warrant further discussion:

1. **Publicity content.** It is necessary to establish which sources of information are available when seeking publicity for a client or an organisation. This information will serve as the content of the message that the publicist will ultimately relay to the media. Publicity content can mainly be divided into two general categories: news and newsworthiness. These terms must be described for the purposes of this discussion, since everyone's idea of what news is may differ. *News* is anything that interests people in general or any smaller section of the public. News is what is new and important. It also implies immediacy, timeliness and urgency. *Newsworthy* information, however, responds to a *created* need identified by an organisation, not to a perceived need. It engages the curiosity of the public in an area in which they may have had no previous interest, or not have known they had interest in. A newsworthy item may be timeless or at least not linked to a specific date. It may involve a human interest story, a profile of – or an interview with – an unusual or important individual, or an assortment of useful tips in an area with which the recipients are concerned. Journalism distinguishes between news and newsworthiness, usually calling them hard or soft news.[27]

2. **Publicity context.** The context of publicity refers to the *setting or situation* in which the content occurs or exists, and the *audience* for whom the content would be of interest. Publicity context supplies the necessary background and determines the angle from which the content should be presented. It must be emphasised that any public relations is linked to the medium to be used in the communication process.

A large number of *publicity techniques* are used by an organisation or its spokesperson in an attempt to communicate with the relevant segment of the public:

▲ **Publicity release.** Some authors distinguish between a press release and a news release. A press release contains information aimed at the press or print media , while a news release contains information aimed at the broadcast or electronic media.[28] Other authors refer only to a *publicity release*, which includes all press and news releases.[29] The latter is a more workable term since it includes all types of information releases to the media and is also known as a publicity technique. A publicity release is used to convey information, news or any important material from the publicist to the media. It can be harmful to the publicist and his or her client or organisation if it is not handled properly. Some media specialist magazines often identify 'bad' publicity efforts, thus harming the image of the organisation.

▲ **Interviews.** The public relations practitioner (or publicist in this context) usually co-ordinates interviews for the media. Irrespective of which medium is utilised, this publicity technique provides a high level of exposure for the organisation concerned. Interviews may take place on an interpersonal level or telephonically, and usually originate from the need of an editor, journalist, author or writer who has a topic in mind and would like to meet the right person by means of an interview.

▲ **Media or news conference.** The terms 'media conference' or 'news conference' are once again preferred to the term 'press conference' because the latter tends to exclude the electronic media. The media are not always positively inclined towards this publicity technique, which may result in antagonism on their part towards the organisation concerned. Media or news conferences are necessary in cases where an important personality pays a brief visit, or for an announcement with strong pictorial possibilities, or to deliver important news that is going to provoke questions from the news media, such as a political candidate's withdrawal from an election, or emergencies, crises and catastrophes. Some recent labour disputes have seen the use of press conferences by both sides to inform and express their views.

Excessive publicity can backfire, however, by irritating the media or creating false expectations and impressions. The public relations practitioner, in his or her role as publicist, must live with the fact that publicity is a two-edged sword. Once an organisation is invested with news value, everything about it becomes newsworthy in the journalist's eye. Publicity items in the media soon become conversation pieces in offices, bars, beauty salons and living rooms. Publicity provides a means of introducing a message into the word-of-mouth communication web.[30]

Media relations

Media relations can be described as a public relations function that involves dealing with the communication media in seeking publicity for an organisation, or responding to media interest in an organisation.[31] Media relations involves targeting the 'gatekeepers' of the mass and specialised communication media to supply information to them about a client or organisation. However, the media are actually intermediate audiences. The ultimate target audiences in media relations are the media consumers.[32] Examples of media publics are shown in table 5.2.

Mass media	Specialised media

Local
• Print publications
  • Newspapers
  • Magazines
• Television stations
• Radio stations
 	
National
• Print productions
• Broadcast networks
• Wire stations
	Local
	• Trade, industry and association publications
	• Organisational publications
	• Ethnic publications
	• Publications of special groups
	• Specialised broadcast programmes and stations
	
	National
	• General business publications
	• National trade, industry and association publications
	• National organisational publications
	• National ethnic publications
	• Publications of national special groups
	• National specialised broadcast programmes and networks

Table 5.2 Examples of media publics

In the context of media relations, then, the public relations practitioner or publicist is the intermediary. Both the success of the publicist-media relationship and the publicist's public relations skills are important here. He or she must be trained and educated to give the media accurate, timely and comprehensive information. However, creating and managing successful relations with the media is not solely a job for the publicist. The climate must be right, and there has to be commitment from the top management of an organisation towards open and honest relations with the media.[33] The organisation has to be visible to engage media interest. The publicist is the professional who can assist in creating the effective channels and means, and ensure that opportunities are planned and followed up as far as possible.

There are various aspects of importance to be taken into consideration when dealing with the media:

▲ **Research.** The research process in media relations requires a thorough understanding of the publicist's client or organisation, and of the reason – opportunity or problem – for communicating with the media. Most

importantly, however, it requires knowledge of the targeted media themselves – the nature of the media outlets, the audiences reached, the types
of material used, the specific names and titles of staff contacts, and their
deadlines.

▲ **Objectives.** Media relations require both impact and output objectives. *Impact objectives* represent the desired outcomes of modifying the attitudes
and behaviours of target publics. In media relations, they usually include
statements such as:

△ to increase knowledge of news about the client or organisation among
community media representatives

△ to enhance the client's or organisation's credibility among media people

△ to reinforce favourable attitudes towards the client or organisation on
the part of media representatives

△ to increase favourable client or organisation news coverage.

Output objectives in media relations refer to the efforts made by the publicist on behalf of the client or organisation. These objectives have nothing
to do with the client's or organisation's desired influence on audiences.
Possible output objectives may be:

△ to be of service to the media, both proactively (to provide newsworthy
stories about the client or organisation) and reactively (to be available
for responses to media enquiries)

△ to co-ordinate media interviews with client or organisational officers
and personnel.

▲ **Programming.** Programming for media relations includes a variety of technical aspects:

△ *Writing effective publicity releases*. The material used must be of interest
and value to the audience. The model shown in table 5.3 can be used for
publicity release writing.

A seven-point publicity release formula (SOLAADS)
1 Subject
2 Organisation
3 Location of organisation
4 Advantage – what is new, special or different?
5 Applications – how or by whom can the product or service be used?
6 Details – price, colour, size, specifications
7 Source – full name and address of organisation

Table 5.3 A model for publicity release writing

One of the easiest ways to establish good media relations, therefore, is to supply the media with what it wants, how it wants it and when it wants it. Other ways to keep media relations intact, apart from publicity releases, are photographs and photo opportunities, a media conference, a media reception or a media facility visit.

△ *Dealing with enquiries from the media.* This demands various personal skills. There are some basic guidelines: if a publicist receives a call from a journalist, he or she must make sure of the name of the journalist, who the journalist is working for, the details of the journalist's enquiries, how soon an answer is needed, and his or her telephone number.

△ *Corrections.* Only in the most exceptional and extreme circumstances should a correction or retraction to a newspaper or broadcast piece be sought. If it is simply a case of correcting incorrectly published facts, a brief letter to the editor marked 'For publication' will stand a good chance of publication.

△ *Media relations in a crisis.* Much has been written and said about the subject of crises in public relations. This brief discussion only pertains to dealing with the media in such a situation. The success of any organisation in dealing with its responsibilities in a major emergency is quite likely to be judged largely by the effectiveness of its media relations. If these are successful, the media can work to an organisation's advantage in an emergency and can offer great assistance by publishing or broadcasting essential information and advice. However, poor media relations can have disastrous results. Accurate, up-to-date information and the unquestioning co-operation of the management with already strenuous roles are absolutely vital.

A major emergency or crisis can attract massive and instant interest for national and possibly international news media. It is quite likely that the media will hear of a major emergency some time before an organisation's emergency procedures are fully set up. Even if uncertain about the degree of media interest, the publicist must be briefed immediately so that he or she is prepared for dealing with the media. Irrespective of the type of crisis or emergency that arises, it is vital for the organisation to keep the media informed. It is best to be as honest and straightforward as possible with the media. The public will also tend to forgive a mistake more easily than lies and cover-ups.

▲ **Evaluation.** Evaluation of media relations always refers to the programme's stated objectives. Impact objectives are generally measured through publicity placement, circulations and audience data, computer tracking of messages, and content analysis. The accomplishment of output objectives can be simply determined by counting or otherwise observing the desired outputs as they are set in motion. In essence, however, the effectiveness of media relations always comes down to media placement, that is obtaining the desired publicity for the client or organisation.[34]

Case study

Persuading people to use less water

When water consumption in Hermanus topped 2.8 million cubic litres in 1995, the alarm bells rang. Ten years ahead of schedule, the town had attained the volume projected for 2005. Hermanus had two options: either build a R40 million dam or reduce water consumption. With money short, the second option looked more appealing. The result was a communications programme that has attracted international interest and yielded a 20% decline in consumption so far. The three-year target is 30%. Bea Whittaker of Milkwood Communications managed the programme. She produced a monthly newsletter, wrote articles for magazines, issued dozens of press releases, and gave talks to civic organisations, clubs and on the radio. Residents responded enthusiastically to the call to fit water-saving devices, and to suggestions on a fact sheet entitled 'Ten ways to save water'.

(*Source:* Website: http//secure.financialmail.co.za/97/0808/admark/awards.htm
Date of access: 19 August 2002)

Conclusion

This chapter began with an introduction to characterising media in terms of controllability. There are two types of media, namely controlled and uncontrolled media. In controlled media, the practitioner has control over the content of the message in the media. In uncontrolled media, the practitioner has no control over content. The different types of media were then discussed, namely media for internal publics, mass communication media, privately created media and 'oramedia'. Examples of specific media types within each of these categories were also explained and highlighted. The contexts within which these media can be used for public relations purposes were also discussed, and examples given for each of the different types of contexts.

Questions for self-evaluation

1. Differentiate between controlled and uncontrolled media and give examples of each.

2. Identify the different internal media tools and explain how each could be used to achieve communications objectives.

3. Discuss the different mass media choices available to a public relations practitioner. Identify possible advantages and disadvantages of each.

4. Privately created media and 'oramedia' are increasingly being used by organisations.

   (a) Can you explain why?

   (b) How would this type of media assist in achieving organisational communication goals?

5. Discuss the public relations opportunities that are available for a business considering using sponsorship in its communication programme.

6. Explain the different types of corporate advertising that a firm could undertake. Give practical examples of each.

7. Explain the difference between publicity content and publicity context.

8. Explain the activities involved in programming for media relations.

9. In the case study:

   (a) Evaluate the media choices made by Bea in terms of the campaign.

   (b) Assume you were asked to assist Bea in terms of deciding on media choices for the next year. What specific recommendations would you make?

Endnotes

1 Cutlip, SM; Center, AH and Broom, GM 1994. *Effective Public Relations.* (7 Ed.) Upper Saddle River, USA: Prentice Hall:259.

2 Puth, G and Lubbe, BA 1996. *Public Relations in South Africa: A Management Reader.* Johannesburg: Heinemann:143.

3 Adapted from Puth and Lubbe, op. cit.:143–144.

4 Seital, FP 2001. *The Practice of Public Relations.* Upper Saddle River, USA: Prentice Hall:12.

5   Kotler, P 2000. *Marketing Management: The Millennium Edition*. Upper Saddle River, USA: Prentice Hall:435.

6   Cutlip et al, op. cit.:267.

7   Adapted from Seital:381–383.

8   Ibid.

9   Based on Puth and Lubbe, op. cit.:144–148.

10 See Seital, op. cit.:386.

11 Ibid.:388.

12 Ibid.:390.

13 Rensburg, R 1996. Public relations communications media. Chapter 9. In Puth and Lubbe, op. cit.:120–172. Used with permission of Heinemann.

14 Cutlip et al., op. cit.:370–371.

15 Jefkins, F 1982. *Public Relations Made Simple*. London: Heinemann:126.

16 Ibid.:141.

17 Johnsson, H 1990. *Professional Communications for a Change*. New York: Prentice Hall:290.

18 Skinner, C and Von Essen, L 1998. *The Handbook of Public Relations*. Johannesburg: ITP:285.

19 Jefkins, F and Ugboajah, F 1986. *Communication in Industrialising Countries*. London: Macmillan:33.

20 Jefkins, op. cit.:172.

21 Jefkins, F 1985. *Advertising*. Plymouth: Macdonald & Evans:101–102.

22 Skinner and Von Essen, op. cit.:270.

23 Moriarty, SE 1991. *Creative Advertising: Theory and Practice*. (2 Ed.) Englewood Cliffs, New Jersey: Prentice Hall:371.

24 Rayfield, RE; Acharya, L; Pincus, JD and Silvis, DE 1991. *Public Relations Writing: Strategies and Skills*. Dubuque: WCB.

25 Fedorcio, D; Heaton, P and Madden, K 1991. *Public Relations for Local Government*. London: Longman:48.

26 Moriarty, op. cit.:387.

27 Rensburg, RS and Bredenkamp, C 1991. *Aspects of Business Communication*. Cape Town: Juta:109.

28   Cohen, PM 1987. *A Public Relations Primer.* Englewood Cliffs, New Jersey: Prentice Hall:119; and Seital, FP 1989. *The Practice of Public Relations.* Columbus, Ohio: Merrill:199, 255.

29   Weiner, R 1978. *Professional's Guide to Publicity.* (2 Ed.) New York: Richard Weiner:5; Simon, RS 1980. *Public Relations Concepts and Practices.* (2 Ed.) Columbus, Ohio: Grid:318; Winston, MB 1982. *Getting Publicity.* New York: John Wiley & Sons:87; and Newsom, D; Scott, A and Turk, JV 1989. *This is PR: The Realities of Public Relations.* (4 Ed.) Belmont, California: Wadsworth:212.

30   Cutlip et al., op. cit:359.

31   Newsom et al., op. cit.:506.

32   Hendrix, JA 1992. *Public Relations Cases.* (2 Ed.) Belmont, California: Wadsworth.

33   Fedorcio et al.:33.

34   Hendrix, op. cit.:61.

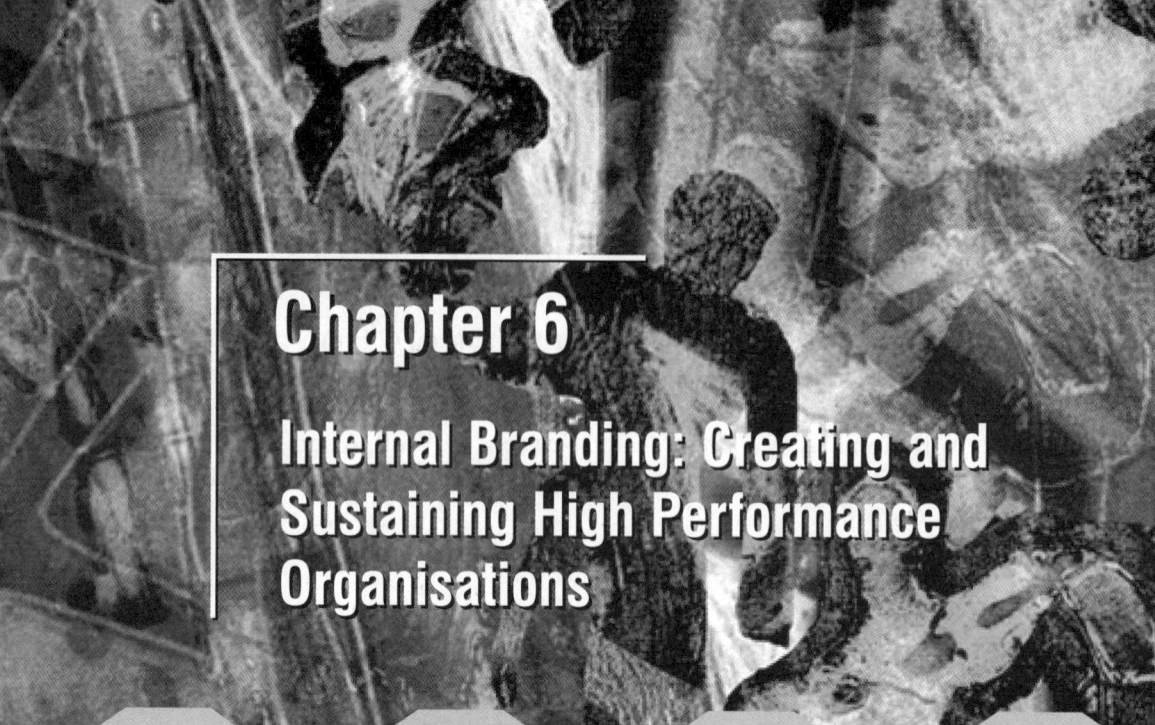

Chapter 6

Internal Branding: Creating and Sustaining High Performance Organisations

LEARNING OUTCOMES

After studying this chapter, you should be able to:

▲ show an understanding of the relationship between internal service delivery and external service quality

▲ provide an overview of the key factors that determine high performance marketing and service cultures

▲ demonstrate an understanding of internal marketing as a process

▲ demonstrate the importance of internal branding in creating a coherent brand identity

▲ illustrate how internal brand mechanisms can be utilised to establish a coherent brand identity

▲ give an overview of current trends in internal branding.

> Our employees should be our best sales force. If they do not
> understand the brand positioning, the brand campaign, what we
> are trying to communicate to our customers, then we've failed.
>
> *(Scott Helbing, Dell Computers)*

Introduction

A sustainable organisation is one that thrives over the long term. An organisation's ability to compete effectively in a particular market is increasingly seen as being dependent on its ability to deliver offerings, which comprise a competitive bundle of benefits or value to the consumer. In order to create good perceived quality of a service, an organisation must manage the service process, as well as the resources needed in that process. Grönroos (1998:330) views this as an open process, where the customer not only sees and experiences how the process functions, but also takes part in it and interacts with resources that the organisation controls directly. To earn a reputation for service quality, an organisation must meet or exceed customer expectations. A recent empirical study by Formburn and Rindova (1998) with leading US and UK companies found that those companies with a more positive reputation appeared to project their core mission and identity in a more systematic and consistent fashion than companies with lower reputational rankings. Furthermore, these companies tried to impart significantly more information, not only about their products, but also about a range of issues relating to their operations, identity and history. According to Puth and Ewing (1998:113), in the highly competitive battle for superior positioning and performance in the marketplace, management must effectively implement a service culture.

Tosti and Stotz (2002) note that a company's marketing can attract customers, but only a positive customer experience that matches the brand promise can capture and retain customers over time. Internal branding translates the company's brand promise into internal behaviours and systems that support people in turning the promise into the reality of customer experience. A company's brand is more than the image it presents to customers through marketing and marketing communication. It is also the experience customers have of a company and its products. The success of a marketing communication message depends not only on its appeal, but also on how well it aligns with the delivery of the actual promise to customers.

Alignment refers to the process whereby the role elements in individual and organisational behaviour are aligned by replacing preconceived concepts and behaviour with new ways of thinking and doing. This is maintained until the new way of thinking and doing becomes resistant to change efforts. Personal leadership behaviour should be directed at attaining the organisational vision. In order to achieve this vision, organisation members must be empowered, and the internal and external alignment of the organisation must be accomplished. Managers must align organisational members through the organisation's vision and strategy, which is required to meet the demands of a continuously changing organisational environment. In itself, this will lead to higher levels of organisational empowerment. When a clear direction is communicated to all employees, lower-level employees can initiate actions without experiencing a high level of vulnerability. Organisations that work internally towards the same goals experience less conflict during the process of goal attainment. This results in increased individual empowerment.

Such focused organisations achieve high levels of organisational integration. This is evident from:

▲ a clear understanding of the organisational mission

▲ shared values

▲ attention to fundamental business aspects

▲ combatting bureaucracy and encouraging innovation

▲ thinking like clients

▲ emphasis on the motivation and development of human resources.

Organisational integration starts with the establishment of shared values and culture.

Sustaining high performance organisations through organisational alignment

Responsiveness to the marketplace, to leadership and employee behaviours, and to infrastructure design and deployment serves to create an organisation's culture. According to Owen, Mundy, Guild and Guild (2001:11), culture represents the shared beliefs and experiences that define the identity of the organisation and serve to guide the perception of what is important (value), what is possible (opportunity), and what is real (reality). Culture evolves over time and these sets of beliefs come to be expressed through organisational routines that are reinforced through the review processes of the organisation. Through organisational recognition and reward systems, culture becomes a normative measure that reinforces desired behaviours, and discourages undesirable behaviour. Because organisational culture serves to identify appropriate sets of beliefs and behaviours that will allow the organisation to fit its internal operating efficiencies with its problems of existence in its environment, the organisation is able to remain responsive to marketplace expectations and to develop and sustain the behaviours required to meet these expectations.

According to Parasuraman, Zeithalm and Berry (1985), customers' expectations of a particular service shape their assessment of the quality of that service. When there is a discrepancy between consumer expectations and management's understanding of these expectations, perceived service quality will suffer. Service quality can only be improved through efforts aimed at enhancing employees' ability and willingness to provide service by creating an organisation that supports service quality in every area. In other words, organisations must create a role environment (culture) that builds a strong belief in the organisation, and inspires a belief in the importance of an individual's contribution and discretionary effort. Zeithalm, Parasuraman and Berry (1996:31) contend that 'the issue of highest priority today involves understanding the impact of service quality on profit and other service outcomes'. According to Rapert and Wren (1998:223), when organisations build a reputation for providing quality service, and make this a top strategic priority, they encourage not only short-term increases in net operating income and revenue growth, but future returns as well. This approach suggests that organisations which are adept at service quality could build competitive positional advantages. Barney (1991) suggests firms with deeply ingrained service quality orientations often develop both an intrinsic *culture* and an extrinsic *reputation,* which tend to be highly sustainable. This link is well illustrated in figure 6.1 on the next page.

Tapping into the service-profit chain

It is important to realise that the fundamental difference between services on the one hand and products on the other is that consumption of a service is *process* consumption rather than *outcome* consumption. *Process consumption* can be distinguished from *outcome consumption* because the consumer or user perceives the production process as part of service consumption, not just the outcome of that process (as in the traditional marketing of physical goods). When consuming a physical product, customers make use of the product itself, that is, they consume the outcome of the production process. In contrast, when consuming services, customers regard the consumption of the service process as a critical part of the service experience (Grönroos, 1998:322).

In essence, the service-profit chain (SPC) is a model, which integrates perceived value from three key stakeholder perspectives: customers, shareholders and employees respectively. Within each of the three stakeholder groups, an interaction based on an exchange of values is assumed. Even more important is the indication that these value-based interactions are also related to one another. The service-profit chain, as formulated by Heskett, Jones, Loveman, Sasser and Schesinger (1994:166), is represented in the model in figure 6.1.

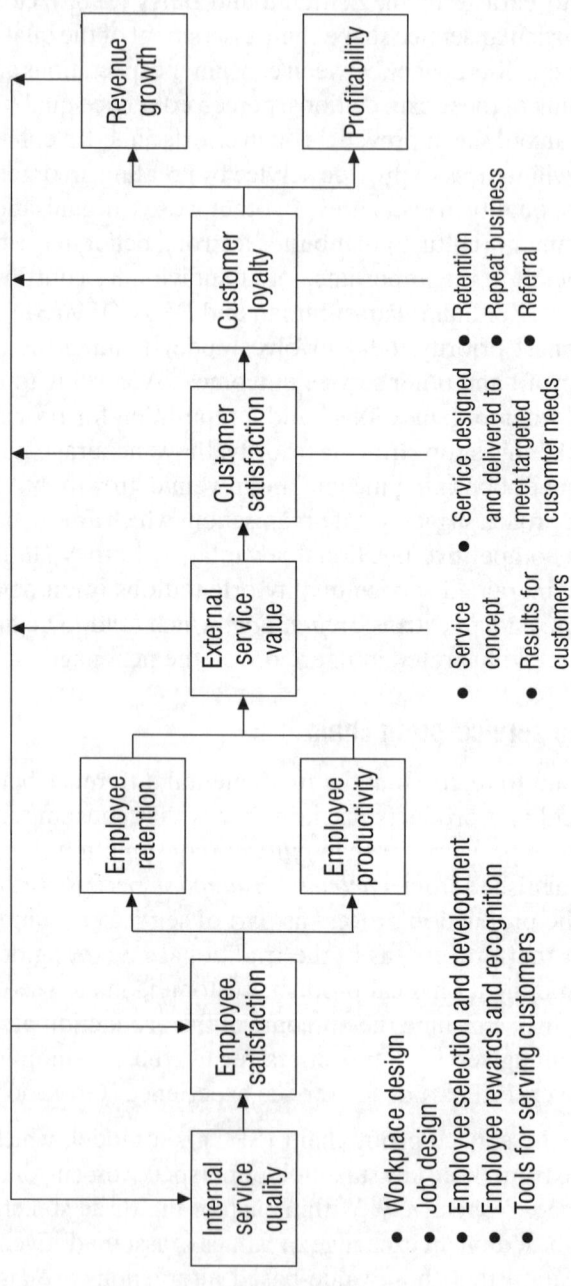

Figure 6.1 The service-profit chain

In developing this model, Heskett et al. (1994, 1997) set out the following propositions which establish relationships between profitability, customer loyalty, and employee satisfaction, loyalty and productivity:

▲ **Profit and growth are stimulated primarily by customer loyalty.** According to Lau (2000:426), loyal customers account for an unusually high proportion of the sales and growth of a service organisation. Serving experienced customers can contribute to the productivity gain of the service delivery system because customers have become familiar with the system, are more liable to make suggestions for improvement, and are generally more co-operative in their service interactions. Heskett, Sasser and Schlesinger (1997) emphasise the importance of evaluating the lifetime customer value of a customer in a relationship through the three *Rs* of marketing: *retention, related sales* and *referrals*. Reicheld and Sasser (1990) studied the effect of customer loyalty on profitability and determined that customer loyalty is a more important factor of profit than market share.

▲ **Customer loyalty is a direct result of customer satisfaction.** A number of studies discuss the link between customer satisfaction and customer loyalty (Yi, 1990; Rust & Zahorik, 1991; Gummeson, 1993; Jones & Sasser, 1995; and Hallowell, 1996). Although a number of studies have established a link between customer satisfaction and loyalty, a distinction must be drawn between attitudinal and behavioural loyalty. *Attitudinal* loyalty refers to the customers' overall attachment to a product or service. *Behavioural* loyalty refers to purchasing habits from the same provider, thereby increasing the scale and scope of a relationship. According to Lau (2000:426), the service-profit chain represents the behavioural side of customer loyalty, which can only be reinforced by increased customer satisfaction.

▲ **Customer satisfaction is largely influenced by the value of services (external service value) provided to customers.** Service value is an important concept in service industry management. Heskett et al. (1997) define service value as a ratio of perceived results and quality relative to price and customer acquisition costs. Put simply, this refers to perceived value for money. Service value is often hard to estimate, but can be perceived by most customers as service value by comparison or past experience. Through their long tenure in serving specific groups, loyal employees make it easier to acquire and create increased profits through enhanced services, reduced costs in acquiring customers, and lower customer price sensitivity (Reicheld & Sasser, 1990).

▲ **External service value is created by satisfied, loyal (retained) and productive employees.** Through their long tenure services, loyal employees tend to develop personal relationships with their customers. According to Lau (2000:426), these relationships serve as the foundation for a reinforcing cycle of positive interactions between the service employees and customers. Retention of employees is critical because a high employee turnover means more than a loss of productivity and decreased customer satisfaction. It may often result in the loss of a customer since many customers may choose to follow the departure of dissatisfied employees. Shermwell, Cronin and Bullard (1994) found trust and affective commitment to be important in building customer relationships because the higher these levels were perceived to be, the less the perceived risk inherent in the relationship, and the greater the probability that the relationship would continue over the longer term. Heskett et al. (1997) stress the importance of recruiting and retaining the right employees as the first step in ensuring productive employees.

▲ **Employee satisfaction is the result of high quality support services and policies that enable employees to deliver results to customers (internal service quality).** Heskett et al. (1994) refer to *internal service quality* as the quality of the work environment that contributes to employee satisfaction. Employee satisfaction (also referred to as job satisfaction) is defined by Locke (1976:1300) as a pleasurable or positive emotional state, resulting from the appraisal of one's job or job experiences. According to Lau (2000:424), many similarities exist between customer and employee satisfaction processes. Customer needs and wants are satisfied when they perceive goods and services to have value that meet or exceed their expectations. Likewise, employee needs are satisfied when they perceive that the rewards from the organisation, including compensation, promotion, recognition, development, and meaningful work, meet or exceed their expectations (Hackman & Oldham, 1990).

The service-profit chain model also suggests that the marketing culture (the organisational process of creating an external identity and 'presence' for itself and its products or services) of an organisation is directly related to the internal organisational culture (Harris, 1998:355–360). In this model, however, there are also inherently at least two potential 'gaps' – the internal service quality gap and the external service quality gap. Grönroos (1998:326) summarises the main assumptions of the service-profit chain model by stating that, from the customers' point of view, the solution to their problems is presented by a set of resources needed to create a good customer-perceived service quality and value. In addition, the organisation must have competencies to acquire and/or develop the resources required, and to manage and implement the service processes in such a manner that they create value for each customer. Thus, a governing system is needed for the integration of the various types of resources and for the management of the service process. Grönroos (1998) contends that instead of a traditional approach where continuous product development is used to prepare an appropriate set of resources, internal marketing and continuous development of the competencies and resource structure of an organisation are needed. This process is much more complicated and requires decisions and actions in a number of departments – internal marketing as well as investments in people and equipment, and the development of all areas of the interactive and support parts of the service system.

Alignment through high-performance cultures

Alignment reflects the extent of an individual's emotional investment in the organisational purpose, defined as the meshing of organisational purpose with organisational practice. Fineman (1993:13) notes that organisations are 'sites where individuals make meaning for themselves and have their meanings shaped'. In essence, this occurs when individuals have internalised organisational values and beliefs (in terms of their most fundamental meanings), and can act instinctively in accordance with these values. According to Dehler and Welsh (1994:6), alignment occurs when vision is used by management to infuse work with spirituality and meaning through transformational leadership and intrinsic motivation. This results in employee behaviours that enhance organisational performance, thus reinforcing and re-energising the fundamental vision. Contemporary organisations require a greater focus on meaning because a sense of purpose can excite and mobilise members of the organisation to work in greater alignment with one another. Aligned individuals or teams understand their contribution and see it as consistent with the organisation's greater purpose. Energising behaviour through purpose, instead of tangible rewards, affords employees greater opportunity for self-management.

Owen et al. (2001:11) identify five key factors that require alignment and determine the ability of an organisation to sustain high performance:

1. a senior leader's perceptions of the marketplace

2. a shared vision, mission, values, and strategies, which are aligned with the realities of the marketplace

3. leadership practices, which are congruent with vision, mission, values, and strategies

4. enabling infrastructures, which support and reinforce the vision, mission, values and strategies

5. employee behaviours that meet customer needs.

According to the sustainable high performance culture model (Owen et al., 2001), the organisation's ability to provide quality products and services and to create value is determined by bringing about the alignment of these five key factors. The model further indicates that there is a cause-effect relationship among these factors. When these factors are aligned, business performance improves measurably. The cause-effect relationships can be managed by creating and sustaining the alignment of the five key success factors. Often there may be a gap between what is and what needs to be, with respect to the five performance factors, as is shown in figure 6.2. These gaps may have various causes, and require different methods for identifying and eliminating them.

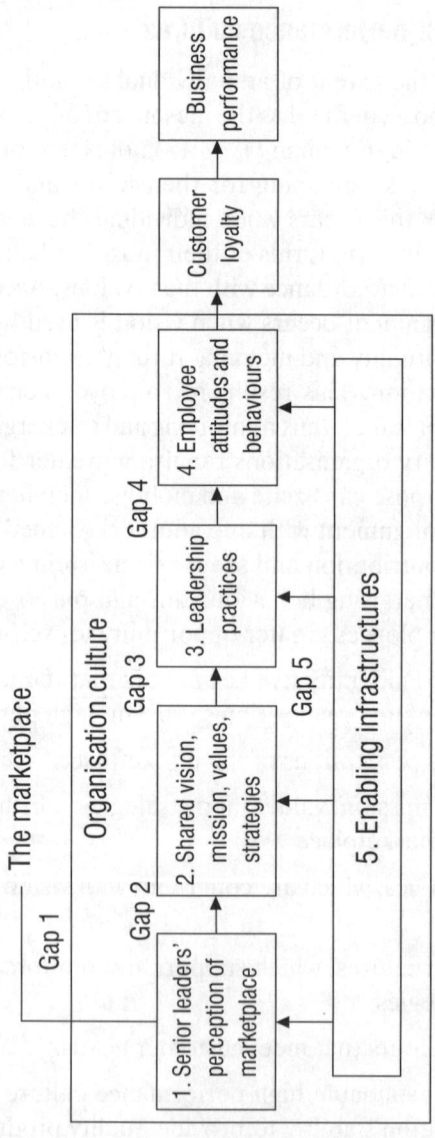

Figure 6.2 Sustainable high performance culture model

(*Source:* Owen et al., 2001:12)

A senior leader's perceptions of the marketplace

Organisations produce sustainable performance as long as senior leaders understand and effectively respond to their markets. Markets change over time because of factors such as competition, technological change, and the economic environment. Sucessful organisations are able to anticipate and adapt to these changes. To excel, organisational structures, processes, and behavioural patterns must continually be aligned with the type of market the organisation is designed to serve. According to Owen et al. (2001:10), when leadership does not have an accurate understanding of the market, leaders may fail to translate the organisation's vision, mission, and values into the strategies and processes that will enable the organisation to compete sucessfully. As a result, the organisation's culture, systems, and infrastructures may not be adequately aligned with the realities of the marketplace.

A shared vision, mission, values and strategies that are aligned with the marketplace

To build a high-performing organisation requires the leaders to create structures and develop processes that are aligned with the market it is striving to capture. The organisation's vision, mission, values and strategy statements are the foundations on which these structures and processes are built. Research by Baum, Locke and Kirkpatrick (1998) has shown that the way in which the vision and values of an organisation are framed and communicated impacts on the organisation's bottom line. Those companies whose vision statements were specific, targeted towards specific strategic intent, and emphasised growth and learning, outperformed (in terms of market share, perceived market value and return on investment) those companies whose visions were less carefully crafted and communicated. In a definitive article on future direction of service quality, Coulson-Thomas (1992) reported that most companies researched acknowledged that, although the sharing or communicating of the organisational vision is regarded as important, the process can generally be much improved throughout the organisation. This is because organisation systems and processes often fail to support organisational vision and strategy. Owen et al. (2001:10) point out that if an organisation lacks strategic focus, it may measure organisational performance in ways that may not recognise or hold people accountable for specific behaviours that are required to respond to customer needs.

Leadership practices that are congruent with vision, mission, values and strategies

According to Owen et al. (2001:12), the term 'leadership practice' describes what managers do on every level of the organisational hierarchy. Studies on sustainable performance have consistently shown that effective managers in high-performing cultures demonstrate these behaviours by:

▲ ensuring clear expectations

▲ promoting belonging

▲ fostering employee involvement in decision making and problem solving

▲ placing emphasis on and reinforcing the importance of quality

▲ promoting consistent focus on meeting customer needs and requirements

▲ encouraging and rewarding learning and skills development.

A recent study by Buckingham and Coffman (1999) indicates that the behaviour of immediate supervisors was the most powerful determinant of employee engagement, productivity, and customer satisfaction and loyalty. Owen et al. (2001:10) note that often the behaviours required to implement the business strategy successfully are out of alignment with customer and marketplace requirements. This may hold true for both leadership and employee behaviours. Leadership behaviour may typically be directed at unilateral control and decision making, when the kind of behaviours required to create sustainable high performance should be directed at empowerment, responsiveness and accountability at the lowest level possible.

Levering and Moskovitz (1999) report that, according to *Fortune* magazine, there are five distinct characteristics that set the 100 best companies it listed apart from the others. These are:

1. more employee participation

2. more sensitivity to work/family issues

3. more two-way communications

4. more sharing of wealth

5. greater enjoyment of work.

In the context of human resources development, good customer service often comes down to effective management of customer service personnel by developing a cohesive, loyal, and dedicated workforce. This requires management and resource strategies aimed at increasing financial performance through sound human resources practices that effectively increase the extent and degree of employee satisfaction. In new global contexts, managers should place emphasis on creating visions that will inspire employees and design challenging tasks that will harness their emotional energy. With the increasing importance of speed, quality, and productivity, corporations need employees who can instinctively act the right way and feel inspired because of their emotional commitment to the organisation (Tichy & Sherman, 1993:161).

Enabling infrastructures, which support and reinforce the vision, mission, values and strategy

Perceived service quality is dependent on systems support, management support and physical support from the support system (Grönroos, 1998:331). This is depicted in figure 6.3.

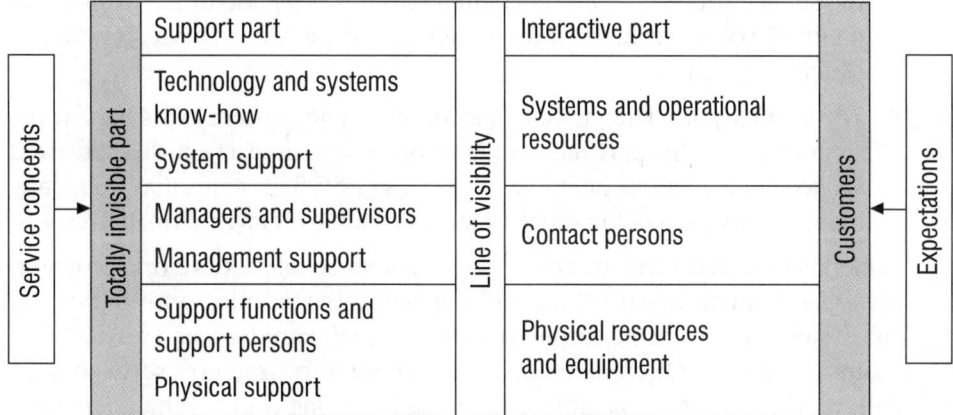

Figure 6.3 The service system

(*Source:* Grönroos, 1998:331)

As illustrated in figure 6.3, according to Grönroos (1998:331), the perceived service quality results from the interaction between four parts of the service system. These are:

1. *Customers:* They should know how to perform within the service system, and have a given amount of time at their disposal, which they expect the firm to use effectively.

2. *The interactive part:* The interactive part of the system is contact persons with certain knowledge of how to perform their tasks and how to interact with customers, systems and operational resources, as well as physical resources and equipment. The contact person's style of performance must match the style of consumption of the customers (Lethinen, 1983). If customers feel comfortable with the systems, resources and personnel, these resources are probably service-oriented and will produce a positive service quality perception. However, systems and physical resources, as well as customers, may have a negative impact on service employees, which in turn can create a negative service quality perception.

3. *The support part:* The support part of the service system produces various types of support to the interactive system. From the user's perspective, it is hidden beyond the line of visibility. Customers seldom see what occurs

behind this line, and often do not realise the importance to the quality of service of the part of the service process that takes place here. Technical quality especially is supported by activities behind the line of visibility. However, there is also interaction between the support part of the service process and the interactive part of the process. Often good technical quality is compromised by the poor functional quality of the interactive part of the service process. The service interaction is often identified as the 'moment of truth', when customers actually experience service (Lewis & Mitchell, 1990).

4. *The invisible part:* The invisible part of the service system exists behind the support part. This part has no direct or indirect impact on the perceived service quality and its outcome. Grönroos (1998:332) notes that frequently there are few parts of the service system that are truly invisible in this respect.

Enabling infrastructures are thus the systems which select, develop, recognise, reward, terminate, and protect people, as well as the technical and operational sub-systems which enable employees to produce the products and services that customers desire (Owen et al., 2001:13). These infrastructures serve to keep culture, climate, and tasks fully aligned and working towards the attainment of organisational goals. Owen et al. (2001:13) note that this includes goalsetting systems, organisational monitoring systems, performance management systems, leadership evaluation systems, and reward and recognition systems.

Employee behaviours that meet customer needs

Sustainable high performance is possible only when the organisation recruits, appoints, trains and retains competent employees. Owen et al. (2001:13) contend that this entails three aspects:

1. Identify the strengths of the individual employee.

2. Capitalise on the individual competence and capability of each employee.

3. Engage the employee through emotional commitment to the organisation.

The concept of service, according to Johns (1999:5), commonly carries a connotation of personal attentiveness. Service interactions must include a certain amount of discretion and must empower employees to use their best judgement in interactions with customers. Bowen and Schneider (1988:63) emphasise that service organisations need to create and sustain cultures that enhance employee commitment to organisational service goals. They maintain that service employees and service encounters function as a 'service trinity': they run the service operation, market the service, and are equated by customers with the service. Johns (1999:5) notes that, in fact, service personnel are often incidental to the delivery of the core service, yet they are equated with the service delivery. For example, the service performance of an air hostess determines the quality of the service encounter, instead of the performance of the pilot who actually delivers the core service. According to Johns (1999:5), there exists considerable evidence in the literature that the interpersonal interaction service personnel provide is the main contributor to customer satisfaction with the service. Narver and Slater (1991) contend that the organisational culture most effectively and efficiently creates the necessary behaviour for the creation of superior value for customers, and thus contiuous superior performance for the business. Schein (1980) presents a view of organisational culture on three levels: on the surface are artefacts, beneath artefacts lurk values, and at the nucleus are basic organisational assumptions. According to Luoma (2000:145), there is a need for organisations to 'compete from the inside out' by finding ways to harness the power of their people-related processes. By harnessing this potential, organisations can build and sustain a competitive service advantage that allows them to outperform their competitors. According to Shapiro (2000:319), an organisational framework is required where each employee contributes to, understands and supports a set of shared values and behaviours.

Owen et al. (2001) distinguish the following behaviours that are required to maintain sustainable high performance service cultures:

▲ competence

▲ cost-effectiveness

▲ commitment

▲ congruence with the organisation's core values

▲ a desire to serve customers.

In terms of the three levels of culture distinguished by Schein (1980), a market-oriented organisational culture can be analysed in terms of basic assumptions, values and artefacts:

▲ **Underlying assumptions:** According to Harris (1998:363), the three pillars of the marketing concept (profitability, customer focus and integration) are clearly founded on bedrock of deeper, more fundamental assumptions that include:

△ interdependence between the organisation and its environment

△ the ability of the organisation to analyse and react to environmental influences, as well as to determine market prospects

△ the possibility of satisfying customer needs, wants and demands in order to ensure long-term profitability and sustainability of the organisation

△ the fact that organisational dissonance will reduce organisational efficiency and effectiveness.

▲ **Marketing culture values:** The application of value dimensions specifically to market-oriented culture can be summarised to include values such as:

△ innovation, stability, people, outcomes, details, teams and aggression (O'Reilly, Chatman, & Caldwell, 1991)

△ a positive team orientation (Jaworski & Kohli, 1993)

△ a highly competitive output orientation (Slater & Naver, 1994)

△ an emphasis on market orientation (Deshpande & Webster, 1989)

△ a high internal/external orientation (Bruning & Lockshin, 1993)

△ an employee-oriented value system (Webster, 1994)

△ an aggressive marketing belief (Keith, 1960).

▲ **Marketing culture artefacts:** According to Denison (1990), the artefacts of an organisation are those more tangible creations of culture – verbal, behavioural or physical. Day (1994) defines the artefacts of market-oriented culture as the sum of those physical outside-in process capabilities and competencies that inform inside-out processes. In this sense, marketing artefacts can be viewed as the sum of the physical, behavioural and verbal artefacts that are geared towards the market. Because marketing artefacts are context specific, they vary from organisation to organisation. They represent a substantial element of the organisation's make-up, including the systems, strategies and structure of an organisation and the behavioural patterns and norms, as well as the subtle influence of organisational language.

In order to create a positive perception of service quality, an organisation must manage the service process, as well as all the resources that are required in this process. This entails the management of systems, as well as the attitudes and skills of employees. In the past, supervisors and managers concentrated on the *outcome* of the service process (a product orientation). What is required, however, is an understanding of how to support and manage the service *process*. Such a service orientation requires that organisational alignment be achieved through internal marketing processes, which are aimed at establishing service values that would ensure a more customer-oriented performance in the service process.

Internal marketing as a framework for organisational coherence

According to Varey and Lewis (1999:1), the essence of the concept of *internal marketing* is not new. What is new is that service orientation and the need for greater organisational effectiveness have become major features of debate about sources of competitive advantage and the future form and purpose of business enterprise. The relationship between marketing and quality, and how to gain a sustainable competitive advantage through a customer orientation, is embodied in a number of current management issues, which require strategic treatment (Lambert, 1995). Varey and Lewis (1999:2) regard these issues as contained within the broadened concept of internal marketing:

▲ The retention of skilled people in the organisation should not be counter-acted by declining management standards and by failing to provide clear corporate and personal direction.

▲ Relationships with the management team, who share objectives, experience and skills, can build, release, and mobilise individual motivation for economic recovery.

▲ A proper understanding of the need for quality and competitive service delivery in a changing economic, social, political and technological environment is essential.

▲ A corporate brand, which appeals both to customers and organisational members, should be built.

▲ Communication management, with a clear strategy based on research and evaluation, and personal skills development and responsibility, are required.

▲ Productivity through participation requires leadership, processes and commitment from all.

Christopher, Payne and Ballantyne (1991) note that in the discussion of the literature dealing with the concept of internal marketing, there has been a considerable shift towards a managerial perspective aimed at establishing guidelines for implementing internal marketing, rather than establishing what constitutes internal marketing and its philosophical base. However, internal marketing can be described as an important activity in developing a customer-focused organisation. The fundamental aims of internal marketing are to develop internal and external customer awareness, and to remove functional barriers to organisational effectiveness.

Internal marketing has been proposed variously as a structured approach to strategy implementation, to the diffusion of innovations, to recruiting service-minded staff, to creating a service culture, or to increasing internal service productivity (Varey & Lewis, 1999:7). Maitland (1990) discusses the relationship between internal marketing and organisational theory. He suggests that the human relations approach of McGregor (1960) is most appropriate to this concept because it emphasises the prerequisites of an internal marketing culture: mutual trust, holistic and supportive relationships, and internal networks and self-direction, which enhance commitment, loyalty and motivation.

Implications of internal marketing for managers

The concept of internal marketing may well require managers to rethink their role, and to recognise the processes by which value is profitably created for internal and external customers. Thomson (1990) draws a distinction between people and organisational issues:

▲ *People issues* are concerned with maximising relationships within the organisation, where individuals, teams, managers and leaders are seen as *internal* target customers with needs, who can be satisfied through the generation of *internal* products and services.

▲ *Organisational issues* include practices, plans, structure, vision, mission, and values, and are concerned with maximising the effective utilisation of resources.

According to Varey and Lewis (1999:10), the adoption of the concept of internal marketing has a number of implications for the management of an enterprise:

▲ A shared set of beliefs about the meaning of *customer orientation* is needed. This requires the promotion of a particular interpretation of the marketing concept, and the systems and tools that are necessary to achieve its objective (delivering value to the customer at a profit). The managers of such an approach focus on the understanding and acceptance of a *corporate ideology*, while planning locally for appropriate activities to operationalise it. The skills and attitudes necessary for effective communication and service are central requirements.

▲ The role of the manager shifts from that of *overseer* or *controller* to that of *organiser*. All levels of employees have to understand and agree on what is in the organisation's long-term best interests, and how they can gain individually from this.

▲ Communication is seen as the *mode* of organisation rather than the *means*. The achievement of goals is seen as occurring within relationships, rather than in discrete transactions of discrete individuals or groups. Collaboration means self-regulation of relationships and obligations at work.

Internal marketing as internal relationship management

Vary and Lewis (1999:11) state that internal marketing can also be considered as internal relationship management. *Internal relationship management* is an integrative process within a system that fosters positive working relationships in a developmental way in a climate of co-operation and achievement. They identify a number of key features of an internal customer relationship management system, which have been adapted from the work of Howe, Gaeddert and Howe (1992):

- ▲ The 'voice' of the customer is incorporated into product/service decisions.
- ▲ Customer commitment is earned within a social contract.
- ▲ There is an open exchange of ideas for mutual gain.
- ▲ Employees develop a greater identification with the corporation (just as the corporation must become more customer-oriented).
- ▲ Customers are involved in product design, production and service delivery.
- ▲ There is a close relationship between suppliers and customers.
- ▲ Customers are viewed as individual people and so are value providers.
- ▲ There is continuous interaction and dialogue between suppliers and customers.
- ▲ There is a focus on discovering, creating, arousing and responding to customer needs.
- ▲ Relationships are viewed as enterprise assets.
- ▲ There is a systematic collection and dissemination of customer information (detailing and negotiating requirements, expectations, needs, attitudes and satisfaction).
- ▲ Communication in the internal markets is targeted through segmentation analysis.
- ▲ While external marketing focuses primarily on economic transaction as a result of its managerial bias, the broader internal marketing fosters the democratising potential of a goal-oriented, value-creating enterprise through continuous improvements in the business performance and quality of working life for all.
- ▲ The role of internal branding in creating high-performance cultures is emphasised.

According to Tosti and Stotz (2002:1), internal branding marries organisational alignment with marketing strategy. Internal branding provides crucial alignment. It should not be confused with internal communication, which deals with delivering organisational messages in a clear, compelling way. Internal branding translates the company's brand promise into internal behaviours and systems that support employees in turning the brand promise into the reality of the customer experience. This customer experience is critical if the brand is to support long-term customer retention rather than simply generate one-time transactions. By maintaining a reciprocal learning environment, and by using this continuous relationship to take swift action and improve their service offerings, marketing and management professionals are creating a level of responsiveness that builds long-term trust and loyalty among customers.

Collaboration and co-operation establish alignment with internal and external customers on the policies, products and performance of the organisation. Blumenthal (2001:1) notes that 'companies have become painfully aware that sending the right message to their employees is just as important as making a good impression with customers, vendors, and investors'. Successful internal branding cannot merely be imposed on employees, who would be rendered passive, powerless and organisationally peripheral in what Blumenthal (2001) refers to as 'forwarding the message'. Rather, employees must fully believe in the brand's higher vision that goes beyond the product or service being sold. The idea is to create an organisational system that can transform personalities at the individual level, and the culture at a broader level. This system must be populated by the kind of people whose behaviours will support corporate messages both internally and externally. If employees are convinced that the brand has meaning and value, it follows that delivering on the brand should create a sense of meaning in the employees' lives, and in that sense enhance its quality (Blumenthal, 2001).

According to Insight (2002), market conditions have created new opportunities for employees to move profitably to new employers. Personnel turnover is taking a significant bite out of profits. Insight (2002) states that losing an employee in high-tech companies is estimated to cost $75 000 (R800 000). There is thus a central need to establish a stronger sense of loyalty among employees, to increase job satisfaction, and to create a sense of belonging and accomplishment, resulting in reduced personnel turnover for organisations. Insight (2002) notes that corporations are discovering the term 'brand loyalty' – traditionally associated with external marketing – is taking on a new meaning for internal communications. Tosti and Stotz (2002) contend that one of the best ways for a company to ensure that service quality is achieved is to make certain that it attains *internal* service quality. They refer to this as the *Janus Effect*, which posits that the way an organisation behaves externally is usually a reflection of the way it behaves internally. Freeman and Liedtka (1997), and Helmsley (1998), point to the fact that the role of employees is changing, since corporate marketing increasingly necessitates a planning perspective that addresses the matching of external opportunities with core competencies, and also considers the integration of internal activities to ensure cohesion and therefore consistency in delivery.

According to Rooney (1995:48), today's organisations are using branding as a strategy tool with increasing regularity. Harris and De Chernatony (2001:441) note that managers are focusing on differentiating their brands on unique

emotional rather than functional characteristics. Because employees constitute a powerful interface between a brand's internal and external environments,
they can have a powerful impact on consumers' perceptions of both the brand
and the organisation (Balmer & Wilkinson, 1991). The role of employees in
this process is also changing – they need to be recognised as the brand's 'ambassadors' (Helmsley, 1998). A brand's emotional values are communicated
not just by advertising, but also through employees' interactions with
stakeholders. According to Kennedy (1977), employees represent a source of
customer information, and action needs to be taken to ensure that this is compatible with the way senior management wishes the organisation to be
perceived.

According to Harris and De Chernatony (2001), employees are thus becoming
central in the process of brand building, and their behaviour can either reinforce a brand's advertised values or, if inconsistent with these values, undermine
the credibility of advertised messages. Historically, management has provided
leadership through defining a brand's values. However, according to Harris
and De Chernatony (2001), corporate branding requires a holistic approach
to brand management, in which all members of an organisation behave in accordance with the desired brand identity. With the recognition of corporate
branding, staff have a critical role to play and therefore need to be included in
the internal debate about defining a brand's values. While management are
still required to initiate the process, employees should be encouraged to contribute to the discussions. Externally, managers need to examine the brand's
reputation among stakeholders to ensure that the brand's identity is communicated consistently and outcomes are delivered consistently.

Internal brand definition

According to Blumenthal (2001), internal branding is generally understood as
a programme for encouraging employee behaviours that align with the brand
as a corporate-sponsored, profit-driven, customer-interfacing image. Originally intended to guarantee quality, brands now provide a sense of meaningful
identity that is distinct from the particular product or service being offered.
Brands add value to the service or products that a company offers by imbuing
them with emotional, social, and even spiritual resonance, thereby offering
the buyer or user a sense of meaning or identity. Because every employee is
involved in the process of delivering the brand in some way or shape, this
entails a long-term process of adjusting employee behaviour from the top down
and side to side (Blumenthal, 2001).

An internal branding approach creates the need for ongoing support processes to ensure effective deployment. Focused meaningful communications,
appropriate training and aligned reward systems are necessary to sustain the

internal branding initiative. Internal branding ensures that the entire organisation understands and actively pursues delivery on the brand promise. The Conference Board (2002:3) notes that a distinction must be drawn between corporate branding and employer branding. A *corporate brand* embodies company values and a promise of value to be delivered. It may be used to differentiate a company from its competitors based on its strengths, corporate culture, corporate style and future direction. The *employer brand*, however, establishes the identity of the company as employer. It encompasses the company's values, systems, policies and behaviours towards the objectives of attracting, motivating, and retaining its current and potential employees. Corporate branding entails that all organisational members act in accordance with the corporate brand *identity*.

Corporate *brand identity* is interpreted by Harris and De Chernatony (2001) as an organisation's ethos, aims and values, that create a sense of individuality, and which differentiate a brand. Formbrun and Rindova (1996) define *brand reputation* as a collective representation of a brand's past actions and results, which describes the brand's ability to deliver valued outcomes to multiple stakeholders. In contrast to a brand's *image*, which reflects current changing perceptions, a brand's *reputation* is more stable and represents the distillation of multiple images over time (Fombrun & van Riel, 1997).

A model of brand management

Building on Kapferer's brand-based view of identity, De Chernatony (1999) proposed a model of brand management, conceptualised as the process of narrowing the gap between the brand's identity and its reputation (see figure 6.4 on the next page). De Chernatony's (1999) model of brand management conceptualises brand identity as consisting of six components, which interact and are then presented to reflect stakeholders' actual and aspirational self-images:

1. **Brand vision and culture:** At the centre of brand identity are brand vision and culture. Managers need to communicate clearly their brand's purpose to employees to inspire and assist them to understand how their roles relate to it. It is also important to convey the brand's core values internally because these guide employee behaviour. Each brand has a unique set of values that are relevant to the target market. The consistency of these values, as well as the nature of these values, are important characteristics of brands. The organisation's culture encompasses employees' values and assumptions, which guide their behaviour. Therefore, organisational culture must be aligned with brand values. Because culture must be adaptive and appropriate to the needs of stakeholders, managers need to agree on a number of core corporate values that will remain unchanged, and on less central values that need to adapt to changing circumstances.

Brand identity

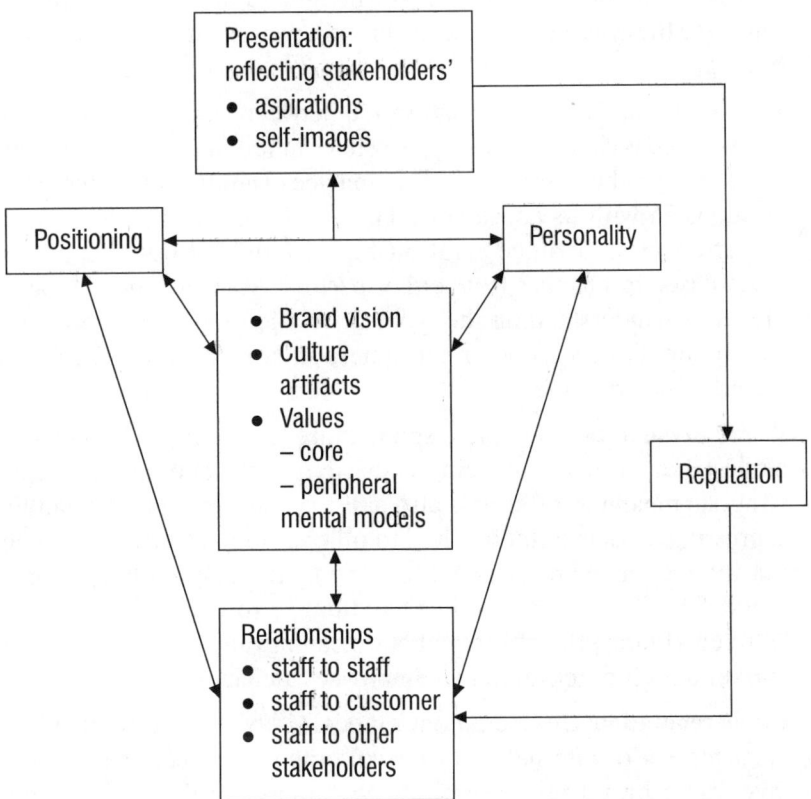

Figure 6.4 The identity-reputation gap model of internal brand management
(*Source:* De Chernatony, 1999:450)

2. **Brand positioning:** The coherence between a brand's vision and core values and its positioning must be determined. A brand's positioning sets out what the brand is, its target market, and what it offers. A set of functionally distinct capabilities that differentiate a brand should be derived from the brand's core values. The brand's positioning will be affected by artefacts, which provide cues about the brand's performance characteristics.

3. **Brand personality:** The brand's emotional characteristics are represented by the metaphor of personality which, among other sources, evolves from the brand's core values. Personality traits are further developed through associations with the 'typical user' imagery, and endorsers' and consumers' contact with the company's employees. Managers thus need to ensure that a brand's personality is conveyed consistently by both its employees and

external communication. Another influential source for a brand's personality is the brand's positioning. An integrated approach to branding can reinforce the synergy between the brand's personality and the brand's positioning.

4. **Brand relationships:** The relationship between a brand and its consumers evolves, and is characterised by the values inherent in the brand's personality. Through their interactions, employees significantly affect a brand's relationship with its consumers. The consistency of these interactions is therefore crucial, since relationships continue to evolve and can be destabilised by changes from either partner. Managers need to assist employees in understanding the types of relationships that are appropriate with other employees, other consumers and other stakeholders, based on the brand's core values.

5. **Brand presentation:** People respond more favourably to brands and companies they perceive as being consistent with their self-concepts. The symbolic meanings of brands also assist consumers in understanding and expressing aspects of their selves to others. Both advertising and employees' interactions with consumers contribute to the symbolic meaning of the brand. Thus, managers need to be attentive to the potential incongruity between a brand's desire for symbolic meanings and those conveyed through marketing communication and employees' behaviour.

6. **Brand reputation:** De Chernatony's model (1999) emphasises that successful management of internal and external brand resources should result in a favourable brand reputation. By encompassing the evaluations of all stakeholders, reputation provides a representative indication of brand performance. Managers need to work with staff to reduce gaps between a brand's identity and its reputation by including both internal and external components in the process, and eliminating sources of incongruity.

A model of perceptual congruity and brand performance

This model emphasises the multidimensional nature of the corporate branding concept, which involves the co-ordination of internal resources (functional and communication capabilities, planning, pricing, etc.) to create a coherent brand identity and a favourable brand reputation. Corporate branding relies heavily on an organisation's members holding congruent perceptions about the nature of the brand. People at different seniority levels and in different departments tend to differ in their perceptions of a brand's identity. To build a coherent brand identity, managers need to understand the factors that can affect the congruency of perceptions. Effective corporate branding requires consistent messages about a brand's identity, and uniform delivery across all stakeholder groups to create a favourable brand reputation. Internal consistency and congruency are vital to the successful external communication of corporate identity.

The internal branding process
• **Analysis** – cultural principles and practices that support people in delivering on the brand promise.
• **Orientation programme for senior management** – identify ways in which to demonstrate commitment to the brand promise through action.
• **Mid-management involvement** – how to support the delivery of the brand promise.
• **Tactical planning** – review company marketing strategy to align it with the brand value.
• **Support, assessment and review** – continuous evaluation of existing programmes and actions.
• **Brand camps** – supervisors work with their teams to develop ways to support the brand proposition and link this to meeting business needs.

Table 6.1 Building a brand through internal branding mechanisms

(*Source:* Tosti and Stotz, 2002:4–5)

Increasingly organisations are using branding as a strategy tool. Creating a brand image involves informing customers that the brand exists. However, there is general agreement in the marketing literature that a brand is more than a name given to a product or service – it embodies a whole set of physical and socio-psychological attributes and beliefs. Creating a coherent perception of a company in the minds of its various stakeholders is a major challenge faced by business organisations. Einwiller and Will (2002:100) note that the management process of creating and maintaining a coherent brand image in the minds of each individual stakeholder forms the basis for a favourable overall corporate reputation (branding). Within most corporations, corporate branding is incumbent upon the corporate communication function, of which symbolism or corporate design forms part.

However, corporate communicators can only communicate successfully if corporate behaviour allows for it, and if dimensions such as products and services, financial performance, workplace environment, vision and leadership, social responsibility and emotional appeal permit positive messages to be conveyed. For corporate branding to achieve the desired outcomes, centralisation and team organisation work best. Einwiller and Will (2002:103) believe the functions that are most central to corporate communication, that is internal communication, stakeholder relations and central functions of marketing communication, should be centralised in one department.

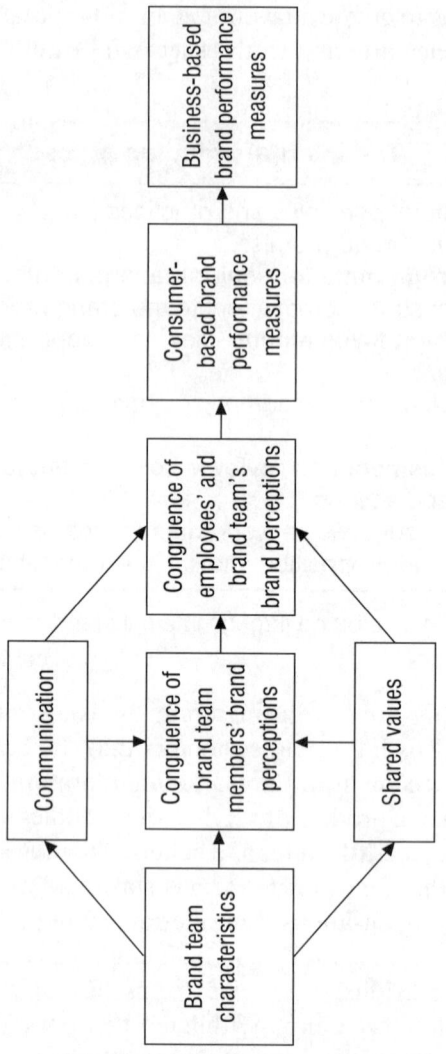

Figure 6.5 The relationships between internal brand
resources and brand performance

(*Source:* Harris and De Chernatony, 2001:455)

Harris and De Chernatony (2001:444) contend that there are three internal brand mechanisms that can be used to create a coherent brand identity:

1. **Similarity of brand team members:** Brand teams are larger for corporate branding and more diverse in their membership. Heterogeneous teams tend to be associated with greater conflict and poorer communication, team integration and consensus building. Therefore, it can be postulated that the greater the similarity of the brand team members, the more congruent

their perceptions about the brand will become. However, the growing team heterogeneity required for corporate branding does offer some benefits because the team has a wider range of skills and knowledge available, and is less susceptible to the effects of 'groupthink'. Harris and De Chernatony (2001:444) suggest that the longer the team tenure of heterogeneous groups, the more congruent their perceptions about the nature of their brand will become. Thus, they recommend that mechanisms be developed to facilitate the surfacing and resolving of incongruent brand perceptions among team members. These mechanisms include:

△ an independent facilitator who collates brand perceptions in a workshop setting in order to reach consensus about brand identity components

△ techniques of strategic decision making (dialectical enquiry and devil's advocacy)

△ the use of object-based metaphors to build shared mental models, for example tallboy as a metaphor for Honda City

△ staff communication programmes that provide and obtain information about brand values, achieve understanding, and gain employee commitment by involving employees in acting as 'brand ambassadors'.

It is suggested that, rather than leaving team tendencies to take effect over time, constructive action should be taken to harness the strengths of the heterogeneous team, while minimising the potential barriers to coherent management of the brand's identity.

2. **Shared values:** People who share similar values tend to perceive things in similar ways. It is important in corporate branding that the brand's and organisation's values are consistent. Shared values play an important part in facilitating congruent brand perceptions and coherent brand actions, both within the brand team and across the organisation. They are also instrumental in communicating the organisation to the outside world. Not only is there better brand performance as the congruence between the values of the organisation and the values of the brand increases, but common values also result in greater consensus and commitment to those values.

In addition to organisational values, personal values also guide behaviour. Harris and De Chernatony (2001:448) suggest that the greater the congruence between employees' personal values and those of the brand, the more likely it is that managers and employees will act in accordance with the corporate brand's values, and the more coherent will be the brand's identity. Managers thus need to agree about the core values to sustain, and the values to adapt as circumstances arise.

3. **Communication:** Communication plays an important role in establishing shared brand perceptions. Balmer (1995) suggests that it fulfils a vital role in surfacing brand perceptions, and in identifying and resolving incongruent perceptions.

△ *Communication at team level.* Communication is easier in teams whose members are similar to one another, or who regularly work together. Homogeneous brand teams are also expected to have more shared perceptions because they are less likely to misunderstand each other. The more frequently team members communicate with each other, the more opportunities they will have to discuss perceptions about the brand's identity and to appreciate other members' perceptions. Harris and De Chernatony (2001:444) therefore contend that the more *similarity* between members of the brand team, the more informal and frequent the communication interactions between them will be. Also, the more *frequent* the interaction between the members of the brand team, the greater the likelihood that they will share brand perceptions. In addition, the more *stable* the membership of the brand management team is, the more likely it is that they will communicate frequently and informally with each other.

△ *Communication at organisational level.* When all members of an organisation understand their brand's identity, they are better able to act in a coherent manner, thereby enhancing the likelihood of their activities supporting the desired identity. The nature and frequency of communication are expected to affect the degree of congruence between the brand team's and employers' perceptions. As two-way communication between the members of the brand team and the rest of the organisation increases, so too does the likelihood that they will share brand perceptions. The brand team must ensure that all forms of communication present the brand identity in a coherent fashion.

Employees' perceptions of the brand are based on what the brand team tells them, but also on their own experience with the brand and brand advertisements. Gilly and Woolfinbarger (1998) note that consumer advertising is an important means of communicating with employees; it affects the way they perceive their service roles. Hence, the brand management team must explain how other forms of brand communication are intended to reflect that identity. Harris and De Chernatony (2001:444) contend that explaining to employees how consumer advertisements are designed to communicate corporate identity will improve the shared perception between the brand team and employees about the nature of the brand.

The five Cs of internal branding	
• **Clarity:**	Give the brand a face and a voice.
• **Commitment:**	Build consensus.
• **Communications:**	Communicate by leader example, high frequency, multiple channels, and environmental management.
• **Culture:**	Build trust.
• **Compensation:**	Reward results.

Table 6.2 The five Cs of internal branding

(*Source:* Blumenthal, 2001:9)

Case study

Elevating brand reputation to new heights

The case study company is the largest repair and maintenance provider for the Scandinavian market. However, its business had been unprofitable for some time and it was losing more service contracts annually than it managed to replace.

Diagnosing the problem

To find out the reasons for the loss of customers, a large-scale survey among the firm's customers was conducted. The result led to a substantial amount of consternation among the top management of the firm, and the marketing and sales group, since they knew the firm was the largest service provider in the market. It had by far the best-trained service technicians, the best possible tools, the best possible equipment for taking care of any repair and maintenance job, and the widest possible assortment of spare parts. No other company could handle an equally large number of repair and maintenance problems. Also, every employee in the firm considered it to have the best product on the market. Thus, they could not understand why the quality of repair and maintenance service was considered low by customers. High prices were easy to understand – as a big company, it had high overhead costs and had to maintain a high price level.

Because top management had trouble accepting the results, a second, qualitative study was initiated. The main interview question could be phrased as 'What went wrong?' The average lost customer expressed the following opinion:

> We realise that you have the best capabilities on the market to repair and maintain elevators, and in most cases you are doing a good job in this respect. However, we do not feel comfortable with the way in

which you are doing the job. We cannot trust your service technicians to start doing the repair or maintenance task according to what has been promised and, quite often, you do not give exact promises about when the job will start. Although some of your people are attentive and show an interest in our concerns regarding elevator repair promises, most of them could not care less about us or the need we sometimes have for information. Sometimes we do not even recognise your employees. Quite often, the service technician just leaves an unfinished job and we do not know for what reason, or when he will be back to finish the job. Because we cannot always trust your way of doing the job, and because it is thus complicated for us to be your customers, we think the quality of your service is low and that we therefore pay too much for it.

In this case study, it is clear that the top management and sales group believed that the company was delivering a product, whereas the customers considered the company to be delivering a service process. Their concerns regarding the repair and maintenance services were associated with the process, and with problems occurring in the process. No coherence existed with regard to the brand's identity or reputation, although the technologies and knowledge required for creating a positive outcome for the repair and maintenance processes already existed.

The interventions

▲ **Systems and operational resources:** Previously the supervisor of a local or regional service group allocated the repair and maintenance tasks to the service technicians available every morning, without considering the history or relationship between the customer and service technician. In this way, no customer relationship could ever develop and the service technicians did not develop a knowledge of, and responsibility for, any of the customers. This was changed to give each technician long-term responsibilty for the same customers. A back-up system to be used in case the regular technician fell ill was also developed.

▲ **Physical resources and equipment:** In the past, technicians carried limited stock of spare parts. This resulted in them having to leave the job to collect the missing part or spare tool from the depot. This left the customer wondering why the technician had disappeared. A decision to invest in new and bigger vans, and to keep more spare parts and tools, was taken. This made it possible for the technicians to finish almost all jobs without interruption. By changing the technology used, the company created additional systems support that made it possible for the technicians to perform in a more customer-oriented fashion.

▲ **Contact persons:** Clearly service technicians were more preoccupied with the outcome of repair and maintenance tasks than with customer interactions and relationships. In addition, the operational systems and management support from supervisors had not been directed at the service interaction. As a result, a study of the internal marketing process was initiated, with the objective of focusing the interest of the service technicians, as well as their supervisors and upper-level managers, on the quality perceptions of customers, especially on the importance of functional quality perception of the process. The reasons for the changes in the systems and equipment were explained. By an internal marketing process, management aimed to change the attitudes of all categories of employees towards their jobs so that a more customer-oriented service process would be achieved. A process perspective was taken, supported by internal marketing. Management support by supervisors and upper-level management was thereby created. In the back office, functions responsible for information about customers already existed. Through increased customer-oriented market research, more accurate physical support in the form of better customer information was achieved.

▲ **Customers:** The new service system was intended to make it easier for customers to interact with the service technicians. Customers could feel that their viewpoints were recognised, and that they could ask any questions they might have and receive satisfactory answers immediately. In addition, the customers' time was used more effectively because unnecessary halts in the maintenance and repair jobs were avoided.

The results of the development of the service system were positive. The customer defection rate went down, while the company managed to maintain its premium price level. The business turned profitable.

(*Source:* Adapted from Grönroos, 1998:332–335)

Conclusion

The importance of internal branding in current organisational management is paramount, and it is evident that brand orientation is also recognised as a potentially powerful resource for creating shareholder and long-term value. When a company is already customer focused, and sees itself as a service company, internal branding may be relatively easy to accomplish. The deployment of an internal branding process is critical to achieving results. Without both a well-designed plan and the expertise and persistence to execute it, an organisation will achieve minimal results. Effective communication and motivational elements that keep employees engaged and give them tools for success, are essential to the effective implementation of an internal branding strategy.

Although there is growing awareness of internal branding strategies, many corporate cultures are still driven more strongly by measures of internal operating efficiency rather than by service measures of the customer experience. According to the research findings of The Conference Board (2002), companies that rated their corporate branding efforts as highly successful shared a number of traits. They were more likely to:

▲ identify employees as a key audience

▲ have received a new infusion of funds for the employee effort

▲ involve their marketing communicators in strategy setting, as well as execution

▲ identify delivering on the brand promise as a key organisational goal.

It can be suggested that communication plays a pivotal role in corporate brand management. Communication benefits may result from both the amount and frequency of communications, and from a variety of issues about itself that the organisation reveals through its communications. Communication makes the organisation transparent and enables stakeholders to appreciate its operations better, which facilitates ascribing it a better reputation.

This chapter suggests that management must adopt new processes for understanding and managing its corporate brand. A survey by The Conference Board (2002) identified the following trends in corporate and internal (employee) branding:

▲ Internal branding is going through a growth spurt – increasingly more efforts are being focused on internal branding than on corporate branding.

▲ Internal branding is taking place even if no formal internal branding strategies exist in companies.

▲ Human resources and senior management are key players in internal branding efforts.

▲ Corporate and internal brands are closely related. More than 90 per cent of surveyed executives called the alignment close.

▲ Companies treat the relationship between corporate and employee brands in different ways. Internal brands are either built on corporate brands or vice versa. Others claim strong internal brands without corporate brands.

▲ Internal branding is closely identified with human resources management, but few companies associate branding with the more strategic potential of human resources, such as instilling brand values into business processes. Instead, the link is with friendly initiatives, benefits and a physically pleasant workplace.

▲ New communication media, such as the Internet and company intranet, are emerging forces in branding efforts.

▲ Measurement of branding effectiveness is lagging. Only 20 per cent of surveyed executives had metrics for the impact of branding efforts.

Finally, it would appear as if the impetus for branding efforts comes from various sources. These include the need to be competitive, to save costs and to overcome 'identity crises' as a result of mergers, acquisitions, and spin-offs. Regardless of the sources, it is clear from the discussion in this chapter that branding can become a powerful force for integrating change initiatives, and for enhancing an organisation's ability to compete effectively in a particular market.

Questions for self-evaluation

1. What is the relationship between internal service value and external service quality, according to the service-profit chain?

2. Briefly discuss the five key factors identified by the sustainable high performance culture model.

3. List the five parts of the service process identified by Grönroos.

4. Describe marketing culture in terms of the three levels of culture identified by Schein.

5. Define internal marketing and list the implications it holds for management.

6. Discuss the meaning of internal relationship management.

7. Define the following concepts: internal branding, corporate branding, corporate reputation, brand personality, employee brand, and brand reputation.

8. List the six components of brand reputation according to the identity-reputation gap model of brand management.

9. Briefly discuss the three internal mechanisms through which a coherent brand identity can be created.

10. How can communication be used at different levels to create a coherent brand identity?

11. List the most important trends with regard to internal branding.

References

Balmer, JMT 1995. Corporate branding and connoisseurship. In *Journal of General Management,* 21(1):24–46.

Balmer, JMT and Wilkinson, A 1991. Building societies, change, strategy and corporate identity. In *Journal of General Management*, 17(2):20–33.

Barney, JB 1991. Firm resources and sustained competitive advantage. In *Journal of Management*, Vol 17, No 1:99–120.

Baum, JR; Locke, EL and Kirkpatrick, S 1998. A longitudinal study of the relation of vision and vision communication to venture growth in entrepreneurial firms. In *Journal of Applied Psychology*, Vol 83, No 1:43–53.

Blumenthal, D 2001. Internal branding: Does it improve employees' quality of life? International Society for Quality of Life Studies. Website: www.cob.edu/market/isoqls (Date of access: 23 February 2002.)

Bowen, DE and Schneider, B 1988. Services marketing and management: Implications for organisational behaviour. In *Research in Organisational Behaviour*, Vol 10:43–80.

Bruning, ER and Lockshin, LS 1994. Marketing's role in generating marketing competitiveness. In *Journal of Strategic Marketing*, Vol 2:163–87.

Buckingham, M and Coffman, C 1999. *First, Break all the Rules*. New York: Simon & Schuster.

Caruana, A; Money, AH and Berthon, PR 2000. Service quality and satisfaction – the moderating role of value. In *European Journal of Marketing*, Vol 34, No 11/12:1338–1352.

Christopher, M; Payne, A and Ballantyne, D 1991. *Relationship Marketing: Bringing Quality, Customer Service and Marketing Together*. Oxford: Butterworth/Heinemann/CIM.

Coulson-Thomas, CJ 1992. Quality: Where do we go from here? In *International Journal of Operations & Production Management*, Vol 9, No 1:38–55.

Day, GS 1994. The capabilities of market-driven organizations. In *Journal of Marketing*, Vol 58:37–52.

De Chernatony, L 1999. Brand management through narrowing the gap between brand identity and brand reputation. In *Journal of Marketing Management*, 15:157–179.

Dehler, GE and Welsh, A 1994. Spirituality and organisational transformation. Implications for the new management paradigm. In *Journal of Managerial Psychology*, Vol 9, No 6:17–26.

Denison, DR 1990. *Corporate Culture and Organisational Effectiveness*. New York: Wiley.

Deshpande, R and Webster, FE 1989. Organisational culture and marketing: Defining the research agenda. In *Journal of Marketing*, Vol 53:3–15.

Einwiller, S and Will, M 2002. Towards an integrated approach to corporate branding. In *Corporate Communications: An International Journal*, Vol 7, Issue 2:100–109.

Fineman, S 1993. *Emotion in Organizations.* Newbury Park, CA: Sage.

Formbrun, C and Rindova, V 1996. *Who's Tops and Who Decides? The Social Construction of Corporate Reputations*. New York: Stern Business School, New York University.

Formburn, C and Van Riel, C 1997. The reputational landscape. In *Corporate Reputation Review,* 1(1/2):5–13.

Freeman, E and Liedtka, J 1997. Stakeholder capitalism in the value chain. In *European Management Journal*, 15(3):286–296.

Gilly, MC and Wolfinbarger, M 1998. Advertising's internal audience. In *Journal of Marketing*, 62:69–88.

Grönroos, C 1998. Marketing services: The case of a missing product. In *Journal of Business and Industrial Marketing*, Vol 13, No 4/5:322–338.

Gummeson, E 1993. *Quality Management in a Service Organization: An Interpretation of the Service Quality Phenomenon and a Synthesis of International Research.* Carlstadt: International Service Quality Association.

Hackman, JR and Oldham, GR 1990. *Work Redesign*. Reading: Addison-Wesley.

Hallowell, R 1996. The relationships of customer satisfaction, customer loyalty, and profitability: An empirical study. In *International Journal of Service Industry Management*, 7(4):27–42.

Harris, LC 1998. Cultural domination: The key to market-oriented culture? In *European Journal of Marketing*, Vol 32, No 3/4:354–373.

Harris, LC and De Chernatony, L 2001. Corporate branding and corporate brand performance. In *European Journal of Marketing*, Vol 35, Issue 3/4:441–456.

Helmsley, S 1998. Internal affairs. In *Marketing Week*:49–53.

Heskett, JL; Jones, TO; Loveman, GW; Sasser, WE and Schesinger, LA 1994. Putting the service-profit chain to work. In *Harvard Business Review*:164–174.

Heskett, JL; Sasser, WE and Schlesinger, LA 1997. *The Service-Profit Chain*. New York: The Free Press.

Jaworski, BJ and Kohli, AK 1993. Marketing orientation: Antecedants and consequences. In *Journal of Marketing*, Vol 57:53–70.

Johns, N 1999. What is this thing called service? In *European Journal of Marketing*, Vol 33, Issue 9/10:1–13.

Jones, TO and Sasser, WE 1995. Why do satisfied customers defect? In *Harvard Business Review*:88–99.

Keith, RG 1960. The marketing revolution. In *Journal of Marketing*, January:35–38.

Kennedy, SH 1977. Nurturing corporate images: Total communication or ego trip? In *European Journal of Marketing*, 11(1):120–164.

Lambert, A 1995. People in business. Company brochure, London.

Lau, RSM 2000. Quality of work life and performance – an *ad hoc* investigation of two key elements in the service-profit chain model. In *International Journal of Service Industry Management*, Vol 11, No 5:422–437.

Lethinen, JR 1983. *Customer-driven Service Firm*. Espoo, Finland: Weïin Goös.

Levering, R and Moskovitz, M 1998. The 100 best companies to work for in America. In *Fortune*:118–144.

Lewis, B and Mitchell, VW 1990. Defining and measuring quality of customer service. In *Marketing Intelligence*, Vol 8, No 6:11–17.

Locke, EE 1976. The nature and causes of job satisfaction. In Dunette, MD *Handbook of Industrial Psychology*. Chicago: Rand McNally.

Luoma, M 2000. Developing people for business success: Capability-driven HR in practice. In *Management Decision*, 38/3:145–153.

Maitland, D 1990. Introduction to theories behind corporate internal marketing. In Thomson, K *The Employee Revolution: Corporate Internal Marketing*. London: Pitman Publishing:240–259.

Narver, JC and Slater, SF 1991. The effect of a market orientation on business profitability. In *Journal of Marketing*, Vol 54, October:20–35.

O'Reilly, C; Chatman, J and Caldwell, D 1991. People and organisational culture: A Q sort approach to assessing person-organisation fit. In *Academy of Management Journal*, Vol 34:487–516.

Owen, K; Mundy, R; Guild, W and Guild, R 2001. Creating and sustaining high performance organisations. In *Managing Service Quality*, Vol 11, No 1:10–21.

Parasuraman, A; Berry, LL and Zeithaml, VA 1991. Refinement and reassessment of the SERVQUAL scale. In *Journal of Retailing*, Vol 67, No 4:420–450.

Parasuraman, A; Zeithaml, VA and Berry, LL 1985. A conceptual model of service quality and its implication for future research. In *Journal of Marketing*, No 49, April:41–50.

Parasuraman, A; Zeithaml, V and Berry, L 1994. Reassessment of expectations as a comparison in measuring service quality: Implications for further research. In *Journal of Marketing*, Vol 58, No 1:11–24.

Puth, G and Ewing, MT 1998. Managers' and employee perceptions of communication in a service culture. In *Corporate Communications: An International Journal*, Vol 3, Issue 3:106–114.

Rapert, MI and Wren, BM 1998. Service quality as a competitive opportunity. In *The Journal of Services Marketing*, Vol 12, No 3:223–235.

Reicheld, FF and Sasser, WE 1990. Zero defections: Quality comes to services. In *Harvard Business Review*:105–111.

Rooney, JA 1995. Branding: A trend for today and tomorrow. In *Journal of Product and Brand Management*, Vol 04, No 04:48–55.

Rust, RT and Zahorik, AJ 1991. The value of customer satisfaction. Working paper. Nashville, Tennessee: Vanderbilt University.

Schein, EH 1980. *Organizational Psychology*. Englewood Cliffs, New Jersey: Prentice Hall.

Shermwell, JD; Cronin, JJ and Bullard, WR 1994. Relational exchanges in services: An empirical investigation of ongoing customer service-provider relationships. In *International Journal of Service Industry Management*, 5(3):57–68.

Slater SF and Narver, JC. Does competitive environment moderate the market orientation-performance relationship? In *Journal of Marketing*, Vol 58:46–55.

Stratecom. 2002. Insight: Internal branding. Website: www.stratecom.com (Date of access: 23 February 2002.)

The Conference Board 2002. Engaging your employees through your brand: Preliminary findings. Research report 12HB-OT-ES. Website: www.conference-board.org (Date of access: 3 March 2002.)

Thomson, K 1990. *The Employee Revolution: Corporate Internal Marketing*. London: Pitman Publishing:240–259.

Tichy, NM and Sherman, S *Control your own Destiny or Someone Else will*. New York: Currency Doubleday.

Tosti, DT and Stotz, RD 2002. Internal branding: Delivering the brand promise. Website: www.Tosti & Stotzcustomsolutions.com (Date of access: 23 February 2002.)

Varey, RJ and Lewis, BR 1999. A broadened conception of internal marketing. In *European Journal of Marketing*, Vol 33, Issue 9/10:1–14.

Webster, C 1993. Refinement of the marketing culture scale and the relationship between marketing culture and profitability of a firm. In *Journal of Business Research*, Vol 26:111–131.

Yi, Y 1990. A critical review of customer satisfaction. In Zeithalm, V *Review of Marketing.* Chicago, Illinois: American Marketing Association:68–123.

Zeithaml, V; Berry, LL and Parasuraman, A 1996. The behavioral consequences of service quality. In *Journal of Marketing*, Vol 60, April:31–46.

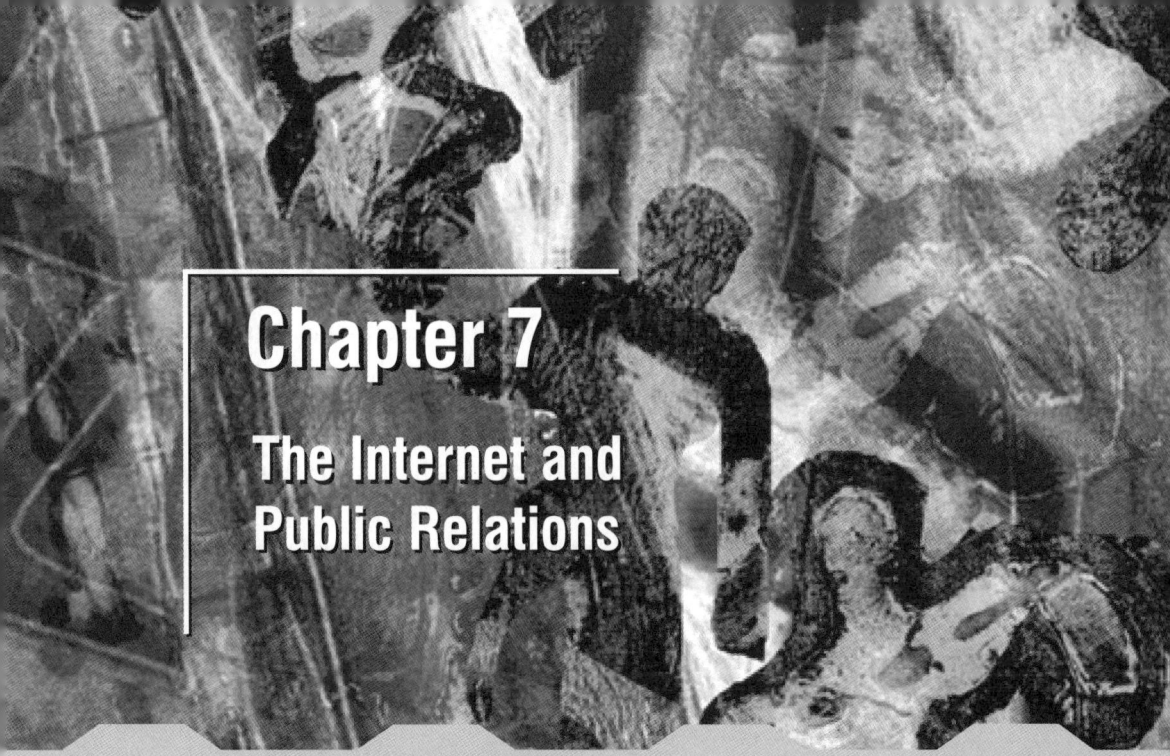

Chapter 7

The Internet and Public Relations

Introduction

Bursting onto the scene in the early nineties, the Internet and its more visible manifestation – the World Wide Web – have together had a significant impact on our business and social lives. With more than 500 million Internet users worldwide already, and the number expected to grow to over one billion in the next decade,[1] the importance of the Internet for businesses should clearly not be underestimated.

The Internet may be defined as a global network of computer networks.[2] The value of linking together the millions of computer networks around the world is embodied in three main benefits. These are:

1. **Communication:** As a communications tool, the Internet enables cheaper, faster and more effective communication between the organisation and its various publics.

2. **Information:** As an information tool, the Internet enables organisations to gather information about their various stakeholders and to share vast amounts of multimedia information with them.

3. **Conducting business:** In this regard, the Internet can be used both as a *marketing tool* in order to advertise products, transact sales, brand a company and research markets, as well as collect information about customers, markets and marketing intelligence, and as a *business tool*, to provide customer support, integrate suppliers and customers into the supply chain, bring about cost savings through automation and integration with back-end legacy systems,[3] improve customer relationships, enable electronic procurement, facilitate electronic billing and payments, and so on.

In the area of public relations, it is really in the first two areas that the Internet has a role to play, that is to *communicate* with stakeholders, and to gather and share *information* with them.

The Internet versus the Web

The Internet and the World Wide Web (or Web for short) are often used in the same semantic context. However, they are essentially different things. The Internet incorporates the networking infrastructure and protocols that allow computers to communicate with each other, while the Web represents a user-friendly, point-and-click environment that serves as an *interface* to the Internet. The Web provides a graphic way of organising and viewing the information available on the Internet. In this chapter we generally use the term 'Internet' to mean both the Internet and the Web.

The Internet and public relations

The Internet serves as the public face of an organisation.[4] Although it is a powerful channel that companies can use to relay their public relations message, the use of the Internet for public relations purposes has not been as high as one would expect. Seitel points out that public relations professionals have been somewhat slow to use the Internet to advance their own messages and those of their clients. But, he argues, this situation is likely to change soon.[5]

The reasons for the expected increase in the use of the Internet as a public relations medium include:[6, 7]

▲ the increasing use of the Internet by the general business community

▲ the relatively low cost of putting out a public relations message on the Internet

▲ the speed with which a public relations message can be put out to interested parties

▲ the interactive nature of the Internet, which allows the targeted audience to provide feedback to the public relations message, making it possible to gauge the feelings and perceptions of stakeholders and other interested parties.

Benefits of the Internet for public relations

Certainly the nature of the Internet offers public relations practitioners many unique benefits. These include the following:

▲ The Internet is a *multimedia environment*, making it possible to present text, video, sound, graphics and animations online. This translates into a powerful business presentation tool, as well as an easy-to-use tool from the user's point of view. The Internet's multimedia features can contribute to a greater impact on the mindset of the press, organisational stakeholders and other interested parties.

▲ It is a *digital environment*, meaning that any information made available on the Internet can be easily reused or adapted for press releases by others.

▲ It is a *hypermediated environment*, making it possible to bring or link together relevant information from other sources spread across the globe. For example, a company experiencing a disaster might link to articles of similar disasters that have happened elsewhere in the world, and to the lessons that have been learnt from these, in order to show that it has taken what are considered to be appropriate steps, given the present circumstances and the current experience.

▲ Large amounts of *information can easily be stored* and updated on the Internet. This information is available to anyone with access to the Internet. This is another powerful feature of the Internet since product details and other marketing information that would normally represent too much information to include in a television, radio or print communique can now be shared with the firm's publics over the Internet. Thus, greater amounts of information that are useful in the decision-making process can be made available to stakeholders and other interested parties over the Internet. It is also possible to provide archived information for referral purposes.

▲ Any information disseminated on the Internet by an organisation is immediately *available to a geographically dispersed audience*.

▲ Information presented on the Internet can be made *interactive*, thereby allowing users to provide feedback. In so doing, the public's perceptions of actions being undertaken by a company can be gauged quickly and easily, and possible follow-up actions or alternative actions can be put into place.

▲ The Internet is an *'always on' environment*, available 24 hours a day, 365 days a year. This makes it possible to deliver a public relations message whenever it is necessary, without having to wait for a newspaper to be published, or for the 8 o'clock news on television.

▲ The Internet is a *flexible environment* – it is possible to add or change information at the last moment, which is often difficult with other media. Again, this makes the Internet a valuable tool for keeping the target audience informed of fast-changing circumstances.

▲ Many *Internet-based services can be automated*, saving the organisation money yet enabling it to serve the customer continually. Automation is also an important component of customisation and personalisation, allowing the organisation to serve customers as individuals.

▲ If well designed, the Internet can serve as an *intuitive and easy-to-use channel* that facilitates interaction between stakeholders and the organisation.

▲ The Internet allows an organisation to *reach the masses* – as mentioned above, there is currently a global Internet market of over 500 million users, which is expected to rise to one billion within the next few years.[8]

Internet-based public relations tools

There are a number of weapons in the armoury of the public relations professional or manager. These include websites, e-mail, e-newsletters, autoresponders, frequently asked questions (FAQs), online archives, discussion forums, bulletin boards, online chat facilities, instant messaging, and SMSs.

Websites

In the growing virtual world, a website is becoming an essential marketing tool in any organisation, be it large or small. A website is little more than digital documentation that has been made available in the virtual realm of the Internet, which the general public can access easily. It serves as a place to post news and to provide information of value to interested parties, thereby generating goodwill.[9]

The advantages of a website have already been pointed out: it is continuously available, incorporates multimedia features that can be used to enhance the message being communicated, offers almost unlimited space within which to communicate a message, makes it possible to provide archived information, and can be quickly put to use or updated.

Websites can be used to:

▲ advertise products and services by providing product descriptions and specifications, photographs, prices, testimonials and case studies

▲ provide corporate information, including company history, the size and growth of the organisation, a list of directors, branches, maps, links to appropriate staff members and contact information

▲ provide investor information, including real-time share price information, financial statements, and growth expectations

▲ provide media information, including the latest news articles that have appeared about the company, archived news articles, company statistics and contact information.

What makes a website – as well as some of the other online facilities discussed below – unique, is that the organisation owns the channel. For the first time it is now possible for an organisation to have absolute control over the channel and message being broadcasted to stakeholders. One of the first contributors to the corporate website is likely to be the corporate public relations manager.[10] This contrasts with the traditional case where an organisation used public channels, over which it had no control, to disseminate a message. The danger of this is that the site owner can make unfettered claims that might otherwise have been challenged in the public domain.[11] Care needs to be taken not to fall into this trap.

E-mail

E-mail is another powerful tool at the disposal of public relations professionals. Most people in the business world now have access to e-mail, so it has reached a critical mass and is today the preferred means of business communication. Indeed, it is expected that by the end of 2002 there will be over

17 billion e-mails sent each day.[12] Although the majority of these may be junk mail (called 'spam'), this still translates into a great deal of e-mail, underscoring the importance of e-mail as a communication medium.

The reasons for the popularity of e-mail are the following:[13, 14]

▲ **Affordability:** E-mail is considerably cheaper than the telephone, fax or post.

▲ **Place:** The e-mail recipient does not have to be tied to a particular physical place, as with a postal address or a physically bound fax machine. The recipient can access his or her e-mail from anywhere in the world.

▲ **Format:** E-mail is in digital format, which allows the recipient to cut and paste content as it is required, without having to retype it; it can also be printed or saved in a file for archiving purposes.

▲ **Avoiding the gatekeeper:** While telephone calls, faxes and post are all normally channelled through a secretary, in the case of e-mail managers often still access their own e-mail, which enables the sender to bypass the 'gatekeeper' and to reach the person they want to make contact with directly.

▲ **Communication processing:** This allows recipients to decide when and if they want to read a particular message. If they are busy with a particular report, for example, they don't have to stop to receive an e-mail as they do with a telephone call. They can read their e-mail when they have time available.

▲ **Mailing lists:** E-mail allows you to create mailing lists (for media, for shareholders, for staff, for customers, for government, etc.) and to send a standard letter to a number of people at the same time (batch processing).

▲ **Interactivity:** While there are more interactive forms of communication, such as the telephone, e-mail provides a degree of interactivity and allows you to include multimedia elements and links to websites that can contain additional follow-up information.

▲ **Management:** Filing and storing e-mail messages is simple and efficient, as everything is in electronic format. Follow-up correspondence is also more efficient as old messages can be re-accessed from appropriate file folders and replied to whenever the recipient wishes, knowing that he or she has the correct e-mail address and the original correspondence at hand.

E-newsletters

An *electronic newsletter* (or *e-newsletter*) uses the same technology as e-mail, that is, it is essentially an e-mail service. The difference is that an e-mail is usually a short, specific and directed message, while an e-newsletter is more 'newsy' in nature. It is usually focused on a particular topic, may consist of several sub-topics and pages, and sent to a number of readers simultaneously, usually based on an e-mail mailing list (such as a customer database). E-newsletters can be powerful tools to keep an organisation's stakeholders informed of developments of a public nature, thereby building a relationship with these stakeholders.

E-newsletters should not be too long because of the information overload we are presently experiencing. They should be highly focused (again, readers have little time to focus on verbose, general newsletters), and must provide useful information to the reader (there must be *value* in the newsletter). Layout and presentation of e-newsletters are important in order to enhance readability. E-newsletters are generally sent out using e-mail servers (called *listservs* or *list servers*), that operate automatically and dispatch large numbers of e-mails or e-newsletters at the same time (much like batch processing). While some companies maintain their own e-mail server, most Internet service providers (ISPs) can provide an e-mail server as part of their service to you.

Autoresponders

Autoresponders are a critical part of modern online communications. They are software programs that filter incoming e-mails, directing these to appropriate persons within the organisation, then sending automated responses to the sender concerned, based on the information contained in the original e-mail. In a world where some companies receive tens of thousands of e-mails daily (or in a disaster situation where a company may suddenly face a deluge of e-mail), an autoresponder service allows public relations managers to deal more efficiently with incoming e-mail, ensuring that it is directed to the right person for attention and that senders receive immediate acknowledgement, informing them of what is happening to their e-mail. This ensures that an enquiry is not left unattended, resulting in an irate customer, journalist, shareholder, or similar enquirer. Not only do autoresponders assist in sending back instant acknowledgements and channelling enquiries to the right persons, they also pre-empt the need for human-generated replies by pointing customers to frequently asked questions and by automatically forwarding press releases to interested parties.

Frequently asked questions (FAQs)

An FAQ service, while somewhat static, is a powerful way for public relations managers to assist their publics. In a public relations or disaster environment, many stakeholders will probably ask similar questions, requiring the manager to keep repeating the same answer. Instead, an FAQ service can be initiated, comprising an online list of commonly asked questions and a corresponding reply for each question. The reply not only provides the required answer, but contains links to a wealth of supporting information, perhaps highlighting other facts, services or contact persons that the enquirer could use or turn to. Providing a swift answer to a problem assists in binding customers closer to an organisation.

Online archives

A powerful public relations service is to make available online all of the public relations and publicity messages that have been sent out by an organisation in an easy-to-browse or search format. Online archives make it possible for interested parties to return to an earlier message or even to compare messages on a self-service basis, a tremendous advantage to journalists, investors, shareholders and similar stakeholders who wish to keep track of an organisation's activities.

Discussion forums

Discussion forums are generally asynchronous communication tools (that is they do not 'talk' to each other at the same time), where one person normally makes a statement and others may (or may not) post a reply, or may choose to initiate a different discussion topic altogether. The posting of the initial statement and of any replies may occur hours, days or even weeks apart from each other. These forums are generally text-based services, where all the discussion messages are listed one beneath the other with any replies they might have received. Readers can browse through the list, choosing to read those messages they are interested in and replying to them if they wish.

Discussion forums are useful in the case of public relations where the public relations manager can initiate and observe a discussion with various stakeholders around a particular topic. While a forum serves a useful purpose in enabling stakeholders to voice their opinions, concerns and frustrations, such forums should be carefully moderated, otherwise an enraged customer might incite other customers to produce a tirade of verbal abuse. The public relations manager or assistant has a veto right as to what may be submitted for others to see.

Bulletin boards

A bulletin board generally functions along the same lines as a discussion forum, except that the communication is usually one-way, directed at readers and customers. It's a useful service for informing customers about regular events or developments. However, you could just as easily use a standard Web page to do this and, for this reason, bulletin boards are not often found on the Internet any more.

Internet relay chat (IRC)

IRC is a form of synchronous, text-based, interactive chat service. Participants access a *chat server*, using their Web browser or some proprietary chat software, and then chat with other people in real time. It is a synchronous service in the sense that, when two persons are chatting with each other, they are physically sitting at their respective computers at that time.

It is possible to create a private chat room and, in so doing, a public relations manager could, for example, arrange a virtual chat session with journalists and other stakeholders at a time of crisis or some other significant event in the organisation's history. The stakeholders would come together at a specific time and be able to chat with the public relations manager interactively, asking questions and receiving answers. IRC can be a powerful public relations channel if used in addition to the traditional press conference. The benefit of such a chat session is that it gives interested stakeholders from afar (for example, from other cities or even from abroad) an opportunity to discuss the matter at hand with the public relations manager.

Newer services include video conferencing facilities that make it possible to show diagrams and pictures or to demonstrate certain actions.

Instant messaging (IM)

Instant messaging, of which ICQ is one of the most well-known types, is a proprietary (there are several such services available), online, real-time communication channel or service, which allows you to register with the service in question (for example ICQ) and then enables you to chat interactively with other people who are online at the same time as yourself, using ICQ. When you go online, you will be informed of who else is online at that moment. You need to tell the ICQ program who you wish to keep track of and, once these people come online, you are informed of this and can then send a message to them if you wish. The message pops up on the person's screen while he or she is online, or is kept in a 'post box' until he or she comes online again. If you know a person's ICQ number, you can send him or her a message that he or she will receive when he or she is next online.

This service can be quite useful for the public relations manager who wants to keep in touch with various stakeholders on an ongoing basis. It could also prove useful in a crisis situation, for example where you want to keep in touch with someone (a journalist for example), but do not have time available to organise a formal online conference. In this instance, as soon as you go onto the Web, you can 'fire' off a batch of messages to your target audience. If they are online at that moment, they will receive the messages immediately and can send back questions immediately for the sake of clarification. The problem is that these other people also need to be users of the IM service concerned (such as ICQ).

Cellular short-messaging service (SMS)

The short-messaging services available on the cellular networks have proved extremely popular among users, with several billion messages being sent daily. The power of this service is the speed and directness with which the message reaches the targeted audience. SMS messages can be sent from the Internet, which is why this service forms part of this chapter. The SMS can be a useful tool for public relations managers and professionals to use, since it is quick and easy to use and can even be automated.

Interested parties would indicate that they want to receive messages of a particular type regularly (for example, if they want to learn about a merger or some other financial event). As soon as such a message is put out by an organisation, an SMS would be sent to the individuals concerned. In this way, it is possible to put out directed messages to stakeholders and, in so doing, build a closer-knit community of interested stakeholders.

Online publics

It is worth briefly mentioning the online publics that the Internet can reach. These include:[15]

▲ consumers

▲ businesses (for example suppliers, intermediaries and service organisations)

▲ the media

▲ government

▲ educational institutions

▲ non-governmental organisations (NGOs)

▲ financial institutions

▲ investors

▲ employees.

Clearly, most of these publics are well represented on the Internet. Certainly most medium to large businesses already have a presence on the Internet, and the media uses the Internet quite intensively for research purposes. But all the other groups are also increasingly using the Internet to learn about potential companies, suppliers, customers and partners, and the Internet is therefore an excellent medium for an organisation to use to reach these various publics.

Public relations models and the Internet

Irrespective of which of the public relations models[16] an organisation uses (be it the press agent model, the public information model, the two-way asymmetrical model or the two-way symmetrical model), the Internet has a role to play.

In the *press agent model*, which sees public relations as little more than a publicity function, the Internet serves as an alternative channel for the press to receive public relations information from an organisation. This could be in the form of a regular electronic public relations newsletter that is sent to the press, keeping them informed of developments related to the organisation and its public activities. Alternatively, it might be an archive of publicity information, including news and reviews, that the organisation makes available online and which press agents can access whenever they wish.[17] The website itself is often a useful source of information on organisations for press agents.

In a similar way, in terms of the *public information model*, which sees public relations as the dessemination of information through the mass media and controlled media, the Internet can also serve as a publicity channel for the public. Stakeholders and interested parties can subscribe to an appropriate e-newsletter with a publicity slant, or visit the website and read up about the organisation, or access archived PR information.

In terms of the *two-way asymmetrical model*, incorporating research into the public relations practice in order to understand the organisation's publics better, the public relations function attempts to bring a research component into the public relations practice. Again, the Internet has a role to play here and is a useful research tool that public relations practitioners can use to learn more about their publics. Also, by bringing Web-based and e-mail surveys into the picture, organisations can learn more about the opinions of their various publics. These types of online surveys, combined with traditional research methodologies, serve as a powerful way of channelling feedback to organisations that, in turn, assists in driving their future public relations efforts and in shaping appropriate messages for their publics.

Finally, in terms of the *two-way symmetrical model*, which describes the public relations efforts of an organisation in terms of its research base combined with the use of communication to facilitate improved and immediate understanding of the organisation's strategic publics, the Internet again has a role to play. Its ability to facilitate one-to-one communications on a real-time basis makes it possible to reach out to an organisation's publics and to gather in personal feedback, and possibly even to dig deeper into the opinions of people through the use of online discussion forums, chat sessions and instant messaging facilities. This can even be done proactively. For example, an organisation can establish a virtual network that brings together selected elements of the various publics the organisation serves (that is, the press, shareholders, clients, suppliers, the general public, government and regulatory authorities), and in so doing, facilitate constant feedback and communication with stakeholders.

This move towards genuine ongoing communication with, and involvement of, an organisation's publics can assist in guiding the organisation on how to manoeuvre in whatever circumstances it may find itself. It also engenders a positive attitude towards the organisation, which may be a crucial advantage to have if disaster strikes. However, this type of intensive interaction with an organisation's stakeholders and publics needs to be carefully managed since it may create expectations that cannot be fulfilled and, once started, can cause frustration and anger if it is not properly carried through.

Publicity for the organisation versus the website

Among other activities, the public relations manager is tasked with generating publicity for the organisation (organisational publicity). At the same time, in the online world, one of the most important tasks of the Web master/Web mistress or other responsible person is to generate publicity for the organisation's website (website publicity) – after all, a website that is unknown is of little value to the organisation that owns it. A publicity campaign is therefore necessary to ensure that the website becomes better known. There is often some confusion between the effort involved in publicising a physical organisation and its activities and using a website in this effort, versus publicising a website in order for the website to become better known.

Of course, these two tasks are related, since a well-known website assists in increasing the flow of publicity to an organisation. In fact, website publicity is almost a subset of organisational publicity and public relations, and requires a separate, focused effort in its own right. Unfortunately, there is no guaranteed method of promoting an organisational website that will ensure its success. Web promotion is only part of the formula for success. Other variables in the equation include content, user value, design, dynamism and ease of use.

Website promotion is essentially a 'bag of tricks' that needs to be drawn from in order to achieve an organisation's objectives. It is a total package of activities that, when used correctly and with perseverance, will contribute to the success of an organisation's online activities in the long run, thereby also contributing to the organisation's broad public relations campaign. Website promotion requires a lot of effort and, too often, organisations give up their promotional efforts and accept a mediocre level of online success that could so easily be a great deal better.

Defining the target audience

It is essential that an organisation reaches the right online audience, that is, an audience comprised of Internet users and potential Internet users who are already customers, or are likely to become future customers, or are part of the publics that the organisation serves (for example investors, shareholders, press, employees). High numbers of online visitors to a website are seldom an objective in itself. Large numbers of visitors alone are only likely to clog up an organisation's Web systems, eating up bandwidth, and possibly causing more problems than they are worth. It is essential, therefore, to concentrate on attracting visitors to the website who are part of the organisation's clearly defined target audience. In the case of public relations, this includes not just customers, but also any person who falls within the various publics that the organisation serves.

Defining a target audience is an important step in the online advertising and marketing process. First, it assists in creating an online service that meets the needs of the target audience; and second, it allows the organisation to focus on reaching its target audience through promotional means.

Awareness of the site

Once the target audience has been defined, the next step in online promotion is to generate awareness of the website among customers and the organisation's publics. This essentially involves planting the website URL (that is, the company's website address) in their minds. The more of the target audience who know the organisation's website address, the better. They may not have used the site, or may not even be planning to use the site, but at least they know that the organisation offers an online service, and what the address is.

Indeed, there are an increasing number of companies, such as M-Web, Kalahari.net (see figure 7.1 on the next page) and Megashopper, which are resorting to extensive television, radio and print advertising in order to inform potential users of their respective online services.

Awareness of what an organisation's website has to offer

Another promotional objective is to inform the target audience of what *value* an organisation's site has to offer them. In the case of the various publics that the organisation serves, this may mean making available regular news articles, frequently asked questions, e-newsletters, archived articles and discussion forums, as well as historic and contact information.

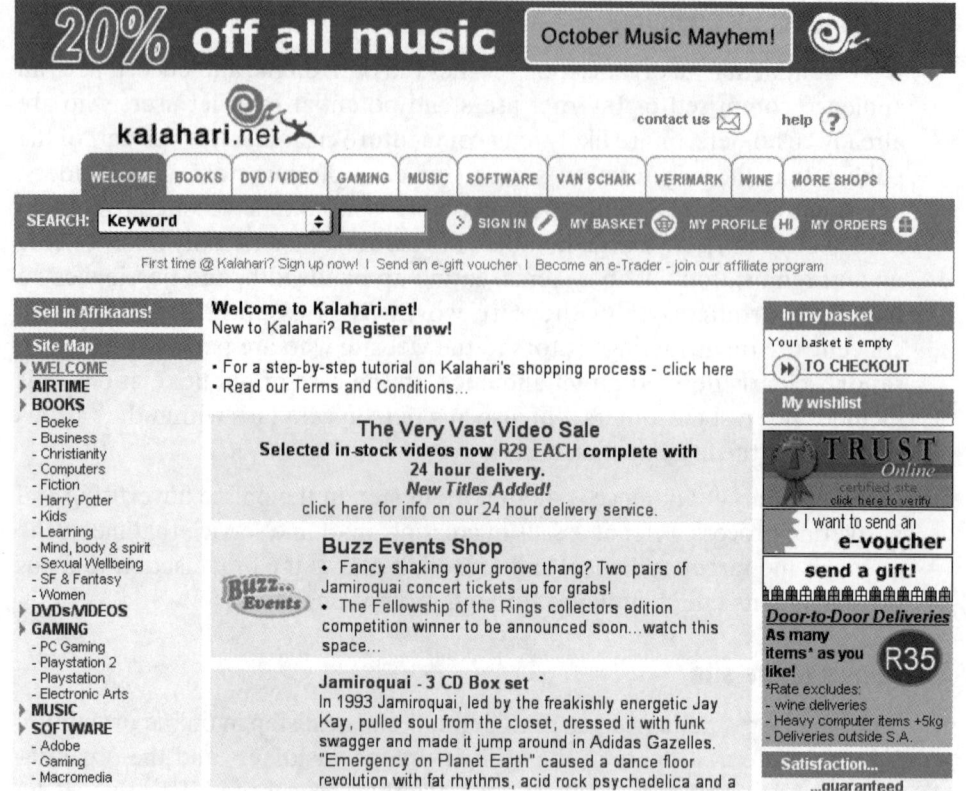

Figure 7.1 The kalahari.net homepage

Marketspace versus marketplace promotion

To reach as many members of the target audience as possible means promoting the organisation's online activities both within the virtual realm (the marketspace) and the physical marketplace. One without the other will only result in missed opportunities.

Those individuals of the organisation's target audience already on the Internet will probably use one or more search engines to find the organisation's website, or may visit a related site that, in turn, has a link to the organisation's website. Registering a site with search engines and arranging reciprocal links with related websites represent two important ways of promoting an organisation's online services in cyberspace – there are others.[18]

Of course, online promotion does not assist in drawing those of the target audience who do not yet have access to the Internet, or who are not yet aware of the organisation's online activities (even if they are connected to the Internet). In order to reach these individuals, the promotion of the organisation's online services in traditional media, for example through presentations, radio and television advertisements, letterheads and business cards is essential.

The total promotional campaign that underpins an organisation's online activities should comprise a blend of both online and traditional media promotions.

Promotional tools

Before an organisation begins its promotional campaign, it should create a number of promotional tools such as blurbs, banners, signature files, buttons, press releases, announcements, and so on. These items should be used over and over again in any promotional efforts. The promotional tools the organisation can use are listed below:[19]

▲ **Signature files:** These are simple text files – the electronic equivalent of a business card – which should be about six to eight lines long and no more than 65 characters wide. They carry the organisation's contact details and a quick introduction to its business, as well as the URL (Web address) of its website. The signature should provide a powerful, concise reason or 'hook' as to why the person reading it should visit the organisation's website.

▲ **Blurbs:** These are short, one-paragraph pieces of text about the organisation or a related topic that can be posted to Usenet newsgroups or pasted into e-mails when required.

▲ **Reports:** These are longer versions of blurbs, detailing the organisation or any other related topic. Post them to selected places on the Internet and send them whenever asked.

▲ **Press releases:** Create professional press releases about the organisation and its website, from new product announcements to site changes. Post them in appropriate places on the Internet and forward them to press release services.

▲ **Announcements:** These are similar to press releases, but are aimed at the general public. They are intended to notify the organisation's various publics of any new developments or events, or any other activities worth publicising.

▲ **Newsletters:** For a wide variety of reasons, it is worthwhile for an organisation to start its own newsletter and to work at enlisting subscriptions, even if they are free. At the same time, the organisation should prepare suitable articles, blurbs and banners for submission to relevant e-newsletters that it, in turn, has subscribed to.

▲ **Links and buttons:** Often other websites agree to include a link to an organisation's site. Generally, they select a word, phrase or short description of their own choosing as the basis for the hyperlink. The words used may not be ideal or may not describe the website effectively. For this reason, it makes sense to create a selection of hyperlinks that best describe the organisation's online activities. When negotiating links with another website, e-mail its representatives a list of possible hyperlinks from which they can choose, together with the underlying page (HTML) coding. Suggest that they use one of these on their site. In addition, it might also be worthwhile creating a selection of button links as an alternative. Amazon.com, for example, supplies partner firms with a range of linked buttons that they can choose from if they intend linking to them.

▲ **Banners:** An organisation needs to ensure that it has professional quality banners of different sizes available for use.

▲ **FAQs:** An organisation should create a few frequently asked questions files about the industry it operates in, or any other related topic. The FAQ files need to be in a question-and-answer format, and should be posted in appropriate newsgroups or e-mailed when necessary.

▲ **Autoresponders:** If appropriate for an organisation, it is a good idea to make use of an autoresponder that is able to read incoming e-mails, and to automatically and instantly send out information files and answers that are appropriate to the query. In this way you can manage thousands of e-mail enquiries on time, without any effort.

▲ **Articles:** An organisation should make the effort every so often to write some good articles related to its industry. These can be contributed for free to various e-zines and websites that may be prepared to flight such articles. This is one of the most effective public relations tools, as it reaches thousands at a time, grabbing their attention for extended periods, and translating into excellent publicity for the organisation concerned.

▲ **Archive support:** The Web allows an organisation to store vast quantities of information online in support of its products and activities, including graphics, photographs, product specification sheets, annual reports, financial statements, full-length press releases, press clippings, street maps, price catalogues, schedules of events, transcripts of interviews, help files, white papers, sound bits, video clips, and so on. This allows the organisation to back up every promotional announcement with a whole package of supporting information.

Online promotion

The need to promote an organisation's activities through both online and traditional media has been emphasised above. Online promotion of websites is a comprehensive and time-consuming task. It includes the following activities:[20]

- ▲ selecting and registering appropriate URLs/Web addresses for an organisation's site
- ▲ registering an organisation's website with local and international search engines and directories
- ▲ negotiating strategic and reciprocal links with relevant websites
- ▲ buying links from major portals
- ▲ developing affiliate and associate programmes
- ▲ advertising on relevant websites using banner ads
- ▲ establishing an e-mail news service
- ▲ publishing an electronic newsletter and/or e-zine, and maintaining mailing lists
- ▲ promoting an organisation's Web services on other firms' e-newsletters
- ▲ making use of Usenet and newsgroups to inform people of an organisation and its products/services
- ▲ arranging online events
- ▲ requesting reviews of an organisation's website
- ▲ encouraging referrals to an organisation's site.

Offline promotion

While online promotion is important, using traditional marketing means to promote an organisation's online activities assists in casting the promotional net as wide as possible. The organisation is probably using several traditional marketing tools already, and these may need to be adapted slightly simply by adding the organisation's Web address to them to begin attracting additional customers to its site.

The traditional media that an organisation can use include:

- ▲ television, radio and print advertising
- ▲ multimedia, CD-Rom and PowerPoint presentations
- ▲ press releases
- ▲ articles in magazines
- ▲ newsletters
- ▲ business cards
- ▲ letterheads and faxes
- ▲ invoices

▲ envelopes

▲ annual reports

▲ classifieds

▲ compliment slips

▲ sales and marketing brochures

▲ price and product catalogues

▲ flyers

▲ T-shirts and promotional gifts

▲ signage such as posters and billboards

▲ packaging.

It is essential today to ensure that an organisation's Web address is on every promotional item that leaves the organisation, or its PR/advertising agent. Printing a Web address everywhere is a great source of free advertising! Not only should an organisation be using its existing advertising and public relations campaign to promote its online activities, but it may want to consider undertaking a dedicated campaign to promote its website (the examples of M-Web, Kalahari.net and Megashopper were mentioned earlier in this chapter).

Third-party public relations portals

Another area where the Internet is being used fairly extensively in the public relations field is to serve as a 'clearing house' for public relations messages and campaigns – also referred to as an *online wire service*. This may be either on an industry level, or as a general public relations forum. In the former instance, a third-party organisation creates a website with a specific industry focus. This website may cover a multitude of topics to do with the industry in question, including general industry news and public relations information. Such public relations information will generally be supplied by the many organisations active in the industry, but may also be gathered independently by the editorial team that runs the website.

Some of these industry portals have become central to the industry they serve, and represent a powerful channel to ensure a public relations message reaches a specific industry-focused target audience. An example of such an industry portal is ITWeb that serves the IT industry in South Africa (http://www.itweb.co.za) as shown in figure 7.2 on the next page.

A derivative of this type of third-party portal is a website that serves as an outlet for any public relations message, irrespective of the industry concerned. More common in the US and in Europe, there are various public relations portals where a public relations manager or professional can submit a public relations message for online publication. The visitors to such public relations portals are journalists and other like-minded individuals who are interested in learning more about the public activities of organisations. An example of such a portal is http://www.prweb.com

Figure 7.2 The ITWeb homepage

The benefit of using a public relations portal is that the editorial which appears on the site tends to be more objective and represents a certain minimum standard. The copy submitted by public relations managers is generally reviewed by the portal editors, who generally require a certain standard to be met and may ask that the message be adapted or rewritten before it is published. As a portal becomes established, it represents a known, central clearing house to which all interested parties can turn in order to exchange messages of a public relations nature. In other words, if an organisation wants to ensure that its message is seen by all, it will publish the message not only on its own website, but will also submit the message to an online clearing house, as described above. This ensures that the message is seen by as many of its various publics as possible.

Finding public relations services on the Internet

The Internet is also a way for companies to find public relations firms and professionals that they can turn to for assistance. Not only are public relations firms using the Internet as a channel to relay a public relations message to the masses, they are also using it as a channel to market themselves! This makes it possible for an organisation that doesn't yet have a public relations service to identify and compare public relations companies before drawing up a shortlist. (Of course, the final decision will only be made once the short-listed candidates have been interviewed.) There are also third-party websites (more common overseas, but you can expect to see them in South Africa soon) that list a wide range of public relations resources that an organisation can utilise. One example is http://www.impulse-research.com/prlist.html and a South African version can be found at http://www.mediaweb.co.za

Case study

The Nando's website: Laying the foundation for publicity

Figure 7.3 The Nando's homepage

Introduction

Nando's is a brand well known to most South Africans, as well as to customers in 15 other countries around the world, reflecting on the growth and success of Nando's. The success of the brand is in part due to the excellent products they sell, but can also be attributed to the effort they put into creative, award-winning advertising and generating good (and sometimes controversial) publicity for the company.

Hatching the idea

This is how Nando's describes its early days: It was in the small suburb of Rosettenville, Johannesburg, in a humble eatery called Chickenland, that a dream was destined to become a reality in a few short years. There, in the heart of the local Portuguese community, chicken was prepared and enjoyed according to a centuries-old, Portuguese tradition – the *delicioso* and well-kept secret of the tightly-knit community. But, Portuguese hospitality being what it is, the secret proved to be one that had to be shared. Fernando Duarte, a member of the community, introduced his close and longtime friend, Robert Brozin, to Chickenland. When Robert tasted the traditional Portuguese-style chicken, he had his first taste of what was to become his *sonho* (dream) – a dream of sharing something this good with the whole world. Fernando and Robert became partners and, embracing all aspects of its Portuguese heritage, Nando's was born in September 1987. Today, the Nando's restaurant chain is a major success story, with stores stretching all the way from Rosettenville to Cape Town, and from Canada to Australia.

The Nando's website

The Nando's website has been around for some time. It is a website that was originally modelled – tongue-in-cheek – on the Windows 98 operating system. Called Nando's 98, the website has a colourful home page that looks like a desktop, but with a strong 'chicken' theme. On this 'desktop' there are several icons that offer the user various options:

▲ The *retail icon* leads users to a Web page that informs them about 'Praiseworthy sauces', 'Ads worthy of praise', 'Delicious recipes' (with links to recipes that complement the Nando's product range), and 'Saucy information' (a short history of peri-peri).

▲ There are *country icons* for the UK, the USA and Australia. Each of these is fairly similar, and tells the user about Nando's in that particular country.

▲ The *Nando's Explorer* – a Windows Explorer lookalike – allows users to:

 △ learn about the history of Nando's

 △ learn more about their overseas operations – here users can visit Web pages that deal with each of the 16 countries in which Nando's operates (in the bigger countries such as South Africa, users can read up on public relations articles that have appeared in the local press, view the ads for that country, and find a listing of stores)

△ download and view some of their award-winning ads

△ access a 'Cluck up' form where one can submit a complaint – a useful customer service

△ access a list of all their stores with physical addresses and contact numbers

△ access a list of competition winners

△ access investor information – where interested parties can access the financial statements of Nando's.

▲ The *outside catering icon* allows customers to learn more about the catering services offered by Nando's.

▲ The *franchise enquiries icon* allows potential franchisees to learn more about the Nando's franchise.

▲ The *bird perfect icon* links to a comprehensive list of recipes that users can try on their own (with Nando's sauces).

▲ The *contact icon* opens a small e-mail window, allowing users to send e-mails to Nando's.

▲ The *survey form* allows users to indicate whether Nando's ads (the ads can be selected) are 'hot or not'.

Looking through this website, it is clear that the site is aimed at promoting the Nando's brand, as well as the company as a whole. The site has changed little over the past few years, besides the general maintenance of the information on the site.

What more could Nando's do?

Various points come to mind:

▲ It seems a shame to hide the public relations articles about Nando's so deep in the site. Perhaps Nando's could create a 'brag file'.

▲ A contact number for head office is required for people who don't wish to work through a website to communicate with Nando's – the only available contact on the site is via an online form, e-mail or through the individual stores.

▲ A full menu could be listed to allow users to make a selection before calling a particular store, or to entice users.

(*Source:* http://www.Nando's.co.za)

Conclusion

This chapter looked at the influence of the Internet on the public relations environment. The discussion began by looking at the relationship between the Internet and the Web, and identifying the three main functions of the Internet, namely communications, information and conducting business. The unique advantages that the Internet holds for the public relations field were then highlighted and, because of the control and flexibility that the Internet offers public relations practitioners, it was suggested that the use of the Internet in this field is likely to increase.

Various online tools were then considered, including websites, e-mail, e-newsletters, autoresponders, online chat services and discussion forums, to which public relations practitioners can turn to send out their messages to their respective audiences. A discussion of how the Internet relates to each of the various public relations models then followed. It was also emphasised that not only can the Internet be used as a tool to facilitate an organisation's public relations efforts, but it is essential that the organisation publicises its online activities as well; in other words, organisational publicity differs from website publicity.

The importance of promoting the website as part of an organisation's overall public relations campaign was discussed further, and various ways in which an organisation can promote its website both online and offline were outlined. The chapter ended by explaining what is meant by a third-party public relations portal and the use of the Internet in finding public relations services.

Questions for self-evaluation

1. Explain the relationship between the Internet and the Web.
2. Identify the three main functions of the Internet.
3. List the advantages of the Internet as a channel for public relations.
4. Explain why it is expected that the use of the Internet as a channel for public relations is likely to increase.
5. Identify and discuss the various online tools that are at the public relations manager's disposal.
6. Discuss how the Internet relates to each of the various public relations models mentioned.
7. Explain how organisational publicity differs from website publicity.

8. Discuss the importance of promoting the website as part of an organisation's overall public relations campaign.

9. Describe how to promote an organisation's website both online and offline.

10. Explain what is meant by a third-party public relations portal.

11. Discuss how an organisation might use the Internet to identify public relations resources.

12. Answer these questions on the case study above:

    (a) Why can the Nando's website be described as a public relations website?

    (b) Why does a company such as Nando's have a public relations website rather than an advertising or transactional website?

    (c) Is the Nando's website only aimed at generating publicity, or does it have other functions as well? If so, what are these functions?

    (d) Does the Nando's website effectively support the organisation's real-world advertising and public relations activities? Explain your reasoning.

    (e) What more could Nando's do to improve their website, besides what is mentioned in the case study?

    (f) Visit the following websites that also have a publicity/public relations slant and discuss how they differ from or are similar to the Nando's website:

    ▲ http://www.samint.co.za

    ▲ http://www.avmin.co.za

Endnotes

1 NUA Internet Surveys 2002. *How many online?* Website: http://www.nua.ie/surveys/how_many_online/index.html (Date of access 25 July 2002.)

2 Bothma, CH 2000. *E-commerce for South African Managers*. Pretoria: Interactive Reality.

3 Legacy systems generally refer to older types of IT systems and applications that are mainframe-based and written in Cobol or other first-generation languages. However, they also sometimes refer to more recent server-based technologies and applications that may already have been displaced by newer systems.

4   Mersham, G and Skinner, C 1999. *Communication & Public Relations.* Johannesburg: Heinemann.

5   Seitel, FP 1998. *The Practice of Public Relations.* (7 Ed.) New Jersey: Prentice Hall.

6   Ibid.

7   O'Keefe, S 1997. *Publicity on the Internet.* Toronto: Wiley.

8   NUA Internet Surveys, op. cit.

9   Tiernan, B 2000. *e-tailing.* Chicago: Dearborn.

10 Keyes, J (Ed.) 2000. *Internet Management.* Florida: Auerbach.

11 Chaffey, D; Mayer, R; Johnston, K and Ellis-Chadwick, F 2000. *Internet Marketing.* London: *Financial Times*/Prentice Hall.

12 Schwartz, KD 1998. Improving customer service through e-mail. Datamation website: http://www.datamation.com/PlugIn/workbench/ecom/11serv.html (Date of access 6 December 1998.)

13 Bothma, op. cit.:79–80.

14 Seitel, op. cit.

15 O'Keefe, op. cit.

16 Lubbe, BA and Puth, G 1994. *Public Relations in South Africa.* Johannesburg: Heinemann.

17 Cataudella, J; Sawyer, B and Greely, D 1998. *Creating Stores on the Web.* Berkeley: Peachpit Press.

18 O'Keefe, op. cit.

19 Bothma, op. cit.:3.

20 Cannon, J 2000. *Make your Website Work for You.* Martinsburg: CommerceNet Press.

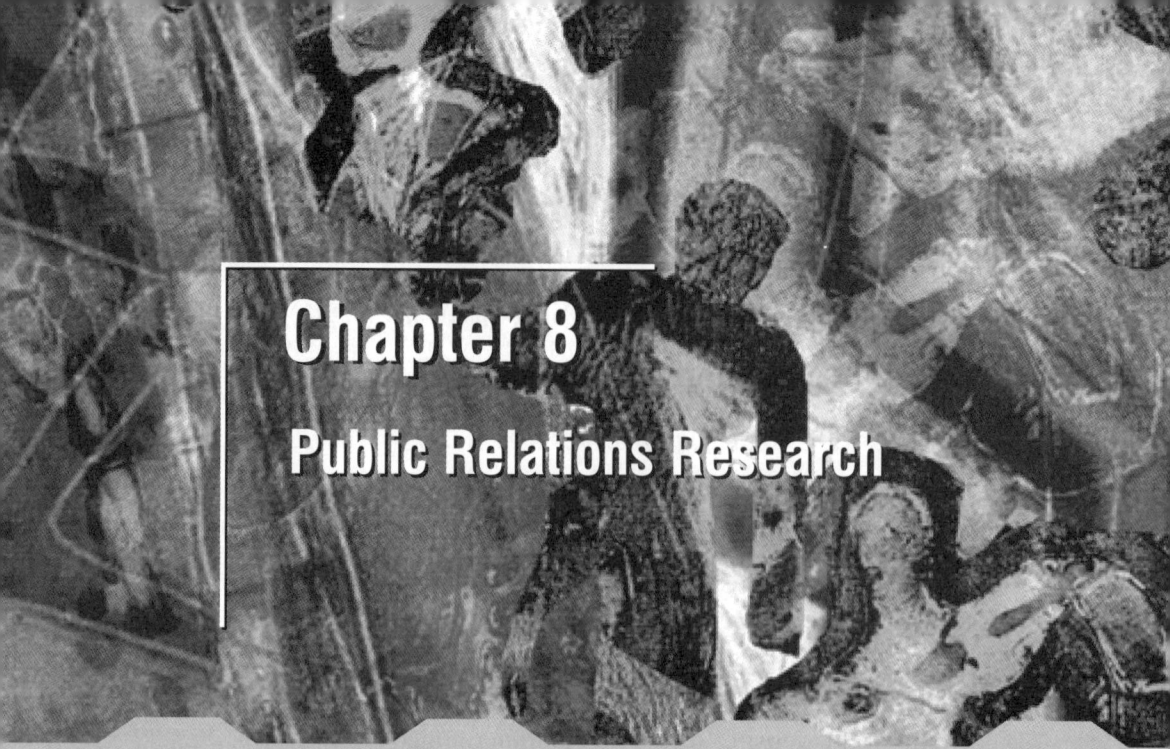

Chapter 8

Public Relations Research

LEARNING OUTCOMES

After studying this chapter, you should be able to:

▲ explain why public relations research is important

▲ explain what public relations research is

▲ explain what the public relations research process is

▲ explain how public relations research objectives are determined

▲ explain what public relations research design entails

▲ explain when to conduct primary research

▲ explain the different methods of primary research

▲ explain how to determine a research frame

▲ discuss the public relations research process

▲ explain the various forms of public relations research

▲ explain what marketing information systems are.

Introduction

To fully understand public relations, we need to have knowledge of the numerous aspects, concepts and theories that relate to public relations. One of these aspects is *public relations research*.

This chapter starts with a brief overview of public relations research. It then discusses public relations research and why it is important in public relations decision making. The formal research process that needs to be followed when conducting public relations research is then considered.

Since it is not always possible to conduct formal research, this chapter will also look at public relations information systems.

Public relations research

Research can be defined as the systematic and objective process of planning, gathering, analysing and reporting of data, which may be used to solve a specific problem or opportunity.[1] It is a tool that links consumers to the marketer through information.[2] The information assists decision makers by reducing the risk and assisting them to make informed decisions.[3] Public relations practitioners are continually faced with tough decisions about public relations campaigns. Before any public relations campaign or programme can be undertaken, however, information must be gathered, data collected and facts compiled.[4] This process is called research. *Public relations research* can thus be defined as a systematic enquiry aimed at providing information to solve public relations problems.[5]

Two kinds of public relations research are identified. The first is used to assess the status quo and to detect problems, and is commonly known as environmental scanning. The second kind of public relations research looks at the planning and implementation of a public relations campaign or programme.[6] Therefore, public relations research is conducted either to identify a problem or to utilise an opportunity to implement a public relations campaign or programme.

Public relations practitioners are not only held accountable by their own organisations but also by the public at large. This means that the success of a public relations campaign or programme reflects directly onto the public relations practitioner. In order to achieve success, the public relations practitioner must make the best possible decisions under all circumstances.

Public relations research has become increasingly important for five main reasons:[7]

1. **The trend towards measurability.**[8] Public relations practitioners are being forced to quantify their results and, in so doing, to justify their existence. This measurability flows directly from research because research is used to measure the results of a public relations campaign or programme in quantitative terms.

2. **Increasing fragmentation of audiences.** Publics are becoming increasingly segmented into groups that have special interests and specific needs. The public relations practitioner needs to understand the publics and to adapt the public relations campaign or programme to appeal to their individual needs.

3. **Increasing isolation of management from the public.** Top management is becoming more and more isolated from the needs of the public and even those of its consumers. Public relations research should bridge the gap between the needs, wants and opinions of the public and consumers and the executive decision makers within the organisation.

4. **Scarcity of resources.** Public relations research can assist organisations in their resource allocation by preventing unnecessary spending on campaigns or programmes that address non-existent problems.

5. **Increasing planning needs.** When planning a public relations campaign or programme, decision makers need to know about the problem or opportunity being faced, the attitudes and opinions of the publics, and which publics require special attention. Public relations research provides the answers to all of these issues.

Public relations research in practice: How public relations restored the Cape's image

Corporate Image Africa, the Cape Town-based public relations consultancy, has won Gold at the Prism Awards for outstanding public relations practice. Their campaign, which sought to position Cape Town as a top investment location, included steps to restore law and order to the city by instituting levies on rates that paid for 150 extra security officers, and to improve the parking management systems. They also provided positive press coverage and in all cases gained public acceptance of the changes. The results of the campaign included R2 billion worth of new construction approved, the return of several high profile corporations to the CBD and a considerable volume of favourable media coverage.

(*Source:* Adapted from the *Financial Mail*, 8 March 2002)

Public relations research has thus become an integral part of public relations decision making, and the process that must be followed when conducting research needs special attention. The next section focuses on the nature of the public relations research process.

The nature of the public relations research process

As mentioned before, public relations research is a systematic enquiry aimed at providing information to solve public relations problems. The steps that define the tasks to be accomplished in conducting a public relations research study therefore refer to the public relations research process.[9] This process provides a systematic and planned approach to conducting public relations research. Thus, it could be said that the *public relations research process* is a sequence of steps involving the systematic collection and analysis of public relations data.

It could be assumed that the public relations research process is like a map because there is more than one path to take to reach the desired destination. The decision on which path to take depends on where the researcher wishes to go, and on the resources available to the researcher. Since there are several paths that researchers can follow during each phase of the research process, it is necessary to explore various paths to ensure that they take the right path to solve the specific public relations problem or to utilise the public relations opportunity effectively.

The phases in the public relations research process are functionally interrelated, and are not performed in isolation. Each phase has a forward and backward linkage to another phase. The next section looks at the public relations research process in more detail.

The public relations research process

The public relations research process is a series of carefully thought-out steps, designed to attain a specific objective. These steps are sequential and interrelated. This implies that any decision made at any stage in the process may affect decisions to be made at other subsequent steps in the process. Also, any modifications made at one stage usually result in modifications at other stages in the process. For the purposes of this chapter, the research process consists of nine steps. These steps are illustrated in figure 8.1 on the next page.

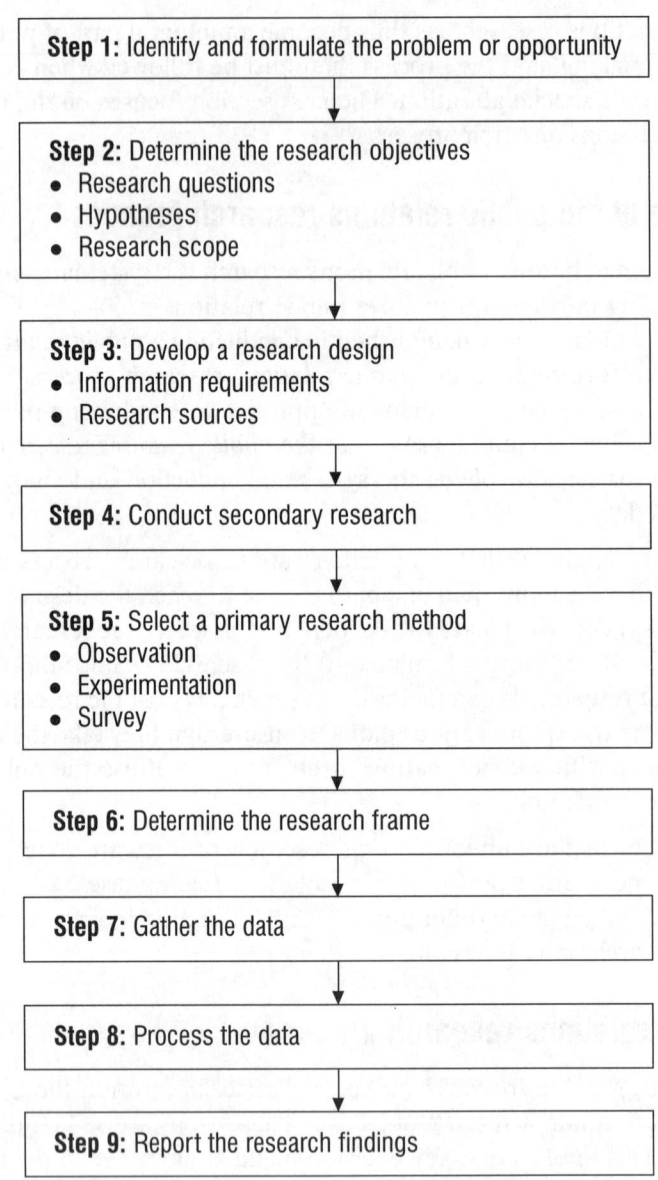

Figure 8.1 The public relations research process

Step 1: Identify and formulate the problem or opportunity[10]

The public relations research process begins when a public relations problem or opportunity is identified. A *public relations problem* refers to situations that might represent real problems to public relations decision makers. A *public relations opportunity* refers to any favourable or unexploited situation in one or more of the public relations environments that can be utilised proactively by decision makers to the advantage of the organisation.[11]

Identifying a public relations problem or opportunity is probably the most important stage in the research process, but is sometimes overlooked by researchers. This stage is crucial because a weak diagnosis of the problem may also lead to an inefficient solution.[12] The public relations problem or opportunity should thus be clearly defined and formulated to ensure that the results obtained by the research are not irrelevant. The research should therefore generate the kinds of answers needed in an efficient manner.

It is important for public relations researchers to fully understand the nature of the problem or opportunity, as well as the environment surrounding it. A prerequisite of defining a problem or opportunity at hand, therefore, is to analyse the environment in which the organisation operates by doing a situation analysis. A *situation analysis* refers to the informal gathering of background information to familiarise researchers with the public relations problem or opportunity.[13]

Public relations research in practice: Making friends with Castle

Faced with a flat beer market, South African Breweries (SAB) planned to reposition its flagship brand, Castle. Repositioning any brand can be a public relations nightmare and, without the proper information, many costly mistakes can be made. In the late eighties, SAB redesigned the label, backing the change with an advertising campaign that emphasised: 'We're changing the label, not the beer.' The resultant loss of half of their market in four months made them wary of any changes to the Castle brand. The new campaign has been widely researched, with SAB representatives conducting more than 80 personal interviews per day, and is accompanied by an extensive advertising campaign emphasising the 'friendship brew'.

(*Source:* Adapted from the *Financial Mail*, 15 February 2002)

To enable researchers to understand the background and nature of the public relations problem or opportunity, they should analyse the factors that have an impact on its definition. These factors may include:[14]

▲ **Secondary data analysis.** This refers to investigations of past information and forecasts. It may include investigating aspects such as sales, market share, public opinion, image, technology, population and lifestyle.

▲ **The resources and constraints of the organisation.** The resources of an organisation include aspects such as its financial resources and its research skills. Constraints may include cost and time available.

▲ **The macroenvironment of the organisation.** This pertains to the legal, economic, social, international, and political environments.

▲ **The technological skills of the organisation.** These refer to the organisation's access to and ability to use adequate technology.

Once public relations researchers have investigated the abovementioned factors, they should carefully consider the findings of the preliminary research so that the problem or opportunity can be clearly formulated and defined. To ensure that the identified problem or opportunity is well formulated, researchers could ask themselves what the purpose of the study is.[15] If the decision makers agree, then the research problem or opportunity is formulated.

Once the purpose of the study has been established, researchers should lay down some primary and secondary objectives that support the purpose of the study and give some direction as to where the process is heading.

Step 2: Determine the research objectives[16]

A public relations research *objective* refers to the specific information that is needed to solve a public relations research problem. In order to do so, researchers should state all objectives in terms of the precise information necessary – as well as desired – to solve the specific public relations problem or opportunity. When researchers determine the objectives for the research study, they should consider the following questions as a broad guideline:[17]

▲ Is additional background information necessary before public relations research objectives can be determined?

▲ What information is needed to make decisions or solve the public relations problem?

▲ How will the information gathered be used?

If researchers are able to answer these questions, they can specify the research objectives for the public relations research study. However, since the determination of research objectives is a crucial part of the public relations research process, researchers should consider three basic aspects when they state the public relations research objectives. These aspects include the specific research question at hand, the development of hypotheses, and the scope or boundaries of the research.

Research question

The *research question* specifies the exact information that the decision maker needs. The public relations research question should be stated as specifically as possible, to ensure that it supports the purpose of the study. If, for example, a clothing organisation identifies that customers are unhappy with the current products that it is offering, the purpose of the study would be 'To determine what aspects of the products displease the consumers'. Research questions could be:

▲ What products are customers pleased with?

▲ What products are customers displeased with?

In the example, the public relations problem of the clothing organisation is customer displeasure with its products. The purpose of the study is to determine how to improve the products of the organisation (solve the problem). The research questions that are specified will provide researchers with the necessary information to solve the problem, namely, the factors that are displeasing customers. Sometimes public relations researchers may have possible answers for the research questions. These are known as hypotheses.

Development of a hypothesis

A *hypothesis* refers to possible answers to stated research questions. These can sharpen the specific aims and directions of the research study. Hypotheses can therefore be tentative solutions or actions for the research problem or opportunity. A hypothesis can be defined as an unproven statement or proposition about a factor or phenomenon that is of interest to the researcher.[18]

To formulate a hypothesis, public relations researchers should speculate on possible answers for the research questions. Researchers could attempt to develop more than one possible hypothesis, so that enough scope will be created to gather the information needed to solve the problem. For instance, in the example, possible hypotheses may be:

▲ Customers are displeased with the quality of the clothing.

▲ Customers are pleased with the organisation's low prices.

▲ Customers seek quality clothing at reasonable prices.

Sometimes the most reasonable statement of a hypothesis may be a trivial restatement of the research question.[19] For example:

Research question: Do customers of store X exhibit store loyalty?

Hypothesis: Customers of store X are loyal.

Therefore, it may not always be possible to develop hypotheses. However, when setting public relations research objectives, researchers must consider the scope and/or boundaries of the research.

Research scope

The *scope* of the research refers to the extent to which it is possible to conduct the research.[20] When researchers consider the scope of the research, they should keep three aspects in mind:

▲ **The target segment of the research.** Researchers should consider who constitutes the subjects of the research study, and whether it is possible to reach them.

▲ **The area under study.** Here researchers should determine what the areas or topics of the investigation are, and whether it is possible to reach these areas.

▲ **The accuracy level.** The desired accuracy of the research results should be determined. In other words, the greater the risk facing the public relations decision, the higher the level of precision should be.

Once the scope of the research has been considered, researchers should assess the resources available for the research study. The value of the information gathered by the research should be greater than the cost involved to conduct the research.

When determining public relations research objectives, it is important to mention, once again, that the public relations research process is not a static process where stages happen in isolation. All stages in this process have a forward and a backward linkage. In the discussion on the determination of research objectives, possible research methods have already been considered. However, since this is a systematic process, research methods can only be established once a research design is formulated.

Step 3: Develop a research design[21]

A *research design* is a preliminary plan for conducting the research.[22] In this stage of the public relations research process, a research plan is developed for the carrying out of the research study. The format of the plan depends on the nature of the research that the public relations researcher wishes to do. The research objectives as determined in the previous stage of the process should therefore be translated into specific data needs. This means that the researchers should specify what information is required from the research and from which sources the information will be obtained.[23]

Information requirements

When considering what kind of information is required to solve the specific public relations problem or opportunity, researchers should define the information needed. By doing this, they can ensure that the data obtained by the research will answer the requirements of the problem or opportunity under consideration. Categories of information include the following:[24]

▲ **Facts.** Facts are data, which are clearly defined and measured, for example the number of Ford light passenger vehicles sold in 2001.

▲ **Levels of awareness.** Awareness refers to what respondents know or do not know about some object or phenomenon. Information on awareness is important in public relations research where, for example, researchers want to determine whether or not respondents are aware of a public relations campaign or programme.

▲ **Opinions and attitudes.** These contain a certain element of judgement and include consumers' ideas, convictions and/or likes and dislikes regarding a certain object or phenomenon.

▲ **Preferences.** These are closely related to opinions or attitudes. However, when research is conducted on preferences, researchers should formulate questions with some ranking procedure.

▲ **Motives.** These are the reasons why people act as they do. Researchers could, for example, ask respondents direct questions to glean information on their motives.

▲ **Behaviour.** This is how people act in the marketplace. Behaviour finds expression in a variety of dimensions contained in such questions as *what*, *how*, *how much/often*, *where*, *when* and/or *in what situation*.

Once researchers have established the information they need, they should consider where to find it.

Research sources

When considering from which sources to obtain information, researchers have two alternatives: data collection methods include secondary research and primary research. *Secondary research* refers to secondary data and/or information that already exists and that has been collected before. *Primary research*, however, refers to primary data that should be collected for a specific purpose. Researchers should always begin their research by exploiting secondary research sources.

Step 4: Conduct secondary research

As mentioned above, secondary research is research that already exists some-where, because it was collected for another purpose.[25] When a public relations problem or opportunity arises, researchers should always begin their research with secondary research, as it might be sufficient to answer the research questions. Secondary research can be gathered by consulting either internal or external sources. *Internal* secondary data sources may include sales invoices, customer complaints, and so on. *External* secondary data sources, however, include libraries, the Internet, books and periodicals, government, media, trade associations, universities, institutes and banks.

Even if the secondary research obtained turns out to be insufficient, it should assist researchers to further define the public relations research problem or opportunity, or to highlight some aspects of the research that need careful consideration. Furthermore, if the secondary research is unable to answer the research questions, researchers should not automatically move on to primary research, which is usually costly. Researchers should first estimate the value of the information that needs to be obtained. If the benefit gained by the research will be greater than the cost, then researchers could pursue primary research. If, however, the cost of conducting the primary research is greater than the benefit sought, researchers should think twice about conducting it and consider using only secondary data. This process is illustrated in figure 8.2.

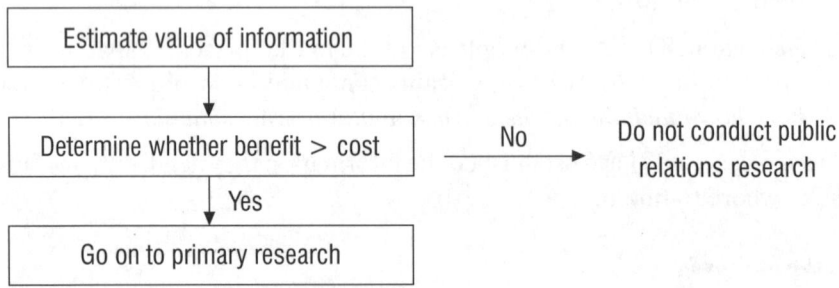

Figure 8.2 Determination of whether or not to conduct primary research

(*Source:* Adapted from Aaker et al., 1998:43)

Once researchers have established that the benefit outweighs the cost of the primary research, they could proceed with the gathering of primary data. This is usually more complicated than the gathering of secondary data. Researchers should first decide on a primary research method.

Step 5: Select a primary research method

As mentioned before, primary research is research that is gathered for the first time to solve a specific public relations problem or to utilise an opportunity. During the research process, primary research begins when secondary research is insufficient to answer the research problem or to utilise the opportunity (step 5), and ends when the information has been collected (step 7).

Broadly, researchers have three primary research methods. No particular method is the best in all cases. Depending on the public relations problem or opportunity, no method, or one, two or many methods may be appropriate.[26] Thus, it is safe to say that there is no right or better research method. The decision to use a specific method depends on the public relations problem or opportunity, as well as the resources available to researchers to conduct the research.

The three different primary research methods are observational research, experimental research and survey research.

Observational research

Observational research is descriptive research that monitors respondents' actions without direct interaction. In other words, researchers watch people and situations. The research can be done either by a machine or a person. Observational research can either be structured or unstructured, disguised or undisguised, direct or indirect, and natural or contrived. Observational research is used, for example, to determine how customers react to a public relations message by observing their physical responses to the message.

Experimental research

Experimental research is conducted research that examines whether one variable causes or determines the value of another variable. Here, one variable (or more) is changed by the researcher, while the effects of the change(s) on another variable are observed. In other words, researchers test something in controlled conditions. This can either be done in a laboratory or by conducting field research. Experimental research is usually used when, for example, an organisation runs a public relations campaign or programme to determine whether or not customer perceptions of an organisation will improve.

Survey research

Survey research is research in which an interviewer interacts with respondents to obtain facts, opinions and attitudes. It is mostly done in a structured manner by means of a formal questionnaire. Survey research can be conducted by means of researchers moving from door to door, intercepting respondents in a mall, having personal interviews with respondents, phoning respondents, mailing questionnaires to respondents, or using the Internet.

When a primary research method has been selected, researchers should decide whether or not to gather the information by means of a questionnaire. For example, conducting research by means of unstructured observation does not require a questionnaire. However, survey research that is conducted by means of door-to-door interviewing does require a questionnaire. The design of the questionnaire will be influenced by the type of research conducted (that is exploratory, descriptive or causal), as well as by the means of conducting the research (that is observation, experiments or survey research).

Once researchers have determined the best research method to gather the information they need, they should also consider who should be part of the investigation. This is referred to as a research frame.

Step 6: Determine the research frame[27]

A *research frame* refers to all the elements from which information can be gathered to solve a public relations problem or opportunity. When conducting primary research, it is important that researchers select respondents who represent all the elements (the total group of people) from whom the information is needed, better known as the *population*.

Depending on the problem or opportunity under investigation, researchers will either conduct the research by means of a census or by using a sample. A *census* is the obtaining of data from or about every member of the population of interest. The national census held in 2001 is a good example of a census. All South Africans were part of the survey. A *sample* refers to a subset of the population of interest. Since census research is costly and complicated, researchers usually draw a sample of the population under consideration.

During this stage of the research process, therefore, researchers should first determine who is to be sampled, then how large a sample is needed, and finally how the sampling units will be selected.

Sample frame

When researchers decide on who should be sampled, it is important to select respondents who will represent the population of interest. If, for example, a research study is conducted to determine whether a specific clothing organisation meets the needs of its customers, the sample frame could not be determined by using the telephone book, since not all of the organisation's customers will be listed there. However, if the same clothing organisation wishes to determine whether or not it gives good service to its customers, it might consider using the account holders as a sample frame. The delivering of accounts on time is also a service, and account holders will be able to comment on the organisation's overall service where non-account holders cannot.

Sample size

The size of the sample is also an important consideration for researchers. *Sample size* refers to how many respondents should be included in the investigation. The size of the sample drawn affects the quality and generalisation of the data. If the sample is too small, the data obtained may not be representative of the population. However, big samples may be too costly.

Selection of sampling method

Researchers have two main alternatives when deciding on the selection of a sample. As illustrated in figure 8.3 on the next page, researchers can draw a sample by means of probability sampling or non-probability sampling. *Probability sampling* occurs when all the subsets of the population have a known non-zero chance of being selected. In other words, all elements have an equal chance of being part of the research. Probability sampling methods include simple random sampling and cluster sampling. With *simple random sampling*, each element in the population has a known and equal chance of being selected in the sample and each element is selected independently from another. With *cluster sampling*, the population is divided into mutually exclusive and collectively exhaustive clusters or subgroups, after which certain clusters are selected for the sample. The researcher includes all of the elements in each cluster.

Non-probability sampling occurs when subsets of the population have little or no chance of being selected in the sample. In other words, elements of the population do not have an equal chance of being selected in the sample. Methods of non-probability sampling include convenience sampling and judgement sampling. In *convenience sampling* the researcher selects the elements. Often the respondents are in the right place at the right time when the sample is drawn. *Judgement sampling* is a form of sampling where elements are selected based on the researcher's judgement.

The determination of the sample frame, the size of the sample, and the way in which the sample is drawn, depend on the nature of the study, as well as on resources available to the researcher. Once the research frame has been determined by the researcher, the gathering of data can begin.

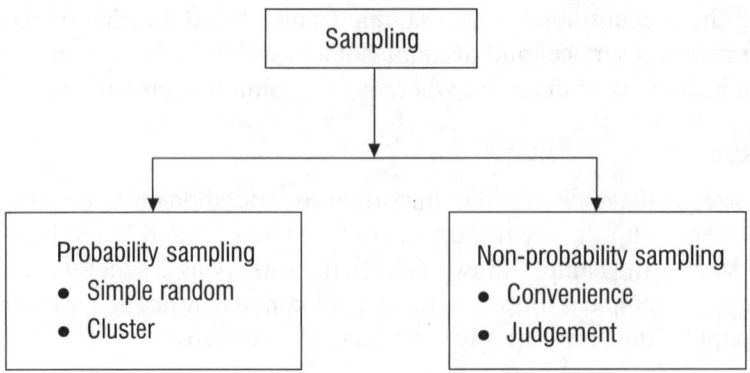

Figure 8.3 Methods of sampling

Step 7: Gather the data[28]

In this stage of the process, the researcher actually collects the data. The survey methodology is finally put into practice and research instruments are completed by fieldworkers. Supervisors have the responsibility of controlling the quality of the fieldwork.

Although fieldworkers are trained and supervised during the collection of the information, possible errors may still occur. These are referred to as non-sampling errors. Non-sampling errors can be attributed to factors other than sampling errors, and may include the following:

▲ the selection of the wrong sample elements to interview

▲ securing subjects who refuse to participate or are not home when the interviewer arrives

▲ interviewing subjects who intentionally give out wrong information

▲ hiring interviewers who cheat and fill out fictitious survey questionnaires.

Since non-sampling errors cannot be measured, researchers should be aware of the sources of these errors. This will enable them to take appropriate steps to limit the occurrence of these errors, for example by hiring fieldworkers with a good track record. Once researchers have gathered the information, it needs to be processed – in the next stage of the public relations research process.

Step 8: Process the data[29]

During this phase of the public relations research process, the data obtained in the primary research phase needs to be converted into a format that will answer public relations management's questions. The data structures should therefore be transformed into information that can be communicated to management.

When data is processed, it is first prepared and then analysed. *Data preparation* is the process of converting data from questionnaires so that it can be read and manipulated by computer software.[30] During data preparation, the data is validated, edited, coded, entered and cleaned. This means that the number or letter codes on the questionnaire are assigned to represent a particular response to each question in the questionnaire. The data is then transcribed or keypunched into a computer by using statistical computer software such as the SASS programme or Microsoft Excel.

Once the data has been entered into the computer, it should be analysed. When data is analysed, it can be tabulated by means of, for example, frequency tables or cross-tabulations. *Tabulation* refers to the simple process of counting the number of observations (cases) that are classified into certain categories. Various statistical tests, such as significant testing, can also be performed. By tabulating the data and conducting statistical tests, researchers can interpret and draw conclusions from the mass of collected data.

If researchers have conducted secondary research and found it to be sufficient because the information gathered solved the problem or utilised the opportunity, then this stage of the public relations research process could still not be overlooked. Researchers still need to process the secondary data by means of tabulations, which make it easier for them to draw conclusions and offer recommendations in the final stage of reporting research findings.

Step 9: Report the research findings

In this phase of the process, researchers should interpret the information and draw conclusions so that they can communicate the findings to the decision makers. A report should then be prepared to formally communicate the conclusions and recommendations to the public relations decision makers.

In the public relations research report, the research process used to conduct the research should be included. Researchers can also make use of tables and graphics to clearly illustrate the findings. In brief, the report should consist of the following:[31]

▲ **A comprehensive explanation of why the research was conducted.** Researchers should motivate why the research was done and give a brief problem statement.

▲ **Research objectives.** Here the main objectives, as well as some secondary research objectives, should be explained.

▲ **A detailed explanation of how the research was conducted.** Methodological aspects, such as how both the secondary and primary research was collected, the sampling procedure and the analytical procedures used in the research, should be discussed.

▲ **A presentation of the research findings.** The research findings can be presented in various tables, cross-tables and graphics.

▲ **Conclusions and recommendations.** Here it is important to show a linkage between the research findings and the conclusions and recommendations drawn from the information. The conclusions and recommendations should not be the opinions of the researchers, but should be supported by the findings of the research.

Researchers could also consider an oral presentation of the research findings. Whatever the policy of the organisation in terms of the communication of research findings, it is important that the findings be communicated to decision makers.

Public relations research in practice: Anglo Alpha Cement

The end of government-sanctioned cement in 1996 presented Anglo Alpha Cement with a need to re-fashion its image as part of a more open society. Gilmark Communications was entrusted with the task of communicationg a new identity, including a new name, for the organisation. Co-ordination advertising, sponsorships and other publicity were all part of the public relations campaign.

Independent research has indicated impressive results from this campaign. Alpha was seen, for example, to be the cement organisation that showed the most initiative in the marketplace, and which best recognised the value of its customers.

(*Source:* Adapted from the *Financial Mail*, 12 September 1997)

To explore possible paths that the research process can take, researchers need some background information throughout the process. Thus, although the research process is formally conducted to gather information to solve a problem or utilise an opportunity, some informal research is also done throughout the process to ensure that the research process follows the right path. Before the steps in the research process are discussed, therefore, the different types of research that researchers can use to conduct formal and/or informal research during the research process should be taken into consideration.

Forms of public relations research

Public relations research is usually rather simple. It can be used to investigate the organisation's environment, to determine public views and opinions, to plan and develop new strategies, and much more. There are different ways of conducting research in public relations.

Public opinion research

Public opinion research investigates people's opinions about an organisation and why they view it in a certain way. Specific stakeholders such as employees or customers can be targeted, and research can be useful in evaluating the effectiveness of the organisation's public relations strategy.

Image surveys

Image surveys determine people's attitudes towards the organisation, its services, prices, employees and practices.[32] They also determine the familiarity of the organisation and its reputation. Public relations practitioners can use this information to determine how effective messages are, and to better the organisation's image.

Needs and perception surveys

Needs and perception surveys are used to develop new public relations campaigns or programmes, or to improve or modify existing ones. Employees, customers, the media, etc. are normally targeted, and these surveys are repeated over time to determine the effectiveness of changed strategies.

Focus-group research

Focus-group research uses a group of seven to ten participants, chosen from the target public, who discuss ideas, products, issues or messages that are of interest to the researcher.[33] A qualified moderator adds to the quality of the research by using active listening methods and initiating the discussion. Focus groups can assist the organisation to identify future problems and opportunities.

Media clipping services

Media clipping services are an important way of evaluating placements of public relations messages in the media. Clipping services allow the organisation to determine how much is being said/written about it, and to ascertain how many sent messages are actually placed. These services simply measure the quantity of messages about an organisation.

Content analysis

Content analysis determines what is said about an organisation in the media. Over time, the organisation can identify trends in media coverage that indicate emerging public issues, opinions, etc.[34] Content analysis measures the quality of the messages about the organisation in the media.

Formal public relations research is not the only option available to managers when decisions need to be made. A sound information system can assist managers to make timely and accurate decisions, provided they have access to such a system. Public relations information systems, and how managers can develop them, is the next focus in this chapter.

Information systems for public relations

Information systems (IS) for public relations assist public relations managers in their task of decision making. An IS is a planned combination of ways and methods for continuous gathering, filtering, storing and flow of relevant information for purposes of public relations decision making.[35] An IS has various characteristics, which include the following:[36]

▲ An IS can be complex, since it can address a wide range of public relations issues.

▲ It can draw on a wide variety of data sources.

▲ The contents of an IS are subject to cost-benefit considerations.

Furthermore, an IS also provides managers with different types of information. Broadly, there are three types of information that managers can obtain through an IS:[37]

▲ **Recurrent information.** This is information that is provided to managers on a continuous basis, and includes information from regular image polls or opinion surveys.

▲ **Monitoring information.** This refers to information that is derived from the regular scanning of certain sources, such as trade association publications.

▲ **Requested information.** This information is developed in response to specific requests by marketing managers. A manager might request the size of a specific market, which is currently not served by the organisation, or the reach of a new medium that has not been used before.

It is important that an information system within an organisation has information that is accurate, timely, adequate, available, relevant, easy accessible and with a low maintenance cost.

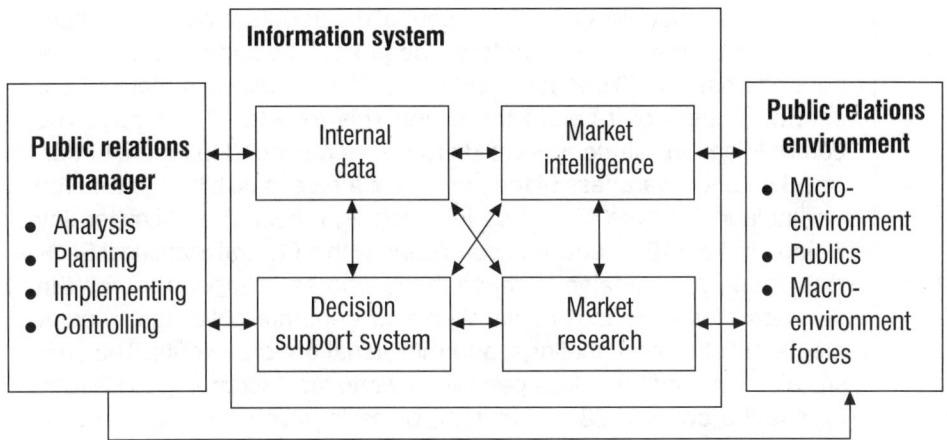

Figure 8.4 A public relations information system

(*Source:* Adapted from Burns and Bush, 1998:12)

From figure 8.4 it is clear that various components play a key role in the development of an IS. These components are internal data, such as previous records of public relations campaigns; market intelligence, which records information about the publics and the immediate environment; market research, which is formalised and follows the steps already discussed; and decision support systems, which are computers used to assist managers in routine decisions.

Information systems make it easier for public relations managers to obtain relevant and timely information for decision making.

Case study

How PR was used to boost the census

The publicity campaign for the 1997 population census was probably the biggest PR-driven marketing campaign ever undertaken in South Africa. As it turns out, it was also one of the best. Ultimately, more than R8 million was spent on it, of which roughly half was on advertising. As the leader of the consortium that won the contract, Baird's Communications was responsible for developing and implementing the campaign, which became the first recipient of the Prism Award for a PR consultancy practice. The award was devised by the consultants' chapter of the Public Relations Institute of South Africa, and sponsored by the *Financial Mail*. An exercise of this type presents huge challenges in a country such as South Africa, where literacy rates are often low, where many people in remote rural areas have never participated in a census before, and where the country's history has left a residue of suspicion among many people. Only 42 per cent of the populace had even heard of a census – any census – before it began but, by mid-census, awareness had risen to 73 per cent. And as for SA Census '96, a mere 17 per cent had heard of it before the event. This rose to 70 per cent. The communications strategy, says Baird's, was designed to create understanding and awareness of the benefits of the census. It began with the official launch of the 'Count us in' campaign, hosted by Minister Jay Naidoo in April 1996, and was concluded with a Central Statistical Services 'mop-up' campaign to reach those who had slipped through the net. Activities included media events to generate coverage, regular media bulletins and briefings, and ministerial endorsements. The census also covered homeless people – a world first, according to Baird's. Across the country, 33 events took place in which homeless people were enumerated and then provided with a celebration and food and warmth.

(*Source:* Adapted from the *Financial Mail*, 24 October 1997)

Conclusion

In this chapter we have looked at the research process and how scientific research methods can be beneficial to the public relations practitioner. There is little doubt that the modern public relations practitioner needs to utilise research and the resulting information in order to make better public relations decisions.

Questions for self-evaluation

1. Explain why public relations research is important to public relations practitioners.

2. Explain the public relations research process.

3. Evaluate the different methods of primary research.

4. Describe in detail the various forms of public relations research.

5. Explain what information systems are, and why they are important to public relations practitioners.

6. In the case study, explain how information systems for public relations played a vital role in boosting the census.

Endnotes

1   Based on Burns, AC and Bush, RF 1998. *Marketing Research*. (2 Ed.) Upper
    Saddle River, New Jersey: Prentice Hall:4; McDaniel, C and Gates, R
    2001. *Marketing Research Essentials*. (3 Ed.) Cincinnati, Ohio: South West-
    ern College:5; and Zikmund, WG 2000. *Exploring Marketing Research*. (6
    Ed.) London: Dryden:3.

2   Gilbert, A and Churchill, JR 2001. *Marketing Research*. (4 Ed.) Orlando,
    Florida: Dryden:7.

3   Ross, R 1977. *The Management of Public Relations*. New York: Wiley:90.

4   Wilcox, DL; Ault, PH and Agee, WK 1989. *Public Relations, Strategies and
    Tactics*. (2 Ed.) New York: Harper & Row:147.

5   Lubbe, BA and Puth, C 1996. *Public Relations in South Africa*. Isando:
    Butterworth:115.

6   Grunig, JE 1992. *Excellence in Public Relations and Communication Man-
    agement*. New Jersey: Lawrence Erlbaum:186.

7   Lubbe and Puth, op. cit.:115.

8   Wilcox, Ault and Agee, op. cit.:148.

9   Malhotra, NK 1993. *Public Relations Research: An Applied Orientation*.
    London: Prentice Hall:25.

10 This section is adapted from Malhotra, op. cit.; Quee, WT 1999. *Public
    Relations Research*. Oxford: Butterworth Heinemann; and McDaniel, C
    and Gates, R 2001. *Public Relations Research Essentials*. (3 Ed.) Cincinnati,
    Ohio: South Western College.

11 Kroon, J (Ed.) 1995. *General Management*. (3 Ed.) Pretoria: Kagiso:143.

12 Strydom, JW (Ed.) 1999. *Introduction to Marketing*. (2 Ed.) Kenwyn:
    Juta:106.

13 Zikmund, op. cit.:117.

14 Gilbert, A and Churchill, JR 2001. *Public Relations Research*. (4 Ed.)
    Orlando, Florida: Dryden:37.

15 Ibid.

16 This section is based on Aaker, DA; Kumar, V and Day, GS. 1998. *Public
    Relations Research*. (6 Ed.) New York: John Wiley & Sons; Cant, MC;
    Strydom, JW and Jooste, CJ 1999. *Essentials of Marketing*. Kenwyn: Juta;
    Steyn, AGW; Smit, CF; Du Toit, SHC and Strasheim, 1999. *Modern Statis-
    tics in Practice*. Pretoria: Van Schaick; Quee, op. cit.; and McDaniel and
    Gates, op. cit.

17 Gilbert and Churchill, op. cit.:37.

18 This section is based on Malhotra, op. cit.; Quee, op. cit.; and McDaniel and Gates, op. cit.:65.

19 This section is based on Malhotra, op. cit.

20 Quee, op. cit.; and McDaniel and Gates, op. cit.:66.

21 This section is adapted from Aaker, Kumar and Day, op. cit.; Cant, Strydom and Jooste, op. cit.; Martins, JH; Loubser, M and Van Wyk, H de J (Eds.) *Public Relations Research: A South African Approach.* Pretoria: Unisa; McDaniel and Gates, op. cit.; and Strydom, JW (Ed.) 1999. *Introduction to Marketing.* (2 Ed.) Kenwyn: Juta.

22 *The Concise Oxford Dictionary* (9 Ed.) Oxford: Clarendon Press.

23 Cant, Strydom and Jooste, op. cit.

24 Martins, Loubser and Van Wyk, op. cit.

25 Kotler, A and Armstrong, G. 2001.

26 Malhotra, op. cit.:185.

27 This section is adapted from McDaniel and Gates, op. cit.; Hair, JF; Bush, RP and Ortinau, DJ 2000. *Public Relations Research: A Practical Approach for the New Millennium.* Singapore: McGraw-Hill; Burns and Bush, op. cit.

28 This section is adapted from McDaniel and Gates, op. cit.; Quee, op. cit.; and Burns and Bush, op. cit.

29 This section is adapted from McDaniel and Gates, op. cit.; Quee, op. cit.; Malhotra, op. cit.; and Zikmund, op. cit.

30 Hair, Bush and Ortinau, op. cit.:480.

31 McDaniel and Gates, op. cit.

32 Lubbe and Puth, op. cit.:118.

33 Grunig, op. cit.:192.

34 Grunig, op. cit.:199.

35 Martins, Loubser and Van Wyk, op. cit.:13.

36 Sudman, S and Blair, E 1998. *Marketing Research: A Problem-solving Approach.* London: McGraw Hill:31.

37 Tull, DS and Hawkins, DI 1993. *Marketing Research: Measurement and Method.* (6 Ed.) Upper Saddle River, New Jersey: Prentice Hall:29; and Martins, Loubser and Van Wyk, op. cit.:15.

Section 3

Current Issues under Scrutiny in the Field of Public Relations

Section 3, the final section, deals with one specific current issue under scrutiny in the field of pubic relations, namely ethics and how it relates to public relations and the practice of public relations in organisations and society.

Chapter 9 begins with a contextualisation of the concept of ethics and describes the relationship between public relations and ethics. The chapter then describes the ancient rhetoric of Plato, Aristotle and Isocrates, and persuasive discourse as the roots of public relations ethics. Various contemporary approaches to public relations ethics are also discussed. The conclusive remarks of this chapter investigate ethics, public relations and responsibility, as well as the complexity of the role of public relations in society.

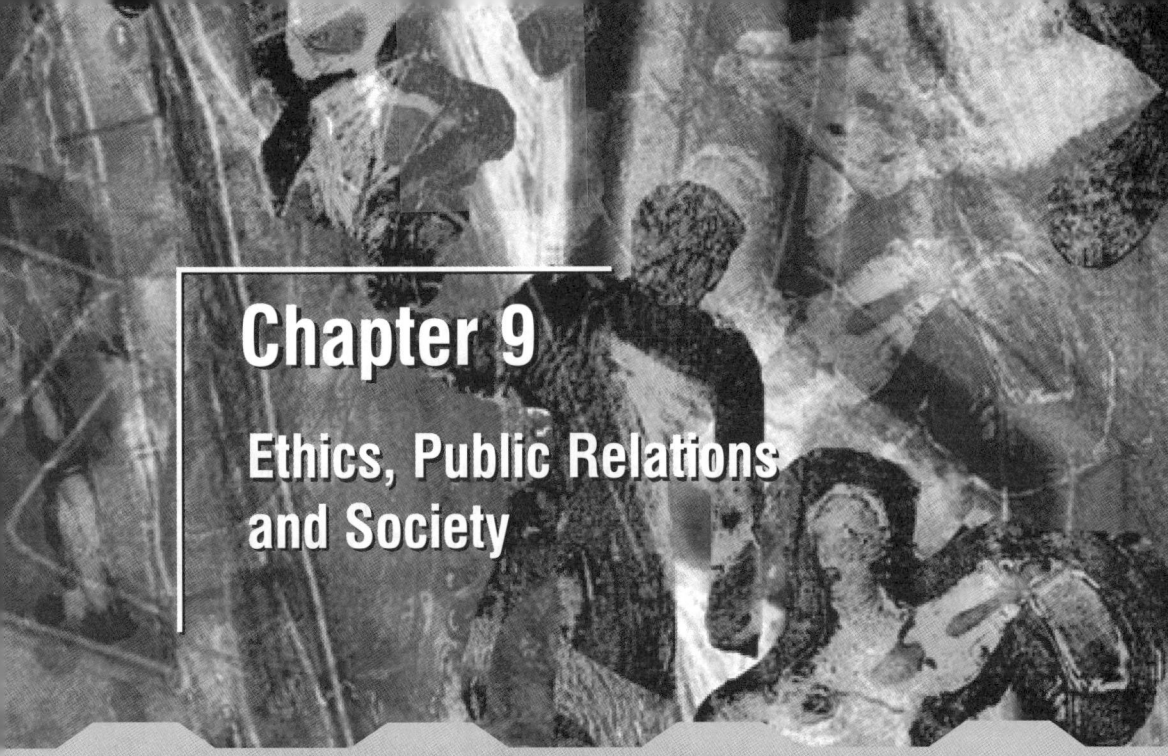

Chapter 9

Ethics, Public Relations and Society

LEARNING OUTCOMES

After studying this chapter, you should be able to:

▲ define and contextualise ethics

▲ describe the relationship between public relations and ethics

▲ discuss the ancient rhetoric of Plato, Aristotle and Isocrates and persuasive discourse as the roots of modern public relations ethics

▲ give a synopsis of the contemporary approaches to public relations ethics

▲ scrutinise the concepts of ethics, public relations and professional responsibility

▲ investigate the complexity of public relations in society.

The truth is rarely pure, and never simple.

(*Oscar Wilde*)

Introduction

The issue of effectively integrating ethics into business decision making is a major area of debate confronting today's corporate leaders and public relations practitioners. Persistent media reports of unethical behaviour by corporations, business executives and government officials highlight the need for effective solutions to the ethics dilemma. The ethics dilemma derives from the perceived conflict between the traditional corporate objective of profit maximisation and the overall desire for increased social welfare. Although ethically responsible business practices are generally desired, opinions about what these practices are, and how they should be encouraged, are diverse. The complexity of the current business environment complicates the development and implementation of resolutions to ethical issues facing industry (Klein, 1992).

A well-considered framework to integrate profit maximisation and social welfare maximisation is necessary to obtain an optimal solution for diminishing unethical actions. Two key factors must be included in this framework:

1. There must be clear understanding of what constitutes acceptable ethical behaviour.
2. There must be an effective mechanism for ensuring that the organisation follows ethical practices.

Defining and contextualising ethics

A contextual definition of *ethics* and *ethical behaviour* is necessary before an effective mechanism to enforce ethical behaviour can be developed. Ethics may be interpreted as the perception by publics of an organisation's standards of behaviour. Ethics involve a moral judgement of the consequences of what the organisation and its employees say and do (Mersham, Rensburg & Skinner, 1995).

Traditionally, an ethic is value-based and stems from socio-economic contexts. The major theoretical approaches to ethics frequently conflict, and the evaluation of ethics may depend more on the framework than the issue.

The *Kantian theory of ethics* involves a *normative ethic*. At a minimum, this ethic is one that all rational people would find acceptable after carefully considering the pros and cons of an issue. This normative approach implies ethical behaviour focused on the rights of others. This approach to ethical decision making allows considerable discretion, as it relies on value-based beliefs and attitudes. Therefore, even within the normative approach, inconsistent decisions can be made about the ethical nature of a business decision.

The *utilitarian theory of ethics* implies that consequences of actions determine ethical behaviour. This approach suggests that outcomes drive the decision, and being responsible for the results of business decisions will promote ethical behaviour. Still, some decisions have unintended consequences, not considered by the decision process. Unethical actions may result from decisions that were initially believed ethical. Conversely, ethical actions may follow unethical decisions.

The *contractual theory of ethics* relies on actual or hypothetical contracts and laws to determine and monitor ethical behaviour. Although the contractual approach is considered more suitable to the general business framework, it relies on external enforcement of the contracts.

The above brief discussion shows that major ethical theories are not precise, and that enforcement of ethical actions relies on individual judgement. Even individuals who are highly trained in the philosophy of ethics do not agree about the application of ethics. The distinction between ethical and unethical behaviour is based on the cultural milieu and is a byproduct of social norms. Therefore, it is extremely difficult to determine ethical behaviour. Mintzburg (1983:50) discusses the diversity and changing nature of social norms that derive from new economic and social situations: 'Every society or culture contains a whole set of social norms, based on its particular history, religions, philosophies, and the nature of its people and the problems they have faced ... While social norms may appear to remain stable being based on long traditions, in fact they are in a continual state of evaluation.'

Conflicting ethical decisions may also arise from conflicting sets of social norms within the same culture. For example, an organisation obtains preliminary test results which suggest that contact with a specific product on their assembly line may result in a low probability of damage to future offspring. The organisation may decide that the ethically responsible action is to remove all women of child-bearing age from contact with the assembly line. However, ethically responsible behaviour prohibits the organisation from denying work based on gender or age. The decision is no longer one of distinguishing ethical from unethical behaviour, but of determining which ethically relevant factor takes precedence.

Before ethical behaviour can be enforced, there must be a clear understanding of *what* should be enforced. Where conflict between organisational and societal objectives exists, the implementation of an effective solution for making ethically charged decisions becomes even more complex.

An effective solution for ethical decision making must consider barriers to implementation besides understanding the nature of ethical behaviour. For example, multinational organisations reside in multiple societies, each with different cultural biases. What is the appropriate method of ensuring that ethical practices are undertaken in a diverse cultural arena? What mechanism exists to guard against the imposition of a particular political view on an organisation in the name of ethics? What power rests with the professional ethicist to settle the conflict between internal profit and power and external social responsibility?

In summary, ethical organisations and people make ethical decisions. Because some ethical decisions must be based on societal norms, business decisions will reflect the ethical tolerances of the environment in which they operate. A 'Big Brother' solution will not resolve an ethical dilemma. Government, through laws and regulation, may assist in establishing the meaning of ethics. However, an effective solution to the dilemma must contain a mechanism in which ethical considerations become a central part of operations. A key component in ensuring ethical performance by modern organisations is the integration of moral reasoning throughout the organisation. Although this task is more difficult than passing a law, the integration diminishes the conflict between ethical practices and acceptable profits. Some organisations in the United States have already undertaken this integration and have developed a comprehensive approach to ethical decision making.

A report published by The Business Roundtable (1988), entitled 'Corporate ethics: A prime business asset', analysed corporate information about ethics and programmes for implementing ethical policies and conduct. This report could serve as a basis for developing a framework for ethical decision making that is both practical and effective. The primary lessons derived from this study are as follows:

▲ Top management must be committed to ethical conduct and must provide constant leadership in attending to and renewing organisational values.

▲ Carrying out ethical behaviour requires a comprehensive ethical perspective that employees on all levels of the organisation understand and use. The code of ethics cannot cover all situations but assists in guiding the judgements and consciences of people making specific recommendations.

▲ A vigorous and continuously renewed process of implementing ethical behaviour is essential.

▲ Employees at all levels of the organisation must be involved and committed to ethical performance.

▲ Results of programmes must continually be assessed.

A successful method of resolving an ethical dilemma should use a practical framework for decision making. This framework should blend the successful experiences of modern organisations with organisational, social and philosophical theories. Externally imposed ethical control through an outside agent is not an effective solution. The ambiguity of what constitutes ethical behaviour makes external control of this behaviour difficult, if not impossible. Problems with implementing the legal requirements for a professional ethics agent also make this type of control impractical. To be effective, the framework must be integrated into the corporate structure of the organisation and supported at all levels. The Business Roundtable provides information on business experiences that could serve as a foundation for developing this framework.

Public relations and ethics

Since the inception of public relations as a discipline and practice, scholars and practitioners alike have battled to come to grips with the ethical considerations of the field. Throughout the brief history of public relations, the partisan efforts of some practitioners have drawn criticism and raised questions regarding the ethical conduct of those who call themselves *public relations professionals*. In some cases, the criticism may be justified because of unprincipled practices. Just like weapons, strategic communication can be used for legal and ethical purposes, as well as for illegal and unethical purposes. Often, however, the criticism results from either a misunderstanding of, or lack of appreciation for, the functions of public relations. The field has always experienced difficulty in defining what public relations professionals do, and in justifying their value and worth to the business environment and society. The result is that public relations practitioners continue to be plagued by charges of unethical conduct.

This current state of the industry is the result of several factors:

▲ The parameters for public relations work have not yet been – and perhaps cannot be – clearly defined. Confusion about the role that public relations practitioners should perform creates further confusion regarding the ethical standards that should define public relations practices.

▲ Public relations has not fully extricated itself from its journalistic or marketing roots. Many still believe that because public relations evolved from journalism – and is still taught primarily in colleges and schools of journalism and communication – public relations practitioners should share their journalistic counterparts' passion for objectivity. When measured by that yardstick, public relations practitioners will never make the grade. Although advocates can be fair, they are seldom objective.

▲ There are no clear and established minimum standards for the practice of public relations. Practitioners or consultants are not required to qualify for a licence before they start practising as consultants or working as practitioners in organisations. In the absence of such regulation, it is left to the industry itself to define standards of performance. Although professional associations across the world have done well in developing codes of conduct for their members, the codes stop short of providing a theoretical basis for ethical decision making.

▲ The values and ethics of the organisations represented by public relations practitioners are often confused with the values and ethics of the individuals who provide counsel on such matters. When an organisation is the subject of public criticism for perceived irresponsible behaviour, the public relations practitioner shares the blame – regardless of his or her involvement in or knowledge of alleged bad acts. This *guilt by association* has become increasingly detrimental to the public relations industry as more and more organisations fail to meet public expectations.

As the consciences of their organisations, public relations practitioners play an important role in corporate ethical leadership. This suggests that corporate ethics is contingent, in large measure, on the ethics of public relations managers. Pearson (1989:128) substantiates this argument: 'Corporate public relations departments, to the extent that they are concerned with how a corporation communicates with its publics, are charged with the responsibility of managing the moral dimension of corporate conduct. This is the core ethical responsibility of public relations from which all other obligations follow.'

Although a number of theories of, or approaches to, public relations ethics have been advanced, few have been fully developed. It can also be assumed that public relations practitioners and educators have different views about the real-world relevance of these approaches to public relations ethics (Pratt, 1994:70). A review of public relations textbooks led one scholar to conclude that: 'There is no accepted conceptual framework from which to study public relations ethics' (Bivins, 1989:39).

To enable public relations practitioners, as strategic communication managers, to respond ethically to potentially unethical organisational actions, scholars and practitioners constantly need to seek an appropriate approach to ethics in public relations. To be able to embark on this road, it is useful to consider the etymology of ethics as rooted in classical rhetoric.

Ancient rhetoric and persuasive discourse and their influence on public relations ethics

As a relatively young profession, public relations seeks a realistic ethics foundation. A continuing debate in public relations has pitted *journalistic/objectivity ethics* against *advocacy ethics*, which may be more appropriate in an adversarial society. As the journalistic/objectivity influence has waned, the debate has evolved, setting the advocacy/adversarial foundation against the *two-way symmetrical model of public relations*, which seeks to build consensus and holds that an organisation itself, not an opposing public, sometimes needs to change to build a productive relationship with its publics (Marsh, 2001:78).

A similar battle between adversarial advocacy and symmetry occurred during the emergence of rhetoric in Athens in the fourth century BC – encapsulated by the work of Plato, Aristotle and Isocrates. Plato and Aristotle favoured adversarial/advocacy rhetoric, whereas Isocrates favoured a symmetrical rhetoric. History shows that Isocrates's symmetrical rhetoric was clearly more effective than its adversarial/advocacy rivals. Recent studies of the two-way symmetrical model concur, indicating that it may well be the most effective foundation for public relations ethics (Marsh, 2001:78).

An individual can barely live through one day without being exposed to some form of persuasive discourse, the main concern of rhetoric. It is therefore easy to assume that rhetoric is the art governing those human relationships that are concluded in the medium of spoken, written and electronic words (Corbett, 1990:164).

The Athens of Plato, Aristotle and Isocrates (400–300 BC) wrestled with developing an acceptable ethical framework for a new art of discourse called *rhetoric*. The comparison to the *new rhetoric* or public relations as it is known today, is not that far-fetched: public relations scholars have long recognised the debt of public relations to Greek rhetoric. In his history of public relations, Cutlip (1994:xi) held that 'persuasive communication is as old as Plato's *Republic*'. Grunig (1992:68) noted that Aristotle is 'often considered the first public relations practitioner'. Seitel (1998:25–26) wrote that the ethical quandaries of public relations might well have begun with the practice of Greek rhetoric in the fifth century BC.

In *Phaedrus*, Plato foreshadowed Baker's (1999) analysis of ethical foundations by outlining three models of rhetoric. In his earlier *Gorgias*, Plato bitterly attacked rhetoric for its immorality, for being 'some device of persuasion which will make one appear to those who do not know to know better than those who know'. In *Phaedrus*, Plato offers an ethical framework for an acceptable rhetoric. Ostensibly about lovers, the three speeches in the *Phaedrus* establish three possible ethical frameworks for rhetoric. These are respectively the *non-lover*, the *evil lover* and the *noble lover*.

The non-lover model

This ironic model is introduced when Socrates repeats a speech by Lysias, who maintains that the best lover is one who does not actually love his partner. Therefore, his actions (the lovers of the dialogue were exclusively male) are disinterested; the relationship is not worth striving for. Weaver (1953:7) maintained that Plato equates this relationship to 'semantically purified speech that communicates abstract intelligence without impulsion. It is a simple instrumentality, showing no affection for the object of its symbolizing and incapable of inducing bias in the hearer'.

This model corresponds to the *public information model of public relations* in which organisations deliver objective information to publics that request it. The organisation makes no other attempt at relationship building. Therefore, the model is often ineffective for public relations. Plato clearly rejects the disinterested non-lover model as an ethical foundation for rhetoric (Marsh, 2001).

The evil lover model

This model encompasses the rhetoric that Plato condemned in the *Gorgias*. The evil lover creates a relationship in which he seeks superiority. Therefore, he naturally tries to make the beloved inferior to himself in every respect. He is pleased if the beloved has intellectual limitations because they have the effect of making him manageable. In brief, the lover is not motivated by benevolence towards the beloved, but by selfish appetite. The speech is on the single theme of exploitation (Weaver, 1953:10–11).

This model corresponds to the *two-way asymmetrical model of public relations*, a model that promotes advocacy and selective truth.

The noble lover model

This is the model that Plato offers as the framework for an ethical rhetoric. The noble lover strives towards improving his beloved. In the words of Plato, noble lovers exhibit no jealousy or meanness toward the loved one, but endeavour by every means in their power to lead him to the likeness of the god whom they honour.

Plato accepted the noble lover model. Aristotle, though, rejected the noble lover model in favour of the evil lover. Isocrates rejected the solutions of both his contemporaries, opting instead for a new definition of the noble lover model (Marsh, 2001).

From the beginning, then, there were in ancient times three characteristic and divergent views on rhetoric. There was the *moral philosophical view* of Plato. There was the *philosophical scientific view* of Aristotle, who tried to see the thing as it really was in itself, and who endeavoured to advise a theory of rhetoric without moral praise or blame for it. Then there was the *practical educational view* of the rhetoricians, from Isocrates to Cicero to Quintilin (Marsh, 2001).

Because Isocratean rhetoricians seek unification and consensus, and because they cannot be certain of a divinely ordained best course of action, they consider the interests and arguments of others in a debate. This is more along the lines of the *two-way symmetrical model of public relations.*

Isocrates's distance from Aristotle can best be seen in his concept of *ethos.* While Aristotle believed that only the appearance of character created during a speech mattered, Isocrates took a much more comprehensive view in his book, *Antidosis*: 'The man who wishes to persuade people will not be negligent as to the matter of character; no, on the contrary, he will apply himself above all to establish a most honourable name among his fellow-citizens; for who does not know that words carry greater conviction when spoken by men of good repute than when spoken by men who live under a cloud, and that the argument which is made by a man's life is of more weight than that which is furnished by words? Therefore, the stronger a man's desire to persuade his hearers, the more zealously will he strive to be honourable and to have the esteem of his fellow-citizens.'

Far then from being an adversarial evil lover whose sole motivation in studying rhetoric is to find the effective means of persuasion, the Isocratean rhetorician seeks to attain objectives by building relationships in which both parties win. Isocrates's motivation to infuse rhetoric with morality may have been his realisation, born of enlightened self-interest, of the persuasive value of true integrity (Welch, 1990:123). Whatever his motivation, though, the results of his philosophy are clear and dramatic. As Marrou (1956: 89) declared: 'In the hands of Isocrates rhetoric is gradually transformed into ethics.'

Isocrates created a moral, symmetrical rhetoric that proved to be more effective, immediately and historically, than its asymmetrical rivals in classical Greece. Were we to cast it as an ethics foundation for modern public relations, it would – at worst – be an enlightened self-interest model and – at best – a social responsibility model. Recent studies support what Isocrates demonstrated and, two millennia later, the Research Foundation of the International Association of Business Communicators (IABC) posited that two-way symmetrical public relations, with its idealistic social role, is the most effective model of public relations. Deatherage and Hazelton's (1998) survey of the Public Relations Society of America members concluded that practitioners who use two-way symmetry build more productive relationships than those who do not (Marsh, 2001).

Public relations need not be adversarial. It need not adopt ethics of asymmetrical advocacy. It can, instead, function admirably by following the foundation of Isocratean rhetoric to form a genuine 'we' out of diversity (Poulakos, 1997:3).

Contemporary approaches to public relations ethics

A review follows of existing contemporary theories of, or approaches to, public relations ethics. They all have their strengths and weaknesses. The role of the public relations practitioner as a *professional* has special obligations attached to the professional status, and such status will influence public relations practice. Note that the contemporary approaches have much in common with the foundations laid down by the ancient rhetoricians.

Attorney adversary

According to this approach, public relations performs the socially necessary role of professional advocacy within the adversary process essential to free enterprise and competition. It is argued that, in the free market system, the public relations advocate functions in the same way as a lawyer who zealously represents his or her client in a court of law (Barney & Black, 1994:233).

▲ **Defence of this approach:** It has been suggested that the public have a responsibility to gather and evaluate information that is relevant to their lives and choices.

▲ **Criticism of this approach:** In a court of law, fairness is presumed. There is no such presumption, however, in the media-driven court of public opinion. This court operates without specific rules of evidence and procedure that, in law, are designed to prevent undue prejudice against either side. When opposing voices are silent or important information is withheld, how will the public obtain information that challenges an organisation's version of the truth? With access to only one version of the truth, how will the public be able to take responsible action?

Enlightened self-interest

According to this approach, '… businesses do well (financially) by doing good (ethically), and it is, therefore, in their bottom-line interest to engage in good deeds and ethical behaviour' (Baker, 1999:7). This standard would allow corporate decisions and actions to be presented as in the public interest, even if their ultimate motivation is the financial benefit of the organisation.

▲ **Defence of this approach:** It is suggested that this form of justification is similar to utilitarian reasoning, in which all of the options are weighed and the costs and benefits to all concerned parties are considered (Whalen, 1998:6).

▲ **Criticism of this approach:** There are several ethical problems here. Representing corporate actions based on 'corporate social responsibility' implies that actions are done out of a sense of duty rather than from selfish motives (L'Etang, 1994:117). Such public relations efforts treat their beneficiaries as mere means to the end of corporate image and profits (L'Etang, 1994:121). Also, representing the organisation's aims in terms of a duty or desire to benefit the community, rather than in terms of marketing strategy, may involve the public relations practitioner in blatant deception of the public (L'Etang, 1994:121). This approach would therefore be insufficient to guide the difficult ethical decisions that public relations practitioners have to make.

Community/communitarian/social responsibility

In contrast with enlightened self-interest, true social responsibility involves taking actions and instituting policies that are morally right for that reason alone, without an ulterior self-interested motive. It is based on values such as honesty, respect, fairness, the avoidance of harm, and justice in the distribution of the benefits and burdens of living together in a democratic society. Social responsibility, or social investment, means first that one recognises, accepts and acts on a general responsibility to those persons who and interests which will be impacted on by one's actions (Fitzpatrick & Gauthier, 2001).

▲ **Defence of this approach:** It would be difficult to find a public relations practitioner who disagreed with the concepts espoused in ethical approaches based on the need for enhanced social responsibility, good citizenship, and improved community relations. All of these concepts focus on the need for public relations to contribute to the betterment of both communities in which their clients and employees operate. Service to society is a pivotal aspect of this approach.

▲ **Criticism of this approach:** Although laudable, approaches to ethics based on the concept of social responsibility are particularly limiting in the effort to develop standards of practice in public relations because the primary focus is on the obligations of organisations, rather than on the ethical obligations of public relations practitioners. Is participation in philanthropic endeavours enough to meet an organisation's obligation to operate in the public interest? And is it the role of public relations to decide on such issues?

Sullivan's partisan values versus mutual values

In 1965, Albert Sullivan set forth a model for public relations that was later reviewed by Pearson (1989). This approach rests on what Sullivan defined as the technical, partisan and mutual values in public relations. *Mutual values* that reflect respect for human rights should be viewed as 'higher' than *partisan values* that can lead to too much commitment and too much obedience (Pearson, 1989:57). Under this approach, partisan values rest on concepts such as commitment, trust, loyalty, and obedience. Sullivan (1965) suggested that, although public relations practitioners' commitment to their organisation or client is important, many take their partisanship to extremes, relying too much on the views of the organisation while ignoring or minimising the viewpoints of others (Pearson, 1989).

▲ **Defence of this approach:** Sullivan certainly identified the thorniest ethical challenge for public relations practitioners, both in the past and now. Balancing the special interests of the organisations represented with those affected by these organisations is the issue that seems to defy resolution. Sullivan's rigorous rejection of zealous advocacy places him among many of today's scholars who call for increased attention to social responsibility on the part of both public relations practitioners and the organisations they serve.

▲ **Criticism of this approach:** An unanswered question is: 'When is it appropriate, if ever, for public relations practitioners to place the interests of others above the interests of the organisations they represent?' This approach does not provide a clear answer.

The two-way symmetrical approach

Previous chapters and this chapter have already referred to the *two-way symmetrical approach* to public relations. Grunig and Grunig (1996) felt that this approach might also be utilised in scrutinising the ethics of public relations. To recap then, this approach rests on principles of mutuality and offers an ethical description of the role of the public relations practitioner. In this approach, public relations practitioners 'play key roles in adjusting or adapting behaviors of [organisational] dominant coalitions, thus bringing publics and dominant coalitions closer together' (Grunig & Grunig, 1996:6). This 'win-win' approach provides an ethical basis for public relations, they argued, because it 'provides a coherent framework for socially responsible practices'.

▲ **Defence of this approach:** Symmetrical public relations provides a forum for dialogue, discussion and discourse on issues about which people with different values generally reach different conclusions. As long as the dialogue is structured according to ethical rules, the outcome should be ethical – although not usually one that perfectly fits the value system of any party.

▲ **Criticism of this approach:** Because organisations most often set the 'rules', this approach raises concerns about the ethics of a process in which the power to establish the operating principles lies in the hands of one party. As Fitzpatrick and Gauthier (2001) indicate, this approach can also be criticised for going too far in requiring public relations practitioners to meet the needs of constituents or publics. As organisational advocates, public relations practitioners represent a particular point of view that may or may not be harmful to those influenced by it. Is the responsibility to ensure that mutual benefit is gained or is it, rather, to ensure that no harm results from an anticipated decision or action? How far should public relations practitioners go in counselling their clients and employers to address the needs of publics? Grunig and Grunig (1992:320) themselves remarked: 'Practitioners of the two-way symmetrical model are not completely altruistic; they also want to defend the interests of their employers – they have mixed motives.'

A normative approach to public relations ethics

Pearson (1989) developed an extensive approach to public relations ethics, based in large part on the theories of the German philosopher Jurgen Habermas (1984). In developing this approach to ethics, however, Pearson also used traditional philosophical theories of ethics and psychological theories of moral development, especially those of Kohlberg (1981) and Gilligan (1982).

Habermas's (1984) theory of ethics rests on his concept of an ideal communication situation – a situation characterised by dialogue. Participants agree on a system of rules to facilitate that dialogue. These rules constitute the formal aspects of ethics.

Pearson (1984:315) explains that people or organisations and publics that follow these rules will not always agree on practical decision making when they have different values or different concepts of what is good. In other words, they often will not agree on the practical aspects of ethics. He notes, just like Grunig and Grunig (1992), that people will have mixed motives – the conviction that they are right and the conviction that other people's opinions should be respected. An approach to ethics that combines 'moral conviction and tolerance' is needed. When people disagree about what is moral, therefore, they debate and attempt to persuade one another. Pearson (1989) states that what is right or wrong, true or false, can only be determined through dialogue and agreement. It cannot be determined only through the evidence of raw organisational data provided by one party or organisation.

Psychologists such as Kohlberg (1981) have shown that people must advance through several stages of moral development before developing the ability to take others into account by accepting the norm of reciprocity. Habermas (1984) and Gilligan (1982) argue that moral development has one more stage, a stage called *interactive competence* or the ability to engage in dialogue. At this stage, people base morality or responsibility not on rights, but rather on the development of a greater sense of interdependence and relationship.

The more ethically developed an individual or an organisation is, the more he, she or it uses the concepts of *reciprocity* and *symmetry* to decide what is moral. These two concepts are crucial components of the ethical world (Pearson, 1989:244). Pearson developed a *normative theory for public relations ethics* based on a premise and two moral imperatives:

▲ **Basic premise:** Ethics in public relations do not fundamentally ask whether it is right or wrong to tell the truth, steal clients from one another, accept free lunches or bribes, or provide information for insider trading, and so on. Rather, ethical public relations practice is more fundamentally a question of implementing and maintaining inter-organisational systems that question, discuss and validate these and other substantive ethical claims.

▲ **Basic moral imperatives:** It is a moral imperative to establish and maintain communication relationships with all publics affected by organisational action. It is also essential to improve the quality of these communication relationships. This is done by increasing the extent of dialogue. This means working towards role and rule identification, clarification and change so that measures of organisational and public understanding of, and agreement on, communication rules become increasingly positive.

According to Fitzpatrick and Gauthier (2001), all of the above-mentioned contemporary models of public relations ethics make significant contributions to an understanding of the ethical challenges encountered in the practice of public relations. However, for various reasons, each falls short of providing a universally acceptable philosophy on which standards of ethical public relations might be based. They then go on to propose what they perceive to be a more comprehensive approach to public relations ethics.

Towards a professional responsibility approach to public relations ethics

Wright (1989:3) observes: 'Central to the importance of ethics in American public relations is the reality that, most of the time, practitioners have the voluntary choice of whether to be ethical or not.' It can be safely assumed that this is the case for practitioners across the globe as well. This argument captures the need for the development of a philosophical foundation for ethical decision making in public relations. Public relations practitioners need some guidelines on which to judge the rightness of the decisions they make. They need ethical principles derived from the fundamental values that define their work as public relations professionals. They also need guidance in reconciling the potentially conflicting roles of the professional advocate and the social conscience.

Bivins (1989:120) poses the following question: 'How can a practitioner advocating a discrete point of view serve the interest of the greater public?' He then goes on to suggest four paradigms:

1. If every individual practising public relations acts in the best interests of his or her client, then the public interest will be served.

2. If, in addition to serving individual interests, an individual practising public relations serves public interest causes, then the public interest will be served.

3. If professionals assure that every individual in need of or desiring their services receives their services, then the public interest will be served.

4. If public relations as a profession improves the quality of debate over issues important to the public, then the public interest will be served.

Noting that none of the above provides the definitive answer, Bivins (1989:121) concludes that: 'In its dual role as mediator and advocate, public relations has the opportunity both to engage in and to encourage public debate. By doing so, it also has the opportunity, and the obligation, to lessen the obfuscation often surrounding the mere provision of information. It must develop clear guidelines and formal mechanisms by which issues important to society are clarified and presented to the public for open, democratic debate.'

Bivins's (1989) focus on the value of ethical communication to open public debate captures the essence of the social role of public relations. By providing voices for special interests, public relations contributes to the harmonisation of diverse points of view and, in so doing, promotes mutual understanding and peaceful coexistence among individuals and organisations.

An approach to public relations ethics based on professional responsibility to specific publics not only assists in resolving the ambiguity of such phrases as 'serve the public interest' and 'social responsibility', but also reflects what recent studies in the field have concluded – 'relationships ought to be at the core of public relations scholarship and practice' (Ledingham & Bruning, 2000:xiii). By emphasising the relationships between an organisation and its publics, rather than an organisation's relationship with or obligation to serve an intangible society, scholars and public relations practitioners can begin to define an organisation's ethical responsibility to its publics. Then only can the standards of performance appropriate to the ethical practice of public relations be defined.

The following three principles might provide the foundation for an approach to professional responsibility in public relations ethics:

1. **The comparison of harms and benefits:** Harms should be avoided or at least minimised, and benefits should be promoted at the least possible cost in terms of harms.

2. **Respect for persons:** Persons should be treated with respect and dignity.

3. **Distributive justice:** The benefits and burdens of any action or policy should be distributed as fairly as possible.

According to Fitzpatrick and Gauthier (2001), a professional responsibility approach to public relations ethics has advantages over other approaches partly because it attempts to reconcile the dual roles of the public relations practitioner as organisational advocate and public conscience for an organisation.

The ethical principles that form the philosophical foundation for the social responsibility approach may also provide more concrete guidelines than do other approaches in resolving ethical dilemmas caused by conflicting obligations to a variety of competing interests. These principles also suggest a series of questions that may assist the public relations practitioner in serving both as organisational advocate and public conscience in a morally responsible way.

Every public relations association across the globe has a code of conduct to guide their members to be professionally responsible. The code of conduct of the Public Relations Institute of Southern Africa (PRISA) can be found in table 9.1.

Declaration of principles

We base our professional principles on the fundamental value and dignity of the individual. We believe in and support the free exercise of human rights, especially freedom of speech, freedom of assembly and freedom of the media, which are essential to the practice of good public relations. In serving the interests of clients and employers, we dedicate ourselves to the goals of better communication, understanding and co-operation among diverse individuals, groups and institutions of society. We also subscribe to and support equal opportunity of employment in the public relations profession.

We pledge:

- to conduct ourselves professionally, with truth, accuracy, fairness and responsibility to the public and towards our colleagues

- to improve our individual competence and advance the knowledge and proficiency of the profession through continuing education and research

- to adhere to the articles of the Code of Professional Standards for the Practice of Public Relations.

Code of professional conduct

1. Definition

Public relations is the management, through communication, of perceptions and strategic relationships between an organisation and its internal and external stakeholders.

2. Professional conduct

2.1 In the conduct of our professional activities, we shall respect the public interest and the dignity of the individual. It is our responsibility at all times to deal fairly and honestly with our clients or employers, past or present, with our colleagues, media communication and with the public.

2.2 We shall conduct our professional lives in accordance with the public interest. We shall not conduct ourselves in any manner detrimental to the profession of public relations.

2.3 We have a positive duty to maintain integrity and accuracy, as well as generally accepted standards of good taste.

2.4 We shall not knowingly, intentionally or recklessly communicate false or misleading information. It is our obligation to use proper care to avoid doing so inadvertently.

2.5 We shall not guarantee the achievement of specified results beyond our direct control. We shall not negotiate nor agree terms with a prospective employer or client on the basis of payment only, contingent upon specific future public relations achievements.

2.6 We shall, when acting for a client or employer who belongs to a profession, respect the code of ethics of other professions and shall not knowingly be party to any breach of such a code.

3. Towards clients/employers conduct

3.1 We shall safeguard the confidences of both present and former clients and employers. We shall not disclose or make use of information given or obtained in confidence from an employer or client, past or present, for personal gain or otherwise, or to the disadvantage or prejudice of such client or employer.

3.2 We shall not represent conflicting or competing interests without the express consent of those involved, given after full disclosure of the facts. We shall not place ourselves in a position where our interests are or may be in conflict with a duty to a client, without full disclosure of such interests to all involved.

3.3 We shall not be party to any activity which seeks to dissemble or mislead by promoting one disguised or undisclosed interest whilst appearing to further another. It is our duty to ensure that the actual interest of any organisation with which we may be professionally concerned is adequately declared.

3.4 In the course of our professional services to the employer or client, we shall not accept payment either in cash or in kind in connection with these services from another source without the express consent of our employer or client.

4. Conduct towards colleagues

4.1 We shall not maliciously injure the professional reputation or practice of another individual engaged in the public relations profession.

4.2 We shall at all times uphold this Code, co-operate with colleagues in doing so and in enforcing decisions on any matter arising from this application.

4.3 Registered individuals who knowingly cause or permit another person or organisation to act in a manner inconsistent with this Code or are party to such an action, shall be deemed to be in breach of it.

4.4 If we have reason to believe that another colleague has engaged in practices that may be in breach of this Code, or practices that may be unethical, unfair or illegal, it is our duty to advise the Institute promptly.

4.5 We shall not invite any employee of a client to consider alternative employment.

5. Conduct towards the business environment

5.1 We shall not recommend the use of any organisation in which we have a financial interest, nor make use of its services on behalf of our clients or employers, without declaring our interest.

5.2 In performing professional services for a client or employer, we shall not accept fees, commissions or any other consideration from anyone other than the client or employer in connection with those services, without the express consent of the client/employer, given after disclosure of the facts.

5.3 We shall sever relations, as soon as possible, with any organisation or individual if such a relationship requires conduct contrary to this Code.

6. Conduct towards the channels of communication

6.1 We shall not engage in any practice which tends to corrupt the integrity of channels or media of communication.

6.2 We shall identify publicly the name of the client or employer on whose behalf any public communication is made.

7. Conduct towards the state

7.1 We respect the principles contained in the Constitution of the country in which we are resident.

7.2 We shall not offer or give any reward to any person holding public office, with intent to further our interests or those of our employer.

8. Conduct towards PRISA

8.1 We shall at all times respect the dignity and decisions of PRISA.

8.2 We are bound to uphold the annual registration fee levied by PRISA, which fee is payable as determined by registered practitioners at the annual general meeting of PRISA.

9. Disciplinary rules

A registered member who, in the opinion of the Disciplinary Committee of PRISA, infringes the Code of Professional Standards shall be informed in writing. The member deemed responsible for such an infringement shall be given reasonable opportunity to state their defence, either in writing or by personal attendance at a meeting of a Disciplinary Committee appointed by the PRISA Board and specially convened for this purpose. Sanctions will take the form of a warning or the practitioner's name will be removed from the register of members. This action will be made public.

(*Source:* Adapted, and used by kind permission of Margaret Moscardi of PRISA)

Table 9.1 PRISA's code of conduct

Ethics, public relations and professional responsibility

Escalation of competition in the marketplace and globalisation do not relieve modern public relations practitioners from ethical responsibilities. They must reckon morally with the use and implications of the notion of *better*. Baker (1999) maintains that there is moral justification for persuasion in public relations. If a public relations practitioner wishes to be at the highest level of the moral menu, he or she must at least be socially responsible and at best exemplify what is called the 'kingdom of ends'. Baker asserts that the second highest level, *social responsibility*, means one has a higher responsibility to community (customers, clients, humanity) than to the self. The highest or most virtuous level for Baker (1999), the *kingdom of ends,* calls for living one's life as if it were the role model for the world. People and actions are treated as ends in themselves, not justifications for unethical means to someone else's ends.

If public relations practitioners wish to be publicly accountable through a *kingdom of ends*, or even to practise social and professional responsibility as described by Baker (1999), they must carefully evaluate their claims to a better product or service or foothold in the marketplace in the ways described below.

Clear definition

Ethical public relations practitioners should not make claims of what is *better* without a definition and clarification to their publics. They must clearly define what their organisations or clients mean by *better*, *bigger* and *the best*.

Scientific evidence

Although *better* is often subjective, as in a better tasting tea, it often implies that there is objective data, such as when a car is said to be better because it is safer. Practitioners should not imply better in an objective sense, unless there is independent, replicable, valid scientific evidence. Failure to reveal the source and current status of full evidence may lead to deception by omission, as can failure to disclose the absence of scientific evidence. Such failure may also lead to lawsuits, loss of credibility and harm to both the consumers and clients.

Context for comparison

Better and kindred terms *faster, cleaner, cheaper, safer, softer, easier*, and so forth, imply a comparative state between a product or service and its competition. Ethically, practitioners ought to declare the answer to the question: 'Better than what?'

Audience sensitivity

Professional practitioners have an obligation to consider the nature of their audiences or publics. A better condom that can be used in a family planning programme may be an oxymoron to audiences who do not condone birth control. The multicultural and mixed-gender nature of most mass media audiences makes many claims of *better* questionable or inappropriate. Thus, ethical practitioners must ask: 'To whom might my product, service or message be objectionable? Offensive? Worse? Better? And why?'

To succeed in today's competitive marketplace requires public relations practitioners to work effectively within an adversarial marketplace, while realising their moral responsibilities to society. Grunig (1993) examined the ethics of two-way communication. In his two-way *asymmetrical model* of public relations, public relations practitioners primarily use feedback and research to persuade publics. In other words, they use communication primarily as a means to the organisation's ends (usually bottom-line profits). In contrast, the two-way *symmetrical model* depicts how publics and organisations may communicate more often in a balanced manner. Publics have the same opportunity to influence organisations as organisations have to influence publics. The public relations practitioner who practises symmetrical communication will be in an optimal position to inform an organisation's management team about those products, services, or ideas that are better from the perspective of the organisation's publics. This public relations practitioner will also be uniquely suited to decide on those claims that are unethical in promoting his or her organisation's competitive advantage in the marketplace (Cooper & Kelleher, 2001).

The following case illustrates how failure to adhere to the principles of *professional responsibility* can lead to unethical behaviour by an organisation.

Case study 1

Failed professional responsibility – Nestlé's infant formula

Clear definition

Infant formula is a substitute for mothers' breast milk, allowing mothers to feed their babies using a mixture of powdered formula and water. Apparently Nestlé does not deceive mothers about the contents of the breast milk substitute itself. However, Nestlé's promotional strategies, which imply that formula is better than natural breast milk, have been a source of controversy. The main points of contention between Nestlé and its critics are how the product is promoted and to whom.

Scientific evidence

The question of whether infant formula is better than natural breast milk has been an issue for decades. However, evidence in favour of natural breast milk is most pronounced in developing countries. In documenting the origin of boycotts against Nestlé, James Post (1985:115–116) described the problems that physicians and established medical organisations such as the World Health Organisation have observed: 'Sanitation and refrigeration are not generally available to the population in many such countries. Water supplies are unpurified, thereby increasing the probability that a formula mixed with local water will produce diarrhoea and disease in the bottle-fed child. Poverty encourages the over-dilution of powdered formula, thereby reducing the amount of nutrition the child receives from each bottle. Once a mother's ability to breastfeed 'lets down', the infant must be fed in an alternative way. If the mother is too poor to afford formula, which is an expensive product, there is the temptation and need to place other products in the infant bottle. These products may range from powdered whole milk (which is unsatisfactory for a infant's digestive system) to white powders such as cornstarch.'

According to Post (1985), the controversy over the use of infant formula has attracted the attention of advocacy groups, health professionals and government agencies throughout the world, and resulted in a 'medical consensus about the desirability of breastfeeding as the best way to provide infant nutrition'. On its website, Nestlé (2000) acknowledges that 'Breast milk is best for babies', and encourages consumers to 'Consult your doctor or clinic for advice' before using formula. However, consumers in developing countries are not likely to purchase Nestlé products based on information delivered via the World Wide Web. In addition, Nestlé's promotional strategies have often contradicted its formal statements.

Context for comparison

Nestlé promoted its products in impoverished areas with advertising that showed healthy, smiling, robust children. They used healthcare systems to distribute samples and posters. 'Milk nurses', who were paid commission by Nestlé, walked the halls of maternity wards in uniform, advising mothers to use formula. Nestlé infant formula was featured in radio jingles, posters, and infant books. The healthy, smiling babies in the advertisements provided a sharp contrast to the undernourished babies of developing populations. 'The advertising created an idealized image of what infants should look like and a clear concept of how the ideal could be achieved by even the most destitute of families' (Post, 1985:116). The implied comparison, then, was that Nestlé's formula was better than natural breastfeeding and other brands of formula.

Audience sensitivities

No evidence was found to suggest that Nestlé considered consumers in developing countries as anything more than a means to profitable ends. These unbalanced relations became an issue Nestlé had to face, however, when activists organised a boycott against Nestlé products in 1977. The boycott remained in effect for many years and 'many key publics' entered the fray, including 'industry members, media, federal authorities, foreign governments, medical experts, and the World Health Organisation' (Heath, 1997:124). Nestlé had hired and fired two public relations agencies to try to change the organisation's image, with no significant change in the organisation's success.

Nestlé eventually co-operated with others in the industry and the World Health Organisation to develop a code of marketing practices. It hired an outside organisation to audit its efforts to improve marketing practices and, by 1984, the major boycotts were lifted. Yet Nestlé's management strategy was far from a two-way symmetrical model of communication and understanding. Nestlé's extended initial resistance to change and eventual compromises with organised activists do not suggest any genuine concern for the mothers Nestlé and other industry leaders target in their developing promotional campaigns. Heath (1997) documented the continuing opposition Nestlé faced in the early 1990s. Taylor (1998) studied and compared marketing practices in Bangladesh, Poland, South Africa and Thailand, and found that violations of the industry codes resulting from the infant formula controversy are still prevalent in developing countries. For example, the surveys revealed that formula organisations still commonly give free samples of breast milk substitutes, infant formula, bottles, or teats to new mothers, and use health facilities as distribution channels for promotional information.

Summary

Nestlé's persuasive promotion of infant formula in developing countries appears to be unethical on all counts. Nestlé failed to encourage mothers to make informed decisions by clearly defining how and when infant formula is better than natural breast milk. Nestlé downplayed relevant evidence that revealed the product's potential for harm. The image Nestlé created to promote its product in comparison to natural alternatives was presented in a distorted and deceitful context. In addition, consumer sensitivities and interests were ignored, that is, the mothers targeted for formula sales were clearly treated as means to profitable ends. Indeed, the public relations and marketing practices employed by Nestlé are far from the ideals of Grunig's (1993) two-way symmetrical model of communication. The result is a case study in how *not* to practise public relations, evident in this case's inclusion in Stauber and Rampton's (1995) *Toxic sludge is good for you: Lies, damn lies and the public relations industry.*

The Nestlé case study demonstrates how unethical persuasion interrupts the process of natural selection in the marketplace. Nestlé's images of robust, healthy babies posted in maternity wards of developing countries promoted formula to impoverished women using strategic images likely to be described as extravagant, even for wealthy consumers. And the strategies worked. Rather that losing profits as a result of controversy, the infant formula industry continued to thrive in developing nations (Post, 1985). Nestlé touts itself as the world's largest food organisation, with products marketed in nearly every country in the world. This level of success, despite persuasive practices that do not meet the afore-mentioned thresholds for ethical behaviour in the marketplace, contrasts with the optimistic thesis that solid business means solid ethics. How-ever, those who observe these ethical thresholds are more likely to enjoy morally sound, long-term relationships with their publics.

(*Source:* Adapted from Post, 1985)

Public relations, ethics and society

According to Kruckeberg (2000), to practise 'strategic ethics' the public rela-tions practitioner must first think strategically rather than tactically in considering ethical dilemmas. Just as contemporary educators have embraced measurements of 'outcomes' rather than relied mainly on process measure-ment of learners' scholarly achievement, practitioners must look strategically at the ethical ramifications of their organisations, as well as of their profes-sional public relations communication practices. Public relations practitioners must strategically assess their organisations' overall impact on their environ-ments, as well as determine the impact of their specific public relations strategies on their publics. Kruckeberg (2000) continues by providing a sample of ques-tions that the practitioner must consider in his or her strategic consideration of ethics:

▲ Does the organisation, in achieving its mission and in its public relations communication practices, irreparably harm the earth, the sea, the sky or any other environmental element on which all life depends? If the organi-sation causes serious harm, is it the organisational policy and its practice to fully repair and restore the environment?

▲ Does the organisation, in achieving its mission and in its public relations communication practices, value the sanctity of human life and assist in en-suring a social environment in which all human life and cultures are respected and enriched?

▲ Is the dignity of the earth and all its life forms both respected and pro-tected by the organisation in achieving its mission and in its public relations communication practices?

▲ Does the organisation, in achieving its mission and in its strategic public relations communication practices, seek two-way symmetrical dialogue and attempt to foster mutual respect in reconciling the base ideological assump-tions of the organisation with those of the indigenous societies that comprise its publics?

▲ Are the images that the organisation's public relations communication strategies portray both accurate and truthful as well as sufficiently complete for publics to form opinions about the organisation based on fact?

▲ Do the mission, goals and objectives of the organisation recognise and take into consideration that organisations are accountable both legally and ethically to society-at-large and that organisations ultimately exist both at the discretion of global society and fundamentally to serve the needs of society?

The right answers to the above questions should be obvious to all public relations practitioners, as well as to the organisations in which they work. Consideration of strategic ethics requires that public relations practitioners look more broadly, more strategically at their role as interpreters, ethicists, social policy makers and environmental scanners in guiding organisational behaviour, and take strategic responsibility in influencing and reconciling public perceptions of their organisations within a local and global context.

Today's range of multicultural perspectives concerning appropriate public relations ethics can be greatly reconciled as public relations continues to professionalise globally. Historically, the personal ethics of any 'professionalised' occupation's culture-bound practitioners have tended to become subsumed into universal professional ethics that have encouraged corresponding universal ethical values (Kruckeberg, 1998:45).

The leading association in the public relations industry defines the purpose of public relations as follows: 'Public relations helps our complex, pluralistic society to reach decisions and function more effectively by contributing to mutual understanding among groups and institutions. It serves to bring private and public policies into harmony' (Public Relations Society of America Foundations, 1991:4). In short, certain aspects of the public relations profession might be universalised, where others will be unique to the specific country or culture in which they function. Public relations ethics might be one aspect that can be universal. As public relations continues to professionalise, multicultural perspectives in public relations ethics will yield to a universal practice in public relations that will be predictably attuned to professional ethical norms.

Public relations has often been viewed by society, including the mass media and intellectuals, with a certain scepticism and sometimes cynicism. In coming to grips with how society views public relations and corporate communication, Ihator (1999) explored the social, cultural, economic and historical contexts under which the communication between organisations and society takes place. Ihator (1999) came to the conclusion that enhanced knowledge of society's moral compass, and the social metaphors and stereotypical images of the business environment, may lead to the mapping and understanding of the cultural space of public relations.

'Spin': The transformation of public discourse into public manipulation?

There has always been a 'mistrust' of public relations as a phenomenon in society. Many practitioners and scholars in the field are themselves not always comfortable with what they do for a living. Stuart Ewen, a leading media scholar, critic and professor of mass communications at Hunter's College in New York, named a recent publication of his *Public Relations! A Social History of Spin*. According to Ewen, 'spin is the transformation of public discourse into public manipulation' (Ihator, 1999).

Case study 2 is an example of 'mixed' public relations 'spin' success with regard to the image building of South African President Thabo Mbeki.

Case study 2

The incredible shrinking president

Despite a rash of bad press and dumb politics, Thabo Mbeki took Britain by storm – reminding the West just how capable he really is. Once famous for his serial seduction of western diplomats, white businessmen, Zulu chieftains and khaki-clad racists, Thabo Mbeki's tenure as South African president has been marred by a string of public relations gaffes. His comments on AIDS, perceived coddling of strongman Robert Mugabe, and attacks on potential rivals have squandered the favourable image he enjoyed on taking office a few years ago. In the run-up to his first state visit to the United Kingdom, the British press summed it up: 'Has Thabo Mbeki lost the plot?' asked *The Guardian*. 'Is this the face of tomorrow's dictator?' inquired *The Times*. Mbeki's mission was clear: he had a reputation to save.

His job was never going to be easy. Asked how it felt to step into Mandela's shoes, Mbeki joked that the old man 'has much bigger feet than me' and his 'shoes are very ugly'. It was a telling joke. Mbeki had grown impatient with the sunny rhetoric of Mandela's Rainbow Nation and anxious that the benefits of democracy could be jeopardised if South Africa failed to create a genuinely non-racial society. 'When the poor rise, they will rise against us all,' he warned. That acid message and a preoccupation with issues of race have done little to win supporters in the media. Mbeki disdains sound bites, appears aloof in a crowd, and operates best behind closed doors. And he is a maverick. Contemporaries from Britain's Sussex University, where he studied economics in the early 1960s, recall that while girls were discovering miniskirts, Mbeki favoured tweed suits, smoked a pipe and developed a lifelong habit of quoting Shakespeare. He wanted to study at Oxford, but fretted that an English education was a distraction from 'the struggle' at home.

The end of that struggle opened a door to cynicism in the developed world. Robbed of its unique place in the canon of liberal fantasy, South Africa confronted a more brutal and racially charged realpolitik. Seven years into democracy, it is portrayed in most of the British media as a beautiful country in peril. It has become synonymous with AIDS, crime and racial invective. The crisis in neighbouring Zimbabwe, where marauding squatters have maimed, robbed and killed white farmers, has simply reinforced the pessimism. 'Zimbabwe today, South Africa tomorrow,' editors brood.

Mbeki's lieutenants rightly recoil at the comparison. The dynamism of the young democracy is worlds apart from Zimbabwe – and, indeed, any other country. But Mbeki's ill-judged comments on AIDS (his backing of the dissidents' view that AIDS is not caused by the HIV-virus), and the friendly greetings that framed his encounters with Mugabe, have confused even sympathetic observers. And that was before he upstaged Mandela's celebrity appearance at a free concert in Trafalgar Square with news that three potential rivals faced investigation for allegedly conspiring against him.

Mbeki has defended his stances, but his case is undermined by the ease with which his actions fit into the old African caricatures of creeping autocracy and paranoia. Most of what is written or broadcast about his country betrays an underlying suspicion that the young democracy is locked on a path of inevitable decline. When, for example, South African teachers denounced as 'racist' a 1986 novel by Nobel Prize winner Nadine Gordimer, embarrassed ministers insisted they apologise. But the story ran in London's *Sunday Times* under the headline: SO NOW THEY'VE COME FOR YOU, NADINE.

This bleak narrative ignores real accomplishments. Next to his role in negotiating an end to apartheid, Mbeki's greatest achievement has been to impose a modern economic policy on a ruling party wedded to the collectivist faiths of its history. In a continent scarred by the failures of multilateral institutions to prescribe economic reform, South Africa is a rare example of a country implementing successful structural adjustment. For the first time in two decades, manufactured exports and per capita incomes are rising. Similar policies underpin the Millennium Africa Recovery Plan, a pan-African initiative Mbeki touted to British ministers. He wants commitments on debt relief and trade before African leaders meet to ratify the creation of a new African Union, a revamped regional grouping to replace the Organisation of African Unity.

Mbeki's bid for a strategic role in global policymaking has borne fruit. After meeting Mbeki at Downing Street, British Prime Minister Tony Blair called the skewed trade regime that blocks African export to the Organisation for Economic Cooperation and Development countries 'a scandal'. During a recent tour of Africa, US Secretary of State Colin Powell assured Mbeki that Washington would take its cue from Pretoria before intervening in African affairs. Asked recently to reveal his biggest worry, Mbeki offered a diagnosis of the uprisings in the Middle East. And he arrived in London ready to advise on race relations in Britain.

Mbeki did not say much in London that he has not said before, but he did say it better. Before he stepped into the queen's horse-drawn carriage on the Mall, selected British journalists were granted private interviews. 'The president has never spoken for so long or in such detail about his views on AIDS,' said a spokesman. Mbeki's argument that – next to HIV – factors such as malnutrition, sanitation and chronic poverty have contributed to Africa's AIDS epidemic seemed to convince even the habitually sceptical *Times*, which judged him 'intimidatingly well briefed'.

And so Mbeki soldiers on alone. His vision of an open, democratic Africa rising to the challenge of global capitalism remains elusive and possibly utopian. If Africa is going anywhere, he conceded, 'it may even be going backwards.' Three days in Britain did not change that, but they did confirm Mbeki as being much more sophisticated than his battered reputation allows.

(*Source:* Adapted from Adhurst, M 2001. The incredible shrinking president. In *Newsweek* (Atlantic edition), 137(26):31.)

Organisations are always communicating with, and relating to, their various publics. Every communication takes place in a cultural, physical and relational context, which seriously constrains what messages are seen as appropriate and effective. Organisations have traditionally been the source of communication and perceived to be the superior partner in their communication and relationship with society. Though some public relations practitioners are now adopting two-way symmetrical communication that permits bi-directional flow of information, public relations has historically been linked by society to publicity, persuasion and media relations, which are essentially unidirectional in nature (Ihator, 1999). The recipients of the organisation's public relations message came into the transaction with their corporate image – good or bad – which comes from the relational history they have had with the organisation. This is illustrated in case study 3.

Case study 3

Public relations and international affairs – effects, ethics and responsibility

On 20 October 1990, during the escalation of the Persian Gulf crisis, a teary-eyed 15-year-old Kuwaiti girl known only as Nayirah testified to the Congressional Human Rights Caucus that she had seen Iraqi soldiers take babies from hospital incubators in Kuwait and leave them on the floor to die. Months later, a piece in the *New York Times*, followed by stories on the television programmes *60 Minutes* and *20-20*, revealed that Nayirah was the daughter of the Kuwaiti ambassador to the United States.

The Hill & Knowlton public relations firm, on behalf of an organisation called Citizens for a Free Kuwait, an organisation funded primarily by the exiled government of Kuwait, had arranged the hearing. In a book on Robert Keith Gray, then head of Hill & Knowlton's Washington, D.C. office, freelance author Susan Trento reported that Hill & Knowlton had provided witnesses for the hearing, coached them, written testimony, produced videotapes detailing the alleged atrocities, and ensured that the room was filled with reporters and television cameras.

Fewer than three months later, the United States attacked Iraq. By that time, Hill & Knowlton had received $10.7 million from Citizens for a Free Kuwait. With the money, Hill & Knowlton – among other things – organised a press conference with a so-called Kuwaiti freedom fighter, 'National Prayer Day' services for Kuwaiti and American servicemen, and 'Free Kuwait' rallies at 21 college campuses. It also promoted an Islamic art tour, produced advertisements and video news releases, arranged luncheons with journalists, and spent more than $1 million polling the American people.

Critics have asked whether or not these extensive and expensive activities by an international public relations firm led the United States to war. The answer is probably no. As Trento put it: 'Hill & Knowlton's efforts succeeded in the United Nations, the Congress and the media because, in each case, there was a receptive audience. The diplomats and congressmen and senators wanted something to point to, to support their positions. The media wanted interesting, visual stories.'

In short, the Hill & Knowlton campaign probably encouraged decision makers and public opinion to move in a direction in which they were already headed. Even though the war probably would have occurred without the campaign, one still must ask whether such campaigns are ethical. As Trento noted: 'In the end, the question was not whether Hill &

Knowlton effectively altered public opinion, but whether the combined efforts of America's own government, foreign interests, and private public relations and lobbying campaigns drowned out decent and rational, unemotional debate.'

When practised ethically and responsibly, public relations provides a vital communication function for organisations, nations, and even the world, helping to develop an understanding among groups and eventually reduce conflict. When practised unethically and irresponsibly, however, public relations can manipulate and deceive. More often, though, such public relations merely makes 'decent and rational, unemotional debate' on issues difficult.

At first glance, asymmetrical – and unethical – public relations seems to have been prevalent in international public relations throughout history, especially during times of conflict. Propaganda – defined here as one-sided, usually half-truthful communication, designed to persuade public opinion – is not a new aspect of warfare or of international politics.

One of the most extensive international communication programmes was conducted by South Africa over several years, aimed at the United States and Western Europe. An extensive covert campaign managed by Eschel Rhoodie, the Secretary of Information, ended in the Muldergate Scandal – named after Rhoodie's superior, Connie Mulder, South African Minister of Information. The programme was aimed at the United States and Western Europe. Among other things, money from a secret fund was used to bankroll an effort to buy the *Washington Star*, in order to counteract the influence of the *Washington Post*. After the secret programme was exposed, South Africa openly tried to cultivate relationships with US opinion leaders to try to promote understanding of the country's problems. Most of the efforts were typical media relations and promotional activities of the asymmetric models – carefully selecting messages that put the best face on the situation, such as arguing that economic sanctions would hurt blacks most. The personal influence model was also used, in the form of sponsoring golfing trips to South Africa for US business executives who might invest there. The effect of the effort was more embarrassment with the scandal than international support. The 'image-polishing efforts' of the entire Rhoodie campaign were almost meaningless in the face of massive global pressure against South Africa's policy of apartheid.

(*Source:* Adapted from Grunig, J 1993. Public relations and international affairs: Effects, ethics and responsibility. In *Journal of International Affairs,* 47(1):137–161)

The impact of the socio-political, economic and religious environment on public relations ethics

It is necessary to look at economic history to become fully aware of the nature and essence of modern capitalism and its motivation. Self-interest is perhaps the dominating factor. According to Adam Smith (Ihator, 1999), 'It is not from the benevolence of the butcher, the brewer or the baker, that we expect our dinner, but from their regard to their own interest. We address ourselves, not to their humanity but to their self-love, and never talk to them of our own necessities but of their advantages.' The cases of Enron, Andersen Consulting and WorldCom offer the most recent examples of the continuation of self-enrichment of the captains of industry and the corruption of government officials with fiscal and political power in hand. These types of scandals are covered in every newspaper on a daily basis. These may be examples of corporate culture that formulates the social image and perception that dominate the psyche of society. This then often leads to society's cynicism regarding organisations and their 'spin doctors'.

Case study 4

Waging the spin war

In the aftermath of the September 11 terrorist attacks on the United States, the president is winning the battle at home, but should he take his message to the Arab world? Whom would you rather see on television speaking out against the forces of world terrorism? George Bush, grey suit, white shirt, blue tie, standing behind a lectern, saying, 'While the threat is ongoing, we are taking every possible step to protect our country,' or a sweat-soaked Bruce Willis, ammo belts crossed on his bare chest, rocket launcher under his arm, saying, 'Yippee ki-yay, bin Laden, baby!'

Version 2 is unlikely to appear on our screens anytime soon. But some think America has been losing the propaganda war against Osama bin Laden in part because the White House has been unable or unwilling to fully mobilise America's opinion-shaping might. 'US video propaganda needs to be put into the hands of message experts in Hollywood and [the] media, as was done in World War II,' says Steve Cimbala, professor of political science at Pennsylvania State University, Delaware County.

And even America's staunchest friend, British Prime Minister Tony Blair, returned recently from a two-day visit to the Middle-East saying the US-led coalition is in danger of losing the public relations war. 'One thing becoming increasingly clear to me is the need to upgrade our media and public opinion operations in the Arab and Muslim world,' Blair said. 'There is a need for us to communicate effectively.'

There is little doubt that bin Laden understands modern media and spin. Within hours of the first US bombs and missiles landing on Afghanistan, he released a video that contained not just the usual diatribes but, to many Arab listeners, a detailed and convincing history of US and Israeli aggression against them.

George Bush, however, has spent so much time reassuring the American people that they will emerge from this crisis safe and victorious – a necessary, even vital task – that he has almost neglected or at least spent relatively little time making the case against bin Laden to the 1,3 billion Muslims of the world.

Never in his entire career has George Bush been lauded as being a great communicator like Ronald Reagan or Bill Clinton. Indeed, Bush's presidential campaign was partially based on the premise that, no matter how lacking Bush was in communication skills, he at least came across better than Al Gore, a man who sometimes appeared to have difficulty communicating with himself, let alone others.

Finding voice

In the first months of Bush's presidency, in fact, he was criticised for barely speaking out at all, avoiding the opportunity to address the nation directly and forcefully on such subjects as the grounding of an American plane in China, riots in Cincinnati, and rising gasoline prices. The White House staff clearly wanted Bush to be able to grow at his own pace into the role of national communicator.

Since September 11, however, the White House has learned that when the crisis is grave, there is no substitute for the one person who can unify, lead, and comfort the American people: the president. And Bush has been riding a media whirlwind since then, making television appearances at events great and small. But his first prime-time news conference demonstrated both the strengths and weaknesses of the US propaganda effort. Bush was forceful, plain spoken, and in command of his material. But those who believed Bush should use such opportunities to build a detailed case against bin Laden were disappointed.

Good vs. evil

Bush sees the war against bin Laden in such stark terms that, in his mind, building a case is hardly necessary. In the 44-minute news conference, Bush used the word 'evil' or 'evildoer' no fewer than 12 times. To Bush, the case is so simple – a cosmic battle of good vs. evil – that those specifics seem hardly worth repeating. Some, however, point to how fragile the coalition is, and say Bush is missing an opportunity on the airwaves. 'If Bush is serious about winning hearts and minds in the Arab world, he probably should go on al Jazeera television, as Tony Blair has done, rather than ceding that particular stage to the Taliban and other anti-American voices,' says *Washington Post* media reporter Howard Kurtz.

While in America support for Bush and his efforts has been overwhelming – humorist Colin Quinn calls this America's 'first politically correct war' – it is a different story in the Arab world, which gets much of its information either from state-controlled media or al Jazeera, often called the 'CNN of the Mideast' which, though it operates with government funding in the tiny oil-rich emirate of Qatar, claims to be free of any government control. Reaching an estimated 35 million people throughout the Arab world through satellite dishes that sit atop everything – from luxury homes in Damascus, Syria, to shanties in Cairo and tents in the Arabian desert, al Jazeera ('the peninsula') has for the past five years featured freewheeling interviews with everyone from bin Laden, whom it has helped make into an international figure, to US secretary of state Colin Powell. And when the White House recently asked al Jazeera to tone down its coverage of bin Laden, the network refused, just as it has refused the demands of Arab nations to change its coverage. 'All these accusations are proof that we are trying to be professionals and do our job the best we can,' says Hamad bin Thamer al-Thani, chairman of al Jazeera's Board.

From the White House point of view, it was asking nothing of al Jazeera that it has not asked of the US media. Bush has spent a lot of what he calls his 'political capital' on trying to control the information flow at home: the White House threatened to cut off intelligence from many members of Congress until lawmakers agreed to stop leaking to the press; and it easily won agreements from the television networks not to blindly carry broadcasts by bin Laden, and said it was likely to ask newspapers to stop printing bin Laden transcripts.

However, some think the US effort to dampen bin Laden at home is misdirected. During World War II, ranting speeches by Adolf Hitler and Benito Mussolini were commonplace in newsreels carried in every movie theatre and they served to strengthen, not weaken, US resolve. Critics say rather than fight the war at home – where hearts and minds are already won – Bush needs to fight for at least the ears of the Arab world. Indeed, the White House is considering putting Bush on al Jazeera for an interview.

(*Source:* Adapted from Simon, R 2001. Waging the spin war. In *US News and World Report*, 131(17))

The recent paradigm shift in organisational employment practice is another element that may have the tendency to breed mistrust from society's point of view. In the South African environment, affirmative action policies and the attempt to correct the inequities of the past – which are noble causes – might create perception problems from society. Retiring productive employees earlier, or retrenching them during the course of organisational downsizing, streamlining, mergers and acquisitions, often makes members of the public think that organisations do not care much about employees' welfare. The new capitalism, as some economists now refer to it, tends to foster employment instability and future uncertainty. In the middle of all of these trends stands the 'messenger of the bad news' – the public relations practitioner who tries to 'sell' the state of corporate affairs to the public.

Religion also may have some part to play in how society views the business environment. Historically, religion has been influential in the life of ordinary citizens. Religion was the benchmark by which standards in other social systems were judged and valued. Mainstream religious denominations were always sceptical and often cynical about the ethos of capitalism. For a long time religion and business were far apart. The secular and the sacred were viewed as mutually exclusive. The culture of capitalism was considered incompatible with orthodox theology. The tragedy of the terrorist attacks of September 11 on the World Trade Centre and the Pentagon in the United States might be an illustration of the resurgence of cultural and religious conflict between nations. In the middle of all of this stands public relations, trying to relay the messages. The 'war against terror' has been seen by many as a 'public relations war' among the United States, Israel and other Western countries against the Islamic countries. Case study 5 illustrates the ethical dilemma with regard to public relations in the ongoing 'war against terror'.

Case study 5

Hearts, minds, and the war against terror

The scoop appeared in the *New York Times* in February 2002. As part of 'a new effort to influence public sentiment and policy makers in both friendly and unfriendly countries,' it revealed, the Pentagon was 'developing plans to provide news items, possibly even false ones, to foreign media organizations'.

According to the *Times*, what had prompted the creation of this so-called Office of Strategic Influence (OSI) was the worry of 'many administration officials' that 'the United States was losing support in the Islamic world after American warplanes began bombing Afghanistan'. And what had prompted the leak of the story? It seems that a number of people inside the Pentagon, whether for reasons of principle or for reasons of turf, were concerned that the new office, by combining the tasks of public relations with those of covert operations, would thereby taint the former. 'It goes from the blackest of black programs to the whitest of white,' an anonymous official was quoted, thus fueling the impression that the office would be peddling lies.

In fact, the US has rarely done anything like this in its history. (The term 'black operations' in this context properly refers to the practice of hiding the role of the government as the source of a given story rather than to the practice of spreading disinformation.) Nevertheless, the *Times* weighed in the next day with an editorial denouncing the new office, which it called 'Orwellian', while the columnist Maureen Dowd contributed her own broadside against what she dubbed the Office of Strategic Mendacity. In no time, scores of other newspapers around the country had registered their indignation, causing Defense Secretary Donald Rumsfeld to protest: 'The Pentagon is not issuing disinformation to the foreign press or any other press.'

But the die had been cast. Within a week of the first *Times* story, Rumsfeld announced he had closed the office down. This aborted mission was not the only effort by the Bush administration to wage a battle for hearts and minds as part of its larger war against terrorism. The State Department had already brought in Charlotte Beers, formerly the head of the giant advertising agency Ogilvy & Mather, as undersecretary for public diplomacy. According to Beers, her aim was to do for the United States what she had done for IBM in the 1990s, namely, to 'rebrand' it. But her new job, she confessed, would be even tougher than her old one – indeed, 'the most sophisticated brand assignment I have ever had'. 'It is almost,' she added, 'as though we have to redefine what America is.'

If the goal sounded ambitious, she could at least count on the full backing of her formidable patron, the Secretary of State. For Colin Powell himself, it turns out, had been keen on the Madison Avenue approach to public diplomacy even before September 11, much preferring it to the more traditional and overly intellectual methods of the now-defunct United States Information Agency (USIA). In congressional testimony soon after taking office, Powell had declared: 'I'm going to be bringing people into the public diplomacy function of the department who are going to change from just selling us in the old USIA way to really branding foreign policy, branding the department, marketing the department, marketing American values to the world.'

In the wake of September 11, and in line with the new spirit, Beers was reported to be considering 'television and radio spots in which sports stars and celebrities [would] talk up the US'. Her office's major product was a shiny and colourful 25-page pamphlet, *The Network of Terrorism,* distributed in 36 languages and featuring vivid photographs of the September 11 destruction, harsh commentary on al Qaeda and the Taliban, and denunciations of terrorism by such world leaders as Kofi Annan, Tony Blair, and Jiang Zemin. By far the most prominent quotations, spread throughout the pamphlet in huge type, were by Muslims – three Arab sheiks, one Indonesian cleric, and the Council on American-Islamic Relations (CAIR) – repudiating the September 11 attacks and the taking of innocent life.

As the war began, the White House also created another agency, the Coalition Information Center (CIC), with offices in Washington, London, and Pakistan. Its purpose was (and remains) to publicise the US side's war aims, and to provide instantaneous rebuttal of enemy claims about civilian casualties or battlefield successes. Widening its writ, the CIC also gave impetus to the 'Afghan Women's Initiative', which pressed for a role for women in post-Taliban power structures, thereby underscoring the humanly liberating aspect of a victory in Afghanistan.

More important than the work of any of these agencies, the hallmark of America's outreach efforts was the activity of George Bush himself. Three days after September 11, the President led an ecumenical service at the National Cathedral where a spokesman for America's Muslims assisted in officiating. A few days later, the President visited the Islamic Center, a Washington mosque, where he proclaimed, 'Islam is peace,' and went on to castigate Americans who had made threatening gestures toward Muslims in the days since September 11. 'Women who cover their head in this country must feel comfortable going outside,' he declared. 'Moms who wear cover must not be intimidated in America.'

Bush's embrace extended beyond American Muslims to Muslims around the globe. In his address to Congress nine days after the attack, he enunciated several themes to which he has returned repeatedly in the months since: 'I also want to speak tonight directly to Muslims throughout the world. We respect your faith. It's practised freely by many millions of Americans, and by millions more in countries that America counts as friends. Its teachings are good and peaceful, and those who commit evil in the name of Allah blaspheme the name of Allah. The terrorists are traitors to their own faith, trying, in effect, to hijack Islam itself. The enemy of America is not our many Muslim friends; it is not our many Arab friends.'

To demonstrate his earnestness in this matter, the president invited a group of American Muslim spokesmen to breakfast at the White House in order 'to discuss ... what our country is going to do to make sure that everybody who is an American is respected'. In November, he also invited the ambassadors of the member states of the Organization of the Islamic Conference (OIC) to pray and break the day-long Ramadan fast at the White House, expressing his esteem for Muslim 'believers [who] built a culture of learning and literature and science' and with whom 'we share the same hope for a future of peace'. Secretary of State Powell held a similar dinner at the State Department, and US ambassadors around the world were instructed to do likewise.

To reinforce Bush's message of openness to the faith whose teachings the September 11 terrorists had invoked in attacking the US, Charlotte Beers's office printed thousands of posters in a series called 'Mosques of America', for distribution around the world. She herself declared: 'We . . . have to be as good at listening as we are at proposing our point of view, so that our interlocutors will understand . . . that they don't need to kill us to get our attention.'

(*Source:* Adapted from Muravchik, J 2002. Hearts, minds and the war against terrorism. In *New York Times.*)

The topic of *ethics* has been discussed since the origins of democratic capitalism. While many countries do not disapprove of capitalism as a pragmatic and proven economic system of creating and distributing wealth, many in society have questioned its ethics. This scepticism adds to the tension between society and business. The questions that are asked in this regard are: 'Can profit-oriented business promote organisational profitability and social value in the Aristotelian tradition at the same time? Does an organisation have to be virtuous?' In his work *Ethics*, Aristotle remarked that every art and every inquiry, and similarly every action and pursuit, is thought to aim at some good; and for this reason the good has rightly been declared to be that at which all things aim (Ihator, 1999). Ethics scholars are asking whether the marketplace, due to its social role, can be regarded as one of the venerable social agents for including virtues, such as family, education and religion. However, technology and the age of science and information, as well as the universal access to information, have modulated some traditional definitions of virtue and truth.

Public relations ethics and the media

A survey by Dean Rotbart, a media and management consultant in Colorado (Ihator, 1999), suggested media's strong and widespread mistrust and contempt for organisational spokespeople. Among the findings of the survey of 225 top United States business journalists, 47 per cent believed public relations people are more of a nuisance than a help, and 46 per cent believed public relations people are not telling the truth most of the time. On a one to ten scale on the best sources of story ideas that are useful, journalists placed public relations at the bottom – with a rating of 3,5. This is not far removed from the view that society in general holds of public relations practitioners.

The integrated marketing communication approach, which combines advertising, marketing, promotion and public relations programmes, as well as internal and external communication, has not been useful, states Ihator (1999). Public relations activities, whose objective theoretically is to create, maintain and nurture relationships through enhanced and credible communication, might now be viewed as a marketing and/or advertising tool. This again leads to a credibility problem and mistrust of public relations by the media and society in general. Once an organisation's public relations communication is seen only as marketing, it becomes even more difficult to engineer a productive, mutually rewarding relationship. Recognising the encompassing power of the mass media, negative coverage makes the effort at revamping the image of public relations in society much more difficult. The 'unfortunate past' of public relations; the multiplicity of communication activities (some mainly technical) that are lumped together as public relations functions; and the poor image that some corporate communicators have given the profession have all contributed to the perception dilemma.

Case study 6

The Enron scandal and public relations ethics

Introduction: Where did it all begin?

Sherron Watkins, an employee, feared that Enron was 'playing too fast' and that it would lose its business. She delivered a letter in August 2001 to Enron's CEO, Kenneth Lay, in which she predicted, 'the business world will consider the past successes as nothing but an elaborate accounting hoax'. Lay ordered an inquiry, but nothing came of it because those who were questioned 'had professional and personal stakes in the matters under review' (Lachnit, 2002).

Enron became an embarrassment to the business industry. It created a spiral effect, with shares becoming unstable and investor confidence being shattered. Again, people were reminded of the power that organisations might have. It is sad to think that one organisation can do so much damage, and that it assumed it would be able to cover it up. Around 4 000 employees lost their jobs, as well as their retirement funds. Former SEC chief accountant Lynn Turner says that the loss will be around $100 billion (Sewer, 2002). The court case that started in February 2002 is currently still running.

What is ethical and non-ethical?

The grey line between right and wrong is becoming thinner. Laws are open for interpretation. Harris Collingwood, *HBR* senior editor, asserts that there are 176 classes of criminal offences in the US that, if committed, are defined as money laundering. But only ten of them are seen as crimes if committed abroad (Baker, 2002). He also states studies estimate that more than $1 trillion in 'dirty money' passes into the West (US) every year, and that a substantial portion of this money is solicited and channelled by Western business.

So where should the line between being ethical or non-ethical be drawn? Gibson, Ivancevich and Donnelly (1988) describe it as follows: 'If power is used *within* the formal boundaries of a manager's authority and within the framework of organizational policies, job descriptions, procedures, and goals, it is really *non-political* power and most likely *does not* involve ethical issues. But when power is *outside* the bounds of formal authority, politics, procedures, job descriptions, and organizational goals, it is *political* in nature. When this occurs, *ethical issues* are likely to be present.' Tim Hindle (2002) states that, at a minimum, good managers have to meet the following criteria: be honest, be frugal and be prepared. Andrew Stark (1993) refers to Joseph Badaracco, who has described ethics, first, not as issues of right versus wrong but as conflicts of right versus right, and second, as navigating those situations where the right course is clear, but real-world competitive and institutional pressures lead even well-intentioned managers astray.

Background and timeline to the scandal

The timeline discussed below attempts to provide a background to Enron's corrupt executives, the US government's involvement, and also some significant times when the media became involved. The media were at first quite cautious about becoming involved, as everyone really believed in Enron. Only after the SEC intervened, did the press become more involved in the debacle.

▲ **November 1997:** Enron buys out a partner's stake in the Jedi organisation and sells it to an organisation it calls Chewco. Both these organisations are names of characters from the *Star Wars* movies. These two organisations were run by Enron executives, who profited richly from them. They were keeping millions of dollars in debt off Enron's books.

▲ **11 December 1999:** Laws change and give organisations the clearing to also make loans to their clients.

▲ **23 August 1999:** Enron reaches its highest stock price at $90 a share.

▲ **November 2000:** Trader James Chanos shorts Enron stock, betting the price will fall.

▲ **15 December 2000:** Congress deregulates the trading of energy futures, giving a boost to Enron.

▲ **June to October 2000:** Thomas White of the Bush administration (former vice-chairman of Enron Energy Service) sells off 400 000 Enron shares with estimated profits of about $12 million. He was one of the people who pushed privatisation for the energy utilities that supply the armed forces.

▲ **17 April 2001:** Enron's CEO, Ken Lay, meets with US vice-president Dick Cheney and other energy policy officials. This was one of six such visits that were held behind closed doors.

▲ **14 August 2001:** CEO Jeffrey Skilling resigns, becoming the sixth senior executive to leave in one year. Skilling tells analysts that he really feels good about the organisation. They do not believe him, and the stock price falls to $39.55. Skilling sold off about $20 million of Enron's stock between January and August 2001. Cliff Baxter, an analyst, apparently complained loudly to Skilling about Enron's unstable books.

▲ **15 August 2001:** Sherron Watkins, Enron's vice-president, writes a memo to Lay about her disapproval of the ethical issues in the organisation. Lay later dismisses these allegations.

▲ **12 October 2001:** Arthur Andersen's David Duncan instructs workers who audit Enron's books to destroy all but the most basic documents – everything is to be shredded. The company argued later that there are no rules about how long documents and records need to be kept.

▲ **16 October 2001:** Enron reports third quarter losses of $618 million. The *Wall Street Journal* links this to the partnerships of Chewco and Jedi.

▲ **22 October 2001:** Enron discloses that the Securities Exchange Commission has opened an inquiry.

▲ **26 October 2001:** Lay has talks with Allan Greenspan, President of the Central Bank.

▲ **8 November 2001:** Enron admits accounting errors, inflating income by $586 million since 1997. It has overstated its income for more than four years.

▲ **29 November 2001:** The Securities Exchange Commission expands its investigation to include auditing organisation Arthur Andersen.

▲ **2 December 2001:** Enron files for bankruptcy and the stock price closes at 26c.

▲ **December 2001:** John Cornyn launches an investigation into the losses and tax liabilities, which has to be withdrawn since, from 1997, he had accepted $158 000 in campaign contributions from Enron.

▲ **10 January 2002:** Arthur Andersen's CEO, Joseph Bernardino, testifies that his organisation had discovered 'possible illegal acts' committed by Enron. Enron paid about $1 million a week for auditing services in 2000. It paid a total amount of $25 million for its audit in 2001 and an extra $27 million for consulting and 'other services'. Arthur Andersen also acknowledges destroying Enron files. Attorney-General John Ashcroft has to withdraw from the investigations because he received $57 499 for his senate campaign in 2000.

▲ **15 January 2002:** David Duncan, former Arthur Anderson partner who had overseen Enron's auditing since 1997, is fired.

▲ **End of Jan 2002:** Cliff Baxter commits suicide by shooting himself in his car. Even though he had mentioned his dissatisfaction about the situation to Skilling, he did nothing about it and, instead of going to the media, just walked away. He cashed in $35 million in stock.

▲ **January 2002:** President Bush receives a lot of media attention relating to his connection with the Enron debacle. A total amount of $312 500 was paid to his pre-presidential campaigns, and an amount of $413 800 to his presidential war chest and inaugural fund.

▲ **2 February 2002:** The Bush administration orders a government-wide review of more than $60 million in federal contracts between Enron and Arthur Andersen.

▲ **February 2002:** New evidence shows that the final draft copy for the energy plan given to Congress for approval in March 2000 was subtly changed when the Bush administration proposed the plan six weeks later to the public. A new section was introduced, calling for increased energy production in India. Enron has a $2,9 billion plant in India that had not been profitable because the prices were too high for the local organisations. Cheney met with Lay on April 17 before the final energy proposals were unveiled.

Main players/groups involved

Five major players were identified in this scandal: first, the corrupt Enron executives who were acting without any ethical standards; second, the Arthur Andersen auditors auditing Enron under David Duncan since 1997, who knew about the scandal, and were probably paid a lot of money to keep it quiet; third, the Bush administrators who realised that they were also involved – even if this realisation only came afterwards; fourth, the media, the SEC and the investigation groups, which really believed that they should intervene to stop this scandal; fifth, the people who actually suffered most – the investors, as well as the rest of Enron's staff who lost all their savings.

Enron's ethical breaches

Information asymmetries

Businesses are there to make profit – there is no doubt about that. But when they do business in such a way that it interferes with the rights of others and starts to have an effect on people's personal lives, then that type of business acts unethically. This is especially true when a person does a transaction with someone else, and knows information that can have a negative effect on the other person. Enron's executives knew the real value of the stock, but Lay still encouraged employees to buy stock. Insider trading is also part of information asymmetries, and a number of the executives were selling off stock just before the stock price started to fall.

Truth and disclosure

Approximately 60 per cent of Enron's plans consisted of Enron's stock (Berenbeim, 2002). Lay failed to disclose anything to investors and employees about possible stock that would be devalued. Thus, while they thought their retirement money was safe in this organisation that apparently was doing so well, they were actually losing money by the minute. Enron also failed to disclose that it was moving money to its two partner organisations, Jedi and Chewco.

Gifts, side deals and payoffs

Government officials, who wanted to become involved to try and unwind this scandal, realised they could not because Enron had already paid so much money into their own bank accounts. Expensive gifts can develop into an ethical issue.

Whistle blowing

If it were not for Enron's vice-president, Sherron Watkins, Enron might still have been up and running. She played the role of whistle blower in this scandal.

Managers and directors: fiduciary duties

The directors had a fiduciary duty towards the shareholders. This duty entailed ensuring that all business practices were sound.

Social responsibility

Enron's employees thought their organisation was focused on social responsibility. They donated $600 000 to the MD Anderson Cancer Centre and $50 000 to the Mercatus Centre (Berenbeim, 2002). Unfortunately, investigations only showed later that Mendersohn and Gramm, from these respective centres, were both part of the Audit Committee of Enron's Board.

Moral standards across borders

Enron had its $2.9 billion plant in India. The energy plan gave it better opportunities, since locals did not want to buy from it anymore.

Business ethics

Business ethics professor Linda Trevino explains that ethics really work best in an organisation when they are woven into the fabric of the organisation, and this is where human resources management is important (Lachnit, 2002). Trevino states that if leaders are trained, sessions on ethical leadership have to be part of that process. Ethics should be a component of the performance review process. Questions such as 'How do employees (and executives) stand up in terms of trustworthiness and honesty?' should always be part of the review. Ethics must be factored into the compensation system. According to a former Enron employee quoted by the *New York Times*, the attitude at Enron was: 'Get it done. Get it done now. Reap the rewards.' Whether the deal made money or even sense was somebody else's problem (Lachnit, 2002).

Organisations with global presence should especially look for recurring patterns, whether they are a series of suspicious claims, rebates paid to the same customer, exceptionally high amounts of agent commission, or payments to charities outside the normal boundaries. Money payments made to banks located in tax havens or jurisdictions known for strict bank secrecy laws should also be investigated.

Conclusion

Enron has been marked as the worst possible corporate scandal to date. This should be a wake-up call for organisations to educate their staff across the board on ethical issues. Organisations should implement open communication systems for employees to report ethical breaches. These channels should be confidential, but should also be trustworthy themselves. Employees should also take a lesson from this to question management decisions that just do not feel right.

Conclusion

This chapter introduced and contextualised the complex issue of *ethics* and how it pertains to public relations in the organisational, socio-political, economic and religious contexts. It also gave a synopsis of ancient rhetoric and persuasive discourse, and their influence on modern public relations. In addition, contemporary theoretical approaches to public relations ethics were covered in this chapter. The ethical and professional responsibility of public relations practitioners, and the role of public relations in the socio-political and economic environments were other issues under consideration. Various case studies were cited to explain and illustrate the complexity of ethics in public relations.

Despite society's scepticism, there has always been and will always be a need for effective business relations, both locally and internationally. Market competitiveness creates the need for effective public relations. Qualified and experienced public relations practitioners are now needed more than ever before. In its career guide, the *US News and World Report* (1997) stated that public relations jobs are expected to grow by 55 per cent by 2006. The need is greater as a result of the intense global market competition and concomitant international public opinion, with its cultural, historical and political complexities.

Public relations practitioners must communicate with society adequately and effectively. There is no other option. From an ethics point of view, honesty is the best policy in spreading the message of the corporate world. The truth must be told as far as possible, and credibility and reputation have to be constructed in a sceptical and sometimes disbelieving world.

Questions for self-evaluation

1. Write an article about the relationship between public relations, its professional responsibility and ethics.

   (a) Are these concepts compatible?

   (b) Can public relations practitioners uphold ethics in their work and professional conduct?

   (c) Refer to recent public relations examples to illustrate the arguments in your article.

References

Adhurst, M 2001. The incredible shrinking president. In *Newsweek* (Atlantic edition), 137(26):31.

Baker, RW 2002. Business's dirty little secret. In *Harvard Business Review*.

Baker, S 1999. The baselines for justification in persuasion. In *Journal of Mass Media Ethics*, 14:69–81.

Barney, R and Black, J 1994. Ethics and professional persuasive communications. In *Public Relations Review*, 20(3):233–248.

Berenbeim, R 2002. Improper corporate behaviour. In *Vital speeches of the day*, February.

Berquest, G and Berquest, GE (Eds.) *Essays on the Rhetoric of the Western World*. Dubuque: Iowa:162–167.

Bivins, TH 1989. Are public relations texts covering ethics adequately? In *Journal of Mass Media Ethics*, 4:39–52.

Cooper, T and Kelleher, T 2001. Of Emerson, ethics, and post-millennium persuasion. In *Journal of Mass Media Ethics*, 16(2 & 3):176–192.

Corbett, EPJ 1990. Introduction to the rhetoric and poetics of Aristotle.

Creedon, PJ 1996. The future of strategic public relations practice in the global marketplace: Building a case for strategic ethics. Paper presented at the Conference for Strategic Planning of the United Arab Emirates University, Dubai.

Cutlip, SR 1994. *The Unseen Power.* Hillsdale, New Jersey: Lawrence Earlbaum.

DeGeorge, RT 1990. *Business Ethics*. New York: Macmillan.

Duffy, M and Dickerson, JF 2002. Enron spoils the party. In *Times*, 4 February.

Fama, EF and Jensen, MC 1983. Separation of ownership and control. In *Journal of Law and Economics*, 26(June):301–325.

Fitzpatrick, K and Gauthier, C 2001. Toward a professional responsibility theory of public relations ethics. In *Journal of Mass Media Ethics*, 16(2 & 3):193–212.

Gibson, JL; Ivancevich, JM and Donnelly, JH 1988. *Organisations*. BPI: Irvin.

Gilligan, C 1982. *In a Different Voice*. Cambridge, NA: Harvard University Press.

Grunig, J (Ed.) 1992. *Excellence in Public Relations and Communication Management*. Hillsdale, New Jersey: Lawrence Earlbaum.

Grunig, J 1993. Implications of public relations for other domains of communication. In *Journal of Communication*, 43:164–173.

Grunig, J 1993. Public relations and international affairs: Effects, ethics and responsibility. In *Journal of International Affairs,* 47(1):137–161.

Grunig, J and Grunig, LA 1992. Models of public relations and communications. In Grunig, J (Ed.) *Excellence in Public Relations and Communication Management.* Hillsdale, New Jersey: Lawrence Earlbaum.

Grunig, J and Grunig, LA 1996. Implications of symmetry for a theory of ethics and social responsibility in public relations. Paper presented to the Public Relations Interest Group, International Communication Association, Chicago, Illinois.

Habermas, J 1984. *The Theory of Communication Action.* Vol 1, translated by McCarthy, T. Boston: Beacon.

Heath, RL 1997. *Strategic Issues Management: Organizations and Public Policy Changes.* Thousand Oaks, CA: Sage.

Hindle, T 2002. Back to basics. In *The Economist.*

Ihator, A 1999. Society and corporate public relations. Why the conflict? In *Public Relations Quarterly,* 44(3):33–41.

Kadlec, D 2002. Who's accountable? In *Time,* 21 January.

Kiplinger, K 2002. Ethics on the ropes. In *Investing,* May.

Klein, LS 1992. Ethical decision-making in a business environment. In *Review of Business,* 13(3).

Kohlberg, L 1981. *The Philosophy of Modern Development.* San Francisco: Harper & Row.

Kruckeberg, D 1998. Future reconciliation of multicultural perspectives in public relations ethics. In *Public Relations Quarterly,* 43(2):45–49.

Kruckeberg, D 2000. The public relations practitioner's role in practicing strategic ethics. In *Public Relations Quarterly,* 45(3):35–40.

Kruckeberg, D and Starck, K 1988. *Public Relations and Community: A Reconstructed Theory.* New York: Praeger.

Lachnit, C 2002. Why ethics is HR's issue. In *Workforce,* March.

Ledingham, J and Bruning, SDJ 2000. Introduction: Background and current trends in the study of relationship management. In Ledingham, J and Bruning, SDJ (Eds.) *Public Relations as Relationship Management: A Relationship Approach to the Study of Public Relations.* Mahwah, New Jersey: Lawrence Earlbaum.

L'Etang, J 1994. Public relations and corporate responsibility: Some issues arising. In *Journal of Business Ethics,* 13:111–123.

Marrou, HI 1956. *A History of Education in Antiquity*, translated by Lamb, G. New York: Sheed & Ward.

Marsh, CWJ 2001. Public relations ethics: Contrasting models from the rhetoric of Plato, Aristotle and Isocrates. In *Journal of Mass Media Ethics*, 16(2 & 3):78–98.

Mersham, GM; Rensburg, RS and Skinner, CA 1995. *Public Relations, Development and Social Investment: A Southern African Perspective*. Pretoria: Van Schaik.

Mintzberg, H 1983. *Power In and Around Organizations*. Englewood Cliffs, New Jersey: Prentice-Hall.

Muravchik, J 2002. Hearts, minds and the war against terror. In *New York Times*.

Pearson, R 1989. Reviewing Albert J Sullivan's theory of public relations ethics. In *Public Relations Review*, 15(2):52–62.

Pearson, R 1989. A theory of public relations ethics. Unpublished doctoral thesis. Athens: Ohio University.

Post, JE 1985. Assessing the Nestlé boycott: Corporate accountability and human rights. In *California Management Review*, 8(2):113–131.

Poulakos, T 1997. *Speaking for the Polis: Isocrates' Rhetorical Education.* Columbia: University of South Carolina Press.

Pratt, CB 1994. Applying classical ethical theories to ethical decision making in public relations. In *Management Communication Quarterly*, August, 8(9):70–85.

PRSA 1991. Public relations: An overview. In *PRSA Foundation Management Series*, 1(3).

Sewer, A 2002. Dirty rotten numbers. In *Fortune*, 18 February.

Sherman, S 2002. Enron: Uncovering the uncovered story. In *CJR*, March/April.

Simon, R 2001. Waging the spin war. In *US News and World Report*, 131(17).

Stauber, J and Rampton, S 1995. *Toxic Sludge is Good for You: Lies, Damn Lies and the Public Relations Industry.* Monroe, ME: Common Courage.

Sullivan, AJ 1965. Values in public relations. In Lerbinger, O and Sullivan, AJ (Eds.) *Information, Influence and Communication: A Reader in Public Relations*. New York: Basic Books:412–439.

Taylor, A 1998. Violations of the international code of marketing of breast milk substitutes. In *British Medical Journal*, 316:1117–1122.

The Business Roundtable 1988. *Corporate Ethics: A Prime Business Asset*. New York: Business USA.

Whalen, P 1998. Enlightened self-interest: An ethical baseline for teaching corporate public relations. Paper presented to the Public Relations Division, Association for Education in Journalism and Mass Communication.

Wright, DK 1989. Ethics research in public relations. In *Public Relations Review*, 15(2):3–5.

Index

A

above-the-line approach 119
accessibility 78
adaptation phase 101
advertising 5
    advocacy 162
    corporate 161–62
    crisis 162
    financial 162
    identity 161
    image 161
    service 162
advocacy advertising 162
advocacy role 69
agencies, stable of 13
American Association of Advertising
    Agencies 7, 116
American Marketing Association 4
analyst relationship value 124
Anglo Alpha Cement 250
announcements 223
annual reports 149
apartheid 44
archive support 224
Aristotle 265
articles 224
attitudinal change 9
attitudinal loyalty 177
attitudinal objectives 100
audience fragmentation 18
audience sensitivity 278, 280
Audit Bureau of Circulations of South
    Africa (ABC) 152
autoresponders 215, 224
awareness 20, 72

B

banners 224
bargaining unit publications 149
behaviour modification campaign 73
behavioural loyalty 177
behavioural objectives 100
behavioural role 69

below-the-line approach 119
blurbs 223
bottom line 17
brand
    building v
    equity v
    identity 193
    image v
    internal resources 196
    loyalty 9
    perception 9
    performance 194–99
    personality 193
    positioning 193
    presentation 194
    relationships 194
    relationships, drivers 13–15
    reputation 192, 194
    team members 196
    value 11
    vision and culture 192
brand management model 192–94
brand messages, strategic consistency
    13, 14
branding, internal 172–208
branding, internal process 195
British Airways 27–28
budget 102
bulletin boards 149, 216
bulletins 148
Business Roundtable 263
buyer partnerships 121

C

campaign planning, interactive model
    98–101
campaigns 72
    appeals 77
    behaviour modification 73
    cause-oriented 73
    criteria for effectiveness 77–78
    definition 76–77
    ideological 73